NOT FADE AWAY

AWAY THE ROLLING STONES COLLECTION

'Well my mother told my father
Just before I was born,
"I gotta boy-child comin'
Gonna be a Rollin' Stone" '.

MUDDY WATERS (1915–1983)

NOT FADE AWAY

AWAY THE ROLLING STONES COLLECTION

GEOFFREY GIULIANO

COLLECTOR AND CONSULTANT
CHRIS EBORN

Paper Tiger

Paper Tiger
An imprint of Dragon's World Ltd
Limpsfield
Surrey RH8 0DY
Great Britain

First published by Dragon's World in hardback 1993
First published in limpback with corrections 1995

British Library Cataloguing in Publication Data
The catalogue record for this book is available from
the British Library.

ISBN 1 85028 216 1 (hardback)
ISBN 1 85028 367 2 (limpback)

EDITORIAL CONSULTANT	Chris Eborn
EDITORS	Diana Briscoe, Michael Downey
DESIGN & ART DIRECTION	Dave Allen
SPECIAL PHOTOGRAPHY	Graham Bush
DESIGN ASSISTANTS	Bob Burroughs, Victoria Furbisher
EDITORIAL DIRECTOR	Pippa Rubinstein

A Note to the Reader
Although every attempt has been made to trace copyright holders of images contained herein,
any unacknowledged copyright holder omitted should contact Dragon's World so that the
situation may be rectified in future editions.

Neither the author nor publishers of this book condone the manufacture, distribution or
sale of so-called bootleg recordings. The bootlegging of material belonging to any group or
individual is both strictly illegal and reprehensible. The bootlegs in this book are included
solely for the purpose of historical accuracy.

Typeset in Bembo by Dragon's World.
Printed in Spain.

CONTENTS

. . . AS YEARS GO BY

It is the evening of the day, and the tears and the years have gone by. . . 'Lady Jane' and 'That Girl' belong to yesterday (and Gene Pitney). . . but yesterday don't matter till it's gone.

Whatever anyone may have thought on 31 December 1959, the sixties didn't start until 1962 – Quant, Sassoon, Stamp, Caine, the Davids (Bailey and Hockney), The Fab Four, and The Rolling Stones. Mr. Berry said come on and we did. John and Paul gave us 'I Wanna Be Your Man', Mick and Keith gave themselves 'Not Fade Away' – thanx Buddy and Bo. Having another hit felt just as good as having a hit and the time was right for more than dancing in the street. And right again in the future when Mick and David would do just that for stayin' alive aid.

The Beat Boom had already claimed the copyright – bequeathed by the bebop dinosaurs of the American fifties – for the clean cut and the cute. So, the media, with a few suggestions and a little help, labelled them everything else and filled our tabloids and screens with tales and visions of decadent deeds. . . as one good turn deserves another. . . would you let your daughter?. . . or have you seen your mother? And we all had fun, fun, fun as the hits, the headlines and the hype spent the night and the sixties together. Exiled from the street to penthouses, chateaux and the beach/high society – the best of both/jet-setting and tumbling thru the seventies into the eighties, the decade financed by Sony and Co, sold by MTV, sponsored by Madison Avenue, and soon belonging to the madonnas, the Michaels, the rockers and the rappers. Til 'Start Me Up' did once again with Mick's emotions mixed for steel wheels, US dollars and the ecus of the urban jungle – you can always get what you want, and the vinyl junkies did for the last time.

Now, rock's best known riff that once sold rebellion on the streets sells chocolate bars on TV.

It's only the Rolling Stones, and as years go by, the world's greatest rock 'n' roll band still are.

Andrew Loog Oldham, 1992

Andrew Loog Oldham enjoying the hard-earned fruits of his work.

INTRODUCTION

Looking back, the manic, involuntary motion of the Rolling Stones was probably closer to the truth of things in the sixties (and maybe even now) than the wide eyed 'all you need is Love, God, Truth and, just to be safe, phenomenal material success' philosophy wrought by the Beatles. Although to a large extent the Stones were publicly what the Fab Four only dared in private, Mick and the boys certainly had balls. At a time when pop/rock culture was turning the corner from its previous sanitary adolescent aura (typified by naughty-but-nice idols like Lonnie Donegan, Billy Fury and the squeaky clean Cliff Richard) the Stones blissfully stuck their fingers in their noses and lashed out at the world with a wildly brazen attitude screaming 'Let's spend the night together' when the Beatles still only dared hold our hands.

Now, for a committed thirty-year Beatle man like myself such an admission is a mighty big leap. Still, if the truth be known, the down and dirty compositions of Jagger and Richards always sounded pretty darn good to me, even at the impossible height of my own deeply felt Hare Krishna/Lysergic acid days of the late sixties. Beyond the musical good vibrations, though, was an engaging lyrical peek at the dark side of the force forged by two men who seemed to ride the razor's edge daily in all they did. The Rolling Stones were slightly dangerous it seemed. They were the people our parents warned us about, their music a rich tapestry of swirling sorrows and forbidden, untamed pleasure. Just what the doctor ordered for a legion of frustrated, dope-smoking youth intent upon pushing forward the barriers of the old folks' post-war world of work-a-day desperation and tired, conformist thinking.

Contrary to what a lot of terminally unaware people have claimed, the Stones weren't really the root *cause* of anything much that went on back then. For all their decadent charisma and charm, they simply provided the soundtrack for the profound madness that was already in the air. As for me, I simply went along for the ride and came back irreversibly and forever 'altered' in the bargain. Where it all came from, however, or what it actually meant is still anybody's guess. Now that we're all grown up you'd think the Stones iron-clad magic would have effectively ceased to

Your author... a man of wealth and taste.

move us as it once did. But even time, it seems, can do little to dull the unpredictable joy we felt riding the piercing riffs of Keith Richards' guitar, Bill Wyman's sneaky bass, Charlie Watts' thunderous, swinging drumming, or Jagger's wildcat vocals.

Like any real magic the Rolling Stones defy examination. The musical experience is itself still the only true barometer with which to judge their meaning. It says a lot, though, that we're still listening to and enjoying the Stones' music after all these years. Three decades later, the music keeps on pushing all the right buttons. As it is, surely, with any great art.

Rock is dead. Long live the Rolling Stones!

Geoffrey Giuliano
'Skyfield'
Lockport, New York
Christmas 1991

'Not Quite Conversational,' by the author. [Collage/pen and ink, 1992]

'She's Like A Rainbow.' [Pastel, 1985] Illustration: Geoffrey Giuliano.

1963-1970

ACT ONE
THE DECCA YEARS

Before the advent of the Rolling Stones there were just two slightly inarticulate little geezers from Dartford, Kent, called Mick Jagger and Keith Richards. Although they were schoolboy friends they didn't really connect until a chance encounter in 1960 at Dartford railway station while awaiting the morning train to London. Still at a loss concerning his professional future, Richards was treading water, ostensibly studying advertising at Sidcup Art College; while young Mick (or 'Mike' as he was known in those days) was intent upon a business career. Attending the prestigious London School of Economics Jagger was a capable student who, in concord with his new-found mate Keith, shared a deep liking for the native Blues of the American South. 'It's strange,' remembers Richards concerning his early association with the gawky Jagger, 'I knew Mick when I was really young. . . 5, 6 or 7. We used to hang out together but then I moved and didn't see him for a long time. I once met him selling ice creams outside the public library. I bought one. He was tryin' to make extra money.'

Musically, the two teenagers had a lot to talk about. From those first awkward moments together it was Mick's collection of hard-to-find rhythm & blues albums from the States that held sway. Poles apart (even today) in temperament, Messrs Jagger and Richards went on to become firm friends, hanging out, rapping, and above all, absorbing the gut-wrenching blues that cemented the lifelong bond between them.

From the moment Keith got it into his head he wanted to play guitar he was hooked. Posing seductively in front of the bathroom mirror he would pout and prance like the real rockers he saw on the telly, 'getting down the moves' (as he put it) long before he ever touched the instrument. 'Keith was always worrying for a guitar of his own,' remembers his mum, Doris. 'When he was 15, I bought him one for £10. From that day, it has been the most important thing in his life. My father, who used to run a dance band before the war, taught Keith a few chords, but the rest he taught himself.'

Mick Jagger, too, was determined to make his mark as a performer, writing a letter to blues man Alexis Korner in 1962 requesting a spot on the bill at the Ealing Jazz Club in west London. Ginger Baker, latter-day Cream percussionist and Korner's drummer, remembers those first, uncertain gigs as 'horrific,' complaining that the pubescent Jagger was not only a very 'tentative' singer but almost completely devoid of any discernible stage presence or charisma.

'I thought he was God-awful,' says Baker. 'He was also a very pushy little git always on at everybody for a gig. I used to back him during the interval with Alexis which, by the way, I resented as it impeded my ability to nip backstage to the boys' room for my customary half-time fix. Eventually I recommended to my mate, Charlie Watts, that he might consider sitting in with these guys if only to preserve my sanity between the sets.' ⇨

Mick, Keith, Brian, Bill, and Charlie circa 1963.

By now this first feeble incarnation of the Stones (known briefly as Little Boy Blue and the Blue Boys) were an ad hoc collective consisting of Keith on guitar, Mick on vocals, and Dick Taylor (a reasonably experienced semi-pro bassman from Bexleyheath, Kent). All that was to change, however when, on 7 April 1962, they ran headlong into elfin guitarist Brian Jones while gigging in Ealing.

Tearing into a red hot rendition of 'Dust My Blues' Jones growled a terse 'good evening' to the whipped-up crowd, and introduced himself as Elmo Lewis after his musical hero, Elmore James. 'He was doing the same as we'd been doing,' remembered Keith Richards about the Stones' bad boy lead guitarist, 'thinking he was the only cat in the world doing it.'

Brian had originally set his sights on becoming a dentist, but later switched gears significantly by embracing music as a career. Trained on the piano from the age of 6, Jones moved on to clarinet and finally, upon leaving school, the guitar. At 17, Brian jetted off to the continent, trekking through several European countries before returning home to Cheltenham briefly before finally moving down to London with his leggy girlfriend Pat Andrews to pursue his art.

Following Brian's initial meeting with Mick and Keith, he invited them to drop by an upcoming gig at a Soho pub where Richards was introduced to Ian Stewart, then playing piano for Jones. 'He blew my mind,' says Keith. 'I never heard a white piano like that before. Real Albert Ammons stuff.' After a few friendly pints, telephone numbers were exchanged and, several weeks later, Brian and Ian formally invited Jagger and Richards to merge the best of the two bands along with Geoff Bradford on guitar, bassist Dick Taylor and a dreary succession of faceless session drummers. Rehearsing together for the first time over the Bricklayer's Arms on Broadwick Street in Soho, Jones even had a name for the fledgling group, 'the Rollin' Stones,' after Muddy Water's 'Rollin' Stone Blues.'

Stone-faced drummer Charlie Watts first picked up the sticks at 14 after his parents bought him his own elementary set for Christmas that year. Playing along to jazz records in the front parlour, Watts dreamed of one day heading up his own big band – rock 'n' roll at that point was still just a faraway sound drifting in offshore from Radio Luxembourg late at night as Charlie lay listening in bed.

Briefly joining Alexis Korner in 1962 Charlie first jammed with Keith and Mick at the Ealing Jazz Club, performing Chuck Berry's 'Around And Around.' Although they received only sporadic applause that evening, they had connected musically. Ironically, it was to be another five months until the reserved percussionist would relent and officially come on board as the Rolling Stones' one and only drummer. 'Honestly, I thought they were mad,' recalls Watts. 'I mean, they were working a lot of dates without getting paid or even worrying about it. And there was me earning a pretty comfortable living, which obviously was going to nosedive if I got involved with the

To conquer America. The Stones at Carnegie Hall, 20 June 1964, during their initial tour of the US (courtesy Dave Peabody.)

Rolling Stones. . . [But] I liked their spirit and was getting very involved with rhythm & blues. So I said, Ok, yes, I'd join. Lots of my friends thought I'd gone raving mad.'

By September 1962 Dick Taylor had effectively called it quits as a Rolling Stone, moving on to study at the Royal College of Art. Without missing a beat Brian placed an ad in the music press announcing the vacancy. On a snowy 7 December, 26-year-old technician Bill Perks (known professionally as Bill Wyman) auditioned for the band at a pub called the Weatherby Arms in Chelsea.

Although the other band members weren't all that impressed with Bill's even, unexciting, working-class persona, they were thrilled with his top-drawer equipment, including a new amp, spare Vox AC30, as well as a booming speaker system. Keith remembers Wyman's early days as a Stone: 'It turned out Bill really could play. At first he was very untogether, then slowly he started to play very natural, swinging bass lines. But Bill wasn't permanent. He played with us and came to rehearsals, but he couldn't make gigs sometimes because he had to work.'

The only married Stone, Wyman enjoyed a level of comfort and stability the other boys could only imagine. Mick, Keith and Brian were almost always broke (Charlie still lived at home with his parents and so was quite well fed) prompting the compassionate bassist to regularly escort the band down to the local Wimpy Bar for a utilitarian meal of egg and chips. 'I still get the shivers whenever I see a tin of cold spaghetti,' Brian Jones once remarked, 'and that was a treat! A lot of the time we lived on whatever we could concoct from flour and water.'

Despite the group's lack of finances they were slowly building a steady following among the rough-and-ready teenage population of Richmond and Twickenham. By April 1963, nineteen year-old Andrew Loog Oldham signed on as the Stones' manager. One of his first official acts was the controversial move of yanking veteran Ian Stewart out of the line-up as the tough-looking Ted didn't sport the right kind of image for the increasingly trendy, modish group. Relegated to playing his keyboards backstage, out of sight of the fans and working as equipment manager, Ian took the surprise demotion in his stride, rationalizing the move as 'vaguely inevitable.'

Oldham was a first class hustler, despite his still tender years, inciting young girls to near riot at the gigs by standing at the back of the house and emitting a very shrill, high-pitched scream. Instantly, this inspired the keyed-up, swooning girls to follow suit almost bringing down the rafters with their raucous, non-stop bellowing.

'The overall hustle I invented for the Stones was to establish them as a raunchy, gamy, unpredictable bunch of undesirables,' says Oldham. 'I decided that since the Beatles had already usurped the cleancut, choirboy image. . . I should take the Stones down the opposite road. . . By the time I got through planting all the negative publicity there wasn't a parent in Britain that wasn't repulsed by the very sound of their name.' ⮑

The Stones posing for the press during their second American tour in 1964.

On 28 January 1963 the Rolling Stones' first official recording session commenced at IBC Studios, London, engineered by Glyn Johns. This session gave us the first take of 'I Want To Be Loved.' On 10 May a second take of the same song, produced by the savvy Oldham, was recorded at Olympic Studios, Barnes, London. Confiding to house engineer Roger Savage that he didn't know a thing about sound recording (or indeed music) the session lumbered on with the group laying down a rather dour rendition of Chuck Berry's 'Come On' and several additional less distinguished rhythm & blues numbers. Submitting the tapes to Decca Records, the company was predictably less than enthusiastic, prompting the Stones to later redo the tracks at Decca's studios in London. This time the A&R people were ready to take a chance, releasing the group's first single 'Come On' backed by 'I Want To Be Loved' on 7 June. Climbing to only number twenty in the charts, the record's modest success nevertheless caught the eye of a London television producer who subsequently booked the 'swinging new combo' on the popular 'Thank Your Lucky Stars.' The next day the *Record Mirror* called the disc 'good' and 'commercial' but added that it 'should make the charts in only a smallish way.' Ironically, Mick Jagger himself later bestowed perhaps the record's harshest review of all, commenting: 'I don't think 'Come On' was very good. In fact, it was shit. We disliked it so much we didn't do it on any of our gigs.' Bill Wyman, too, agreed, later writing in his autobiography *Stone Alone*: '[The Stones] must have been the only group in the world not to play their début single. To anyone who knew the band and its musical roots the song was really a lie.'

It was at this point that the Stones began an exhausting touring schedule that would not wind down significantly until the latter half of 1966. Playing nightly for months on end the six amiable musicians (including Ian Stewart) were stretched to the limit with a back-breaking routine of five-hour gigs that saw them appearing at such off-beat venues as the Corn Exchange in Wisbech, the Richmond Athletic Club, private parties for Britain's uppercrust gentry, and even a two-day stint at a suburban London fairground. Happily, the group's hard work was beginning to pay off. A Rolling Stones Fan Club was formed with over 300 members and individual chapters for each of the boys. Gigging at ever more prestigious venues the band were regularly rubbing shoulders with top acts of the day like the Hollies, Gene Pitney, Bo Diddley, Little Richard, the Everly Brothers and even the Beatles (with whom they went on to become great friends).

Another giant step forward was the national exposure they received from doing popular TV shows such as the now legendary 'Ready Steady Go!' Hostess Cathy McGowan recalls the ruckus: 'We received literally thousands of letters asking to see them again. People who hadn't seen or heard of them before raved about them. Later, older people started writing saying the Stones were disgusting. . . We were told it was a mistake to have put them on the show.' Andrew Oldham's master plan, it seemed, was beginning to work out very nicely indeed.

ABOVE A break in rehearsal for a British TV show circa 1965.
MIDDLE Bill, Mick, and Brian out on the streets of America. Already the Stones were instantly recognizable Stateside (1964).
BELOW The boys recording yet another mid-sixties television show.

The Stones' second single 'I Wanna Be Your Man,' penned for the the group by new-found mates Lennon and McCartney (backed with 'Stoned'), was released by Decca on 1 November 1963 with much attendant hoopla. Initially, the record was set for release in America as well but was pulled by US execs at the last moment for alleged drug references on 'Stoned'. Within a week the high energy forty-five entered the charts at thirty, eventually rising all the way to number nine.

Intertwined in all this was the blossoming of the songwriting team of Jagger and Richards. In December of that year singer Gene Pitney released the obscure 'That Girl Belongs To Me,' credited to Mick and Keith. Even less well known is 'Shang A Doo Lang' from teen songstress Adrienne Poster as well as 'Will You Be My Lover Tonight' and 'It Should Be You' by the now unknown singer George Bean. Once again, Jagger and Richards were listed as composers. After a time even Watts and Wyman got into the act, writing the novelty track 'I Do Like To See Me On The B Side' for the Andrew Oldham Orchestra, released by Decca in February 1964.

Despite the group's rapidly emerging public persona, life as a Rolling Stone was not all wild parties and willing young ▷

women. The unhappy flip side to manager Oldham's campaign of negative publicity was that the Stones were ever having to explain themselves to the media as well as running a manic gauntlet of out-of-control, sometimes violent fans virtually everywhere they went. 'The Stones hype caught on with a sudden fury that carried them beyond my wildest dreams,' Andrew Oldham has said. 'Whatever I hadn't invented about them, the media did, with the result that when they set out on their second British tour early in 1964 they were in constant jeopardy of being trampled, cannibalized and emasculated.' Accordingly, the cheeky Oldham delighted in all the madness (even if often the band themselves did not). Seeking to wreak havoc at various Stones gigs (and thus more good 'bad' publicity) he would very publicly pluck a policeman's helmet from an unsuspecting head at the front of the stage, illustrating how very easy such calculated mischief might be if any of the punters in the audience cared to follow suit. Another favourite trick was to encourage Jagger to throw out a few discreetly placed 'Sieg Heils' while goose stepping arrogantly across the stage during performances in Holland and Germany. 'Talk about

riots', Oldham comments, 'every train leaving Munich was wrecked. They just tore them apart. They tore the town apart.'

Acting out such over-the-top antics inspired not only the group's manager, it seemed, but the devilish Jagger himself. 'When I'm on the road I just go crazy,' says Mick. 'I become a total monster. I don't recognize anybody. I don't even see them. . . I feel guilty about it afterwards, then I laugh, because the whole thing is a joke. But Keith is worse than I am.'

Predictably, the laid-back Bill Wyman often failed to see the humour in this dark side of the Stones' tailor-made persona. The unofficial historian of the band, Bill has press clippings touting news of 'unwashed, smelly' Stones from whose shaggy heads various body lice might be seen 'jumping for safety.' Not surprisingly, band members were regularly turned away at restaurants, pubs and even neighbourhood stores. 'We'd go into a shop to buy a pack of cigarettes and they would refuse to sell us any,' Wyman recalls. ' "We don't serve the likes of you lot in here" they'd shout. "Now sod off." ' Adding insult to injury, the band was verbally accosted by uptight citizens almost everywhere they went, making even a simple trip down the

KEITH MOON THINK-IN—PAGE 7

STONES FOR PALLADIUM

9d weekly

Daily Record
WED JUNE 28 1967
4d SCOTLAND'S NATIONAL NEWSPAPER No. 22,357

ROLLING STONE IS FOUND GUILTY ON PEP PILLS CHARGE

LEWES JAIL

MICK JAGGER WAITS IN JAIL

New LP, single out in

concert

weekly

STONES GAS AUSSIES!

BRIAN JONES PHONES FROM DOWN UNDER

Brisbane: Tuesday

AUSTRALIA is a gas. We didn't think it would be anything like this. I know it must sound like a load of rubbish coming from me, but facts are facts. We're doing marvellously out here — never imagined anything like it.

I'm phoning frim Brisbane and we're on stage in two minutes. From the moment we flew in we've been knocked out—and surprised—by the reaction.

We're all on a par with the Australian people, and they seem to like us. We were worried, to he truthful —we thought it would just be Beatles, Beatles, and nothing. But it's Beatles and Stones.

JAGGER, 23-year-old lead singer of the Rolling Stones, was in jail last night— sentence on a drugs charge.

at Chichester yesterday he was found guilty of possessing four Italian pep pills. were found, the court heard, when police swooped of another Rolling Stone — guitarist Keith Richard.

Souvenirs

Doctor

---

motorway a stand-off between those who dug all that the Swinging Sixties were and those who most decidedly did not.

The good news, of course, was that all this lunacy was pushing record sales in the UK through the roof. On 17 January 1964 the group's first EP (extended play) was released, including classic tracks 'You Better Move On,' 'Bye Bye Johnny,' 'Money,' and the seductive 'Poison Ivy.' Next month 'Not Fade Away' backed by 'Little By Little' was issued as a single. More importantly, though, their first US record, 'Not Fade Away' backed by 'I Wanna Be Your Man,' was released in March.

Another milestone, the band's first certified number one smash, came with the release of *The Rolling Stones* in the UK on 17 April 1964 . The twelve-track LP would remain in the Top Thirty for a staggering forty weeks, eleven of those firmly at the top of the charts.

Finally, the boys were beginning to cash in on their hard-fought-for success. In 1965 Bill Wyman purchased a small house and bought himself a sporty MGB. Brian, meanwhile, moved from his girlfriend Linda Lawrence's home in Windsor to a smart flat at Chester Street, Belgravia. Among his highbrow

neighbours were Lady Dartmouth and several young starlets. All of the Stones, of course, were regulars at the swankiest boutiques in Chelsea, indulging their well-recorded penchant for wearing only the most expensive, trendiest threads. Jones summed up the boys' love of fashion: 'It depends on what we feel like really. Sometimes I'll wear very flamboyant clothes like this frilly shirt. Other times I'll wear very casual stuff. We spend a lot of our free time buying stuff. There's really not much else to do.'

By 1964 Jagger, rock 'n' roll's first real perfomer/ businessman, had a lot on his mind. Despite their achievements at home, the Stones couldn't really feel they'd made it until the inevitable trip Stateside to try their luck in the all important American market. 'Without dee States,' Brian Jones remarked at the time, 'we're just five louts from the suburbs with a local record deal and a van full of tatty equipment.' *England's Newest Hit Makers*, the band's first American album, was issued in the States in May 1964, with the boys following shortly thereafter to commence an ambitious tour.

The group's first gig in San Bernardino was a knockout, with the capacity crowd of screaming young women in bliss over ⇨

the spirited performance of their shaggy heroes. Not so, however, elsewhere as the tour rolled on to San Antonio and a disappointing turnout of about 200 kids at a 19,000-seat venue. Their next stop too, in Omaha, was similarly inauspicious with the local inhabitants turning out in force to jeer violently at this ragtag group of uppity foreigners so at odds with their deeply ingrained, midwestern Bible-belt values. Once again, only about 600 paying customers presented themselves for the show in the 15,000-seat hall. 'The thing that really went down heavy there was the cop scene,' remembers Keith. 'We were sitting in the dressing room, drinking whisky and coke out of paper cups, just waiting to go on when the cops walked in. "What's that? You can't drink whiskey in a public place. Tip it down the bog." "No man, I've just got Coca Cola." I look up and I got a .44 looking at me, right between the eyes. That's when I realized what it could get into. Nobody came to any of the shows. New York and LA were hip to us, and that was it. Meanwhile we had to do a month around the Midwest where we were the lowest of the low. All we heard was, "What are you, a boy or a girl?" You couldn't go into a bar. Suddenly to be stuck in this environment for a month where you're a nobody, even worse than a nobody, you're a weirdo, you're a foreigner. 1964 in Omaha was no joke. They all hated us and wanted to beat the shit out of us.'

Returning home to England on 23 June the Stones were met at Heathrow Airport by thousands of screaming fans, helping to heal the degrading spectacle of their first American tour. Three days later Decca released their fourth single, 'It's All Over Now' backed by 'Good Times, Bad Times.' 'All things considered,' said Mick earlier that week at a *Record Mirror* presentation for Best British Vocal Group, 'I would rather be a hit in Wisconsin.'

That July the Stones embarked upon their fourth tour of the UK. The fifth show in Blackpool was in front of 7,000 delighted kids. Once again there was trouble, with two of Blackpool's finest injured along with thirty fans. In addition, four spectators were arrested for assault and carrying offensive weapons. Finally, Keith Richards lost his temper when a fan spat at him. He lashed out at the offender, kicking wildly from the edge of the stage. This little display kicked off a full-scale riot in which £4,000 damage was done to the hall. As a result an August show scheduled for the venue was cancelled by the promoters. 'Not a bad night really,' said Keith to a friend afterwards.

By now the Rolling Stones had become something of a national obsession in England, a kind of anti-Christ Beatles hell bent on breaking down the barriers between the old-guard stuffiness of their parents' generation and replacing it with a freer, more experimental, less disciplined approach to life. At least that's what Andrew Oldham would have you believe. For Mick and the boys, though, rock 'n' roll was still, basically, just a way to beat the dole. 'When we saw how successful the Beatles were, early on,' says Jagger, 'we thought, "Oh, there's a good job, world travel, screaming women, nice clothes, fast cars, lots of spare cash. Yep, that's the job for us!" '

On 23 October 1964 the Stones flew to New York to begin their second American tour. First there was an appearance ⇨ 22

Rare photographs of the Stones performing on their first
US tour in San Antonio, Texas, in 1964.

on the 'Ed Sullivan Show.' Following the gold-plated success of the Beatles, Sullivan was anxious to book whoever he thought would press the right buttons with America's youth. Coming so close on the heels of the Fab Four, the Stones seemed just the ticket. Much to Ed's regret, however, the normally well-behaved teenage audience got a bit carried away and staged a 'mini' riot. Sullivan, needless to say, was definitely not amused. 'I promise you they will never be back to our show,' he remarked to the *Newark Evening News*. 'If things can't be handled, we will stop the whole business. We won't book any more rock 'n' roll groups and we'll ban teenagers from the theatre if we have to. Frankly, I didn't see the group until the day before the broadcast. . . I was shocked when I saw them.' Of course, if one is going to stage a riot probably the best place ever was on the 'Ed Sullivan Show.' The viewing figures of the celebrated Sunday night staple were astounding, thus assuring maximum coverage across the length and breadth of the land.

One interesting phenomenon relating to the Stones in America was the fact that, while so many young men found the Beatles' overt cuteness and saccharine delivery a little too wimpy, the Rolling Stones' musical rough stuff was considered right on. Oftentimes upon arriving at an airport it would be the guys standing front and centre holding signs and even mimicking Jagger's famous two-foot shuffle for the excited teen queens who swooned at their feet. America's male population was quickly finding that looking even vaguely like one's heroes wasn't a bad way to gain the attention of the opposite sex. Suddenly all over the globe barbershops were reporting an across-the-board slowing of business, prompting a few of the more militant amongst them to commence a nationwide billboard campaign showing a very scruffy looking youth with his hair just molesting his collar reading KEEP AMERICA

BEAUTIFUL, GET A HAIRCUT. Figuring out that here at least was a great way to once and for all piss off just about every parent in the land, America's male youth banished the brushcut forever in favour of this latest European fashion trend.

1965 was a very big year for the Stones. By this time it was down to two players – the Beatles (admittedly still languishing at the top of the charts) and the Rolling Stones firmly at number two. That's not to say, however, that there weren't other popular bands. Dave Clark and his rakish Five were very big for a time, as were Liverpool imitators Gerry and the Pacemakers and stolid Billy J. Kramer. No one at that time, though, came as close to pure rebellion as the Rolling Stones.

As time went by the Beatles and the Stones became increasingly tight. Prior to issuing a new single Jagger would invariably ring McCartney so that the two might co-ordinate their release dates, thus avoiding confusion amongst the teenyboppers over which fab new record to buy. Mixing business with pleasure, the Beatles and the Stones actually spent quite a lot of time together over the years. Mick, for instance, showed up at the taping of the Beatles appearance on the international broadcast of 'Our World' in 1967 (where they performed the classic 'All You Need Is Love') as well as tagging along to spend a contemplative weekend with the Maharishi and assorted Fabs in Bangor, Wales, that same year. John and Paul, in turn, sang back-up vocals on the Stones' 'We Love You' off *Their Satanic Majesties Request* LP, and were pictured on the cover. George Harrison, in particular, became close friends with Brian, but also shared a few good vibrations with Jagger.

Although the Rolling Stones were rapidly becoming something of a national treasure in Britain (among the young), there was still the rest of the world to be convinced. Throughout 1965 the band travelled unceasingly – from

LEFT Keith and Bill in Cardiff in September 1964, during the interval of the last-night show at the Capitol Theatre.
OPPOSITE, TOP LEFT A pensive Keith Richards.
TOP RIGHT Keith at the mixer in the mid-sixties with onlookers Andrew Loog Oldham and Charlie. Ian Stewart takes a break (photograph by Gered Mankowitz).
BELOW Keith and his prized Gibson Firebird (1965).

Singapore to New Zealand. Life on the road was sometimes harrowing but, as Jagger has said, 'it's your own fault if you don't have fun on the road.'

By this time the Stones had been introduced to the illicit pleasures of not only speed and drink but cannabis as well. Always a big party band the boys applied themselves admirably to their own personal pursuit of happiness, with Brian and Keith as the musical collective's naughtiest alumni. Unfortunately, Jones wasn't physically as sturdy as the rest of the lads, having been plagued since childhood with several stubborn afflictions, including chronic asthma.

While the other Stones seemed somehow revitalized by the rigours of their gypsy lifestyle it eventually took its toll on Brian. Charlie Watts remembers: 'I think he liked drink and drugs but they weren't very good for him. . . He didn't know he wasn't strong enough mentally or physically to take any of it and, of course, he did everything. Brian was one of these people who did everything to excess.' So precarious was Jones' health that the previous year he had been admitted to hospital in Chicago with a temperature of 105°F. Although the American papers tried to imply that it was the result of a drug overdose, the British press apparently saw it for what it was, an acute bout of walking pneumonia.

Another problem with Brian was his unpopular penchant for trying to lord it over the rest of the band. Jones felt that since he had invited Jagger and Richards to join up with himself and Ian (and had given the group its name) it was therefore *his* band – a concept that didn't go down well with the rest of the guys. When, later, it was discovered that Jones had been taking a bigger cut of the group's first meagre earnings for himself a wound was cut which never really healed.

On 26 February 1965 the classic single 'The Last Time' backed by 'Play With Fire' was released in the UK to advance orders of over 200,000. Although the plaintive B side is generally assumed to be strictly a Jagger/Richards composition the copyright was registered in the name of 'Nanker, Phelge,' a pseudonym for all five Stones. 'The Last Time,' according to Keith, was the first original Jagger/Richards composition of which they felt really proud. Richards' instincts were right on the money, entering the charts at number eight the ⇨

23

Keith Richards and his pricey Bentley (photo By Gered Mankowitz).

pounding dance track soon shot into the top slot where it lodged itself comfortably for a respectable four-week stay.

The group's first US number one, '(I Can't Get No) Satisfaction,' arguably represented the Rolling Stones at their searing best. Issued Stateside on 27 May, the high-energy sizzler was to the Stones what 'I Want To Hold Your Hand' was to the Beatles. A rebellious anthem of pubescent sexual yearning, 'Satisfaction' dug its way into the minds of America's young and old becoming the ultimate tuneful 'hook' for a repressed society. From that moment on, everywhere the Stones went they were beleaguered with questions about the exact meaning of the song's garbled sexually explicit lyrics and the atomic effect the tune's wall-to-wall success had had on the group.

Reporter: Are you any more satisfied now?
Mick: Do mean sexually or philosophically?
Reporter: Both.
Mick: Yeah, we're more satisfied now sexually.
Reporter: How about philosophically and financially?
Mick: Financially dissatisfied, sexually satisfied, philosophically trying.

Smack dab in the middle of the Stones' roaring success with 'Satisfaction' came what the band laughingly refers to as the 'Romford Incident.' On 1 July the *London Evening News* reported that private summonses had been issued against Mick, Bill and Brian for so-called 'insulting behaviour' stemming from a roadside incident in Forest Gate, London. Bill Wyman explains: 'We'd stopped at a garage and I asked the attendant if we could use the bathroom and he immediately got very uptight and said there was no toilet. So in the end we drove out of the garage, down the side road and just pissed up against the wall. The next thing we were arrested, we had to go to court and were accused of urinating all over the forecourt of the garage, swearing abuse and everything, but the judge fined us only about £5 each, or something silly.'

Albumwise, the Stones were doing as well in America as elsewhere. On 20 March *The Rolling Stones, Now!* entered the charts, reaching number five in the top 200. That summer, the group's fourth American LP, *Out Of Our Heads*, became the number one record in the country, outselling even the Beatles for a time. Now that they had made it, really made it, in America the entire country seemed like a fairyland of golden opportunity. For starters, the States was where the music came from, which offered the boys the chance to become absorbed in the on-going rhythm & blues scene in places like Harlem and Chicago. Further, it was quite simply a better place to work, given the multitude of well-equipped, modern studios and easy access to the kind of committed, talented engineers and session players they preferred. Mick Jagger explains: 'We are recording in the US solely because we believe we can produce our best work there. We can record right through from six o'clock in the morning over there without so much as a tea break, and the engineers are first class.'

At home, news of the Stones' decision not to record in Britain caused considerable controversy, further fuelled when stories began to fly that the boys were planning to reside permanently in the States. Tens of thousands of letters poured in both to Decca and the Rolling Stones Fan Club. 'I think this got started because I've just bought a house in Los Angeles,' said Brian. 'It's purely a business investment and neither I nor any of the others have plans to settle out there.'

Curiously, success for Andrew Oldham seemed to be more in the hunt than the actual conquest. After a time he began to weary of the constant drain of not only managing the group but producing their records and acting as confessor, nursemaid and music publisher. Early on, Andrew was introduced to hard-nose music business executive Allen Klein who told him that if ever

the eventuality arose he would be interested in involving himself in the Stones' management.

By the late summer of 1965 Oldham was ready to take Klein up on his offer and on 24 August, he called a meeting between Klein and the Rolling Stones at the Hilton Hotel in London. Jagger remembers: 'Andrew got a hold of Klein and told us he was going to do this and do that and make better deals. We had a very bad record contract where we got five cents a record or whatever. And Klein said, "Well, that's not enough, I can go in and renegotiate, you're very big now, etc. . ." What Andrew wanted to do was get out of the "business" aspect of the Rolling Stones.'

To the Stones, Allen Klein was larger than life, the all-American Uncle Sam, the unrelenting tough guy who would ride in on a white horse and liberate the boys from their past business mistakes and on-going shitty deal with Decca. While Andrew had managed to make the Stones famous and reasonably rich, they were certainly not the millionaires they aspired to be. From that point on Oldham happily stepped down as the group's business manager and relegated the day to day grind of running the band to Klein. Keith Richards later discussed the controversial move: ⇨

Mick Jagger sitting pretty
(Photograph by Gered Mankowitz).

Keith: Andrew got Klein to meet us, to get us out of the original English scene. There was a new deal with Decca to be made and no one really knew. . . who's actually making the money. [Klein] was managing financial advisor for Donovan, the Dave Clark Five and Herman's Hermits, who were all enormous then. . . The only thing that impressed me about him was that he said he could do it. Nobody else had said that.

Question: Did the Stones decide together to go with Klein?

Keith: I really pushed them. I was saying 'let's turn things around, let's do something' [or] we go down to Decca and tell them to do it with us. . . which is what we did that very day with Klein. [We] just went down there and scared the shit out of them.

Question: You originally signed a two-year contract with [Decca]?

Keith: Yeah, in '63. [Allen] did a good job, man. Andrew told us that Klein was a fantastic cat for dealing with those people, which we couldn't do. So we had to get someone who knew how to do it or someone who'd fuck it up once and for all.

ABOVE LEFT The Stones live in Dortmund, Germany (1 March 1967); **BELOW** Jagger with two of his many famous girlfriends. With Chrissie Shrimpton (left, November 1966), and (right) Marianne Faithfull emerging from Marlborough Street Court, London, after being remanded for possession of cannabis (June 1969); **BOTTOM** Mick during the press conference at Granada Studios, London, after his three-month prison sentence for possession of cannabis was changed to a conditional discharge (July 1967).

On 5 September 1965 the Stones flew off to Los Angeles to begin work on their next single 'Get Off Of My Cloud.' This was backed with 'I'm Free' in the US and 'The Singer Not The Song' in the UK. As a lyricist, Jagger was definitely improving

with 'Cloud's' obtuse, multi-dimensional lyrics stealing the show from Richards' choppy, driving riffs. A few weeks before, Bob Dylan had remarked to Keith that he could have written 'Satisfaction' but doubted seriously if the Stones could have produced anything as deep or lyrically significant as his 'Mr Tambourine Man.' If 'Get Off Of My Cloud' was Jagger's answer to Dylan, then he rose to the occasion admirably. By 4 November, the hard-driving single was simultaneously number one in both America and England. Later that same month the band's new album, *December's Children (And Everybody's)*, was released, reaching number two in the American charts.

Although Brian, Mick and Keith had always had their share of women they were still pretty much all playing the field. At the time, Bill was still happily married to his teen sweetheart, Diane, and Charlie had long been going with blonde beauty Shirley Ann Shepherd (whom he would marry on 14 October 1964). Of the three remaining Stone bachelors, Brian had a fairly steady thing going with model Linda Lawrence, whom he had met in 1962 while gigging with the Stones at a small jazz club in Windsor. Before long, Jones accepted an invitation to stay with Linda and her parents, thus freeing him from the artistic squalor of his Edith Grove flat in Chelsea which he shared with Mick and Keith. 'It was Brian's flat to begin with,' remembers Lawrence. 'He had one room to himself, and Keith and Mick would share the other one. They were all sort of still living at home, but this is where they had a kind of flat, their own independence. No food, and the kitchen was filthy, and these typical boys all living together. After we'd been going out with each other for a few months my parents wanted to meet Brian, so he put on a nice clean shirt and brought them up to Richmond. After that, Brian came down to dinner a few times and loved the family so much that he kind of moved in 'cause his flat wasn't very nice.'

After the couple had been dating for about a year Linda became pregnant. Although her parents weren't pleased they were supportive, something that couldn't be said of Jones' naturally conservative parents. Initially, Brian took the news

TOP RIGHT Keith Richards and Anita Pallenberg perusing the morning paper.
TOP LEFT Keith and Anita in August 1969 with new-born son Marlon.
ABOVE Richards with his Fender Telecaster (1966).

quite well (even considering marriage for a time) but seemed to change his tune after going off to America for the first time with the band. 'I got cards and letters from him saying he loved me. Then Brian took all these strange psychedelic drugs. When he came back, he was like a different person. And Andrew and everyone was saying "Oh, family man," making Brian feel very insecure. He already was, and it didn't help.'

Although Julian Brian Jones' birth (in July 1964) effectively squashed the couple's relationship, Brian was secretly very taken with his new son and felt badly about rejecting his young ⇨

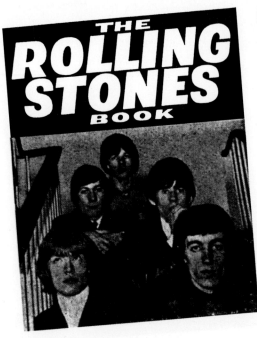

FOR

ROLLING STONES FANS ONLY!

edited by the Stones themselves

No. 1—JUNE EDITION
(editor Mick Jagger)

ON SALE NOW

No. 2 will be published on 10th JULY
Reserve your copy NOW as supplies are strictly limited

Ad for the monthly magazine *The Rolling Stones Book* which ran to 30 issues from June 1964 to November 1966.

family. Linda remembers the last time Julian saw his father. 'Brian was in Richmond Hospital with kidney trouble. It was very strange for both of them because of not seeing each other. That was the last time I saw Brian before he died.'

Mick Jagger's first serious relationship was with office worker Chrissie Shrimpton, kid sister of the famous sixties supermodel, Jean. Chrissie, of course, was with Mick very early on in the game and so vividly recalls Jagger's first poverty-stricken days with the Stones: 'Mick would call at my flat to take me out to the pictures and stand in the doorway, smiling shyly and looking for all the world like a little boy lost. Often I'd ask him if he'd eaten, and he'd airily reel off a list of meals he'd had in the last twenty-four hours. But I soon learned to catch him out. He's the sort of person who can't lie. When this happened, I'd tell him off and fling on my apron and start to cook. I can't tell you how many of our dates have been spent in the kitchen.'

After the Stones' initial wave of success in Britain, Chrissie became something of a celebrity herself. Appearing regularly in all the papers she even penned her own column for *Mod Magazine*. Entitled 'From London With Luv By Chrissie Shrimpton,' she reported featherweight stories of her encounters with the rich and famous and commented on the London music scene. Unfortunately, as with Brian and Linda, there would be no wedding bells for Mick and Chrissie. After dating exclusively for more than three years, in December 1966 they broke up for good. 'We were very much in love,' said Shrimpton at the time, 'but we argued all the time. As time goes on you begin to feel different about life and each other. There wasn't a row. We broke by mutual agreement.' But Chrissie was secretly devastated by the split. Deeply depressed, and alone, she attempted suicide that Christmas. Mick Jagger, meanwhile, kept predictably mum over the incident.

Of the three semi-available Stones, Keith Richards remained the most independent. Although in the early days of Stonesmania he too was steadily seeing model Linda Keith, he was reportedly squiring several other luscious London dolly birds as well. 'We try and encourage our girlfriends not to get too wrapped up in us as we are away on tour so much,' Richards has said. 'I don't know how she can stand me anyhow. I can't really take her out as too many people stop us in the street. Once in a while, though, we make it out for a good continental meal together.'

The ringleader in the Stones' sexual circus, however, had to be blonde German actress and fashion model Anita Pallenberg. Sneaking backstage to meet the band following a 1965 performance in Munich during the Stones' second European tour, Anita immediately made tracks for Brian. Like any self-respecting groupie at the time she invited Brian to smoke a joint with her. And like any self-respecting counter-culture musician he gratefully accepted. Back at the hotel, instead of a steamy one night stand the emotionally frail Jones curled up in Anita's arms and cried all night. Pallenberg remembers her unhappy little boy lover: 'He was so vulnerable, he was so upset about Mick and Keith. They had teamed up on him and I really felt sorry for him. Brian had everything going for him but he was a very complicated person.' After a few months of long-distance dating Brian brought Anita over to England to live with him. Low in the esteem of the other Stones at the time, the boys were suitably impressed with this bewitching blonde and looked up to Brian for his prize catch.

While the other Stones were outwardly very impressed with this exotic, worldly, well-spoken young woman, Mick saw her hard-line approach as a threat to his psychological dominance over the band. Now that the Stones had made it and the whole world saw Mick as the frontman, the last thing he wanted was someone around to further encourage Brian to feel the Stones were still his group. 'Mick really tried to put me down,' says Anita, 'thereby putting Brian down in the process, but there was no way this sort of crude, lippy guy was going to do a number on me. I was always able to squelch him. I found out that if you stand up to Mick he crumbles. He tried to get Brian to stop seeing me, called me poison. He ordered his girlfriend, Chrissie, not to go near me. I figured he was jealous because I was the one close to Brian.'

For the sickly and unhappy Brian, Anita was a God-send. Ill at ease about not only his role in the group but his personal appearance, Anita helped him to relax and take many of the Stones' everyday dramas in his stride. Together the couple soon became fixtures at all the right parties, mixing with the elite of London high society. Among their new-found friends were

Eton-educated art dealer and impresario Robert Fraser, hip photographer Michael Cooper, Guinness heir Tara Browne, Paul Getty, and man-about-town Paul McCartney. '[Brian] had a wonderful curiosity,' Pallenberg recalls, 'he wanted to know everything that was going on, wanted to meet new people, new ideas, learn the new dances. . . The other Stones were more frightened. . . Except for Brian all the Stones at that time were really suburban squares.'

February 1966 saw two new singles out world-wide. The first, 'As Tears Go By' backed by 'Gotta Get Away,' nipped out at the tail end of 1965 climbing up the US charts to a respectable number six, while '19th Nervous Breakdown' (backed by 'Sad Day' in the US and 'As Tears Go By' in the UK) entered the British charts at number two, sliding up easily to number one within just a few days. In April 1966 the all-new album *Aftermath* was released, followed in November of the same year by the intriguing compilation album *Big Hits (High Tide And Green Grass)*. All in all, a dazzling amount of new product to choose from by the discriminating fan. Originally, *Aftermath* was called *Could You Walk On The Water?*, but Decca voted thumbs down, saying: 'We will not issue it with this title at any price!'

Out on the road again that summer the Stones were by now getting quite accustomed to the non-stop lunacy of being the world's number one rock 'n' roll band. Starting the ambitious tour in Lynn, Massachusetts, the entourage moved on to New York where the group's custom-built Vox equipment was lifted from a van parked on the street. Days later, while playing a sold-out gig in Montreal all hell broke loose as the keyed-up fans crashed through several barricades facing the stage. ⇨

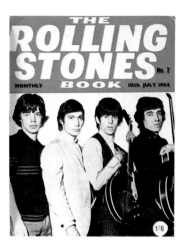
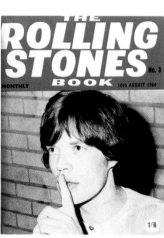
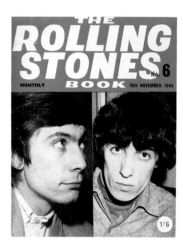
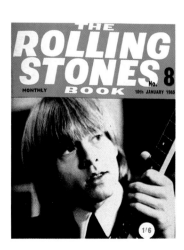
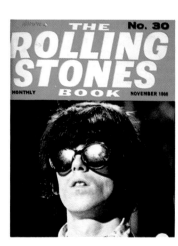

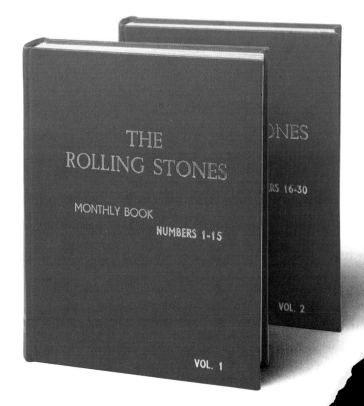

The Stones as the Beatles had their own monthly magazine (from the same publisher entitled *The Rolling Stones Book*. It ran to thirty issues from June 1964 to November 1966. These days a complete set is extremely pricey and hard to find.

Strangely, the Rolling Stones' first appearance on album was not one of their own, but rather on a compilation LP. This was based on the British TV show 'Thank Your Lucky Stars' (1963) and featured a rather raunchy version of Chuck Berry's 'Come On.'

On the success of this album Decca issued a further compilation, this time built around on the British television show 'Ready Steady Go!,' (1964) with the Stones contributing the songs 'I Wanna Be Your Man,' and 'Come On.' Above is Brian Jones on the set of 'Ready Steady Go!' with presenter Keith Fordyce in 1965.

The album *Saturday Club* (1964) was moulded on the popular BBC radio show of the same name, and featured the Stones' scheduled second single 'Poison Ivy' backed by 'Fortune Teller' which Decca, fearing it was too weak, never released.

The compilation *Fourteen,* to which the Stones contributed the song 'Surprise Surprise,' was released by Decca in 1965 with all profits and artists' royalties donated to the Lord Taverner's National Playing fields Association. An American version of *Fourteen* was later issued by London Records titled *England's Greatest Hitmakers* in 1965.

Contributing to the chaos was the fact that the Stones had come on late (nearly midnight) following a long intermission and the kids were predictably edgy. As the group's only protection from their spaced-out admirers melted away the Stones quite reasonably ran for their lives. Longtime Rolling Stones promotion exec Pete Bennett explains what happened next: 'Keith Richards got hit over the head with a flying bottle. Jagger also got hit. I could see in Mick's eyes he was going crazy being chased like that. Charlie took his high hat stand and was swinging it around. I don't know how many people he hit with it before he got away. As it was we ran into the dressing room, and couldn't get out until early the next morning. The only thing we could hear was sirens. Everytime I opened the door, somebody would shout "keep the door locked." Fortunately, there was a nurse with us who took care of Keith and Mick's

cuts, which weren't serious. Brian spent the whole time in the corner, quietly strumming his guitar.'

One of the all-time most unpleasant happenings while traversing the States occurred in Rochester, New York, prior to a performance at the Community War Memorial Arena. Taking the stage for a pre-show sound check, the band hadn't gotten through their first number when the chief of police yelled out: 'Come on, isn't that enough?' A few minutes later several of his underlings stepped forward to try and physically stop the Stones from rehearsing further. 'Why don't you shut your goddam mouth, man!' Keith suddenly screamed at the astounded chief. Bolting up to Richards, the chief positioned himself about six inches from the guitarist's face and screamed: 'What did you say to me?' With that the normally laid back Keith spun around and clobbered the poor old guy over the head. Instantly, every ⇨ 34

TOP Recorded in January and February 1964 at Regent Studios, London, and released on 26 April 1964, the Stones début album, known simply in the UK as *The Rolling Stones* (significantly one of the first albums without a group's name on the front) rocketed to number one in the UK charts and stayed there for an incredible fifty-one week stint. On its release in America that May under the title

England's Newest Hit Makers The Rolling Stones, London Records generously included a free colour poster. Promotional copies of this album (above right) were pressed in England and rushed to the States. Contemporary opinion should perhaps be left to mentor Andrew Loog Oldham who comments on the liner notes: 'The Rolling Stones are more than just a group, they are a way of life!'

Shown above (left) is the classy London label for the first Stones album release in the US, *England's Newest Hit Makers The Rolling Stones*. To the right is the white label for the London promotional release of this first US album (ironically stating 'Made in England').

BELOW With the introduction of the cassette, an exciting new format was made available to the record-buying public. Not to be left out, the Stones' first two albums were issued as cassettes by Decca in 1965

LEFT An extremely rare copy of the first UK album signed by each of the five Stones.

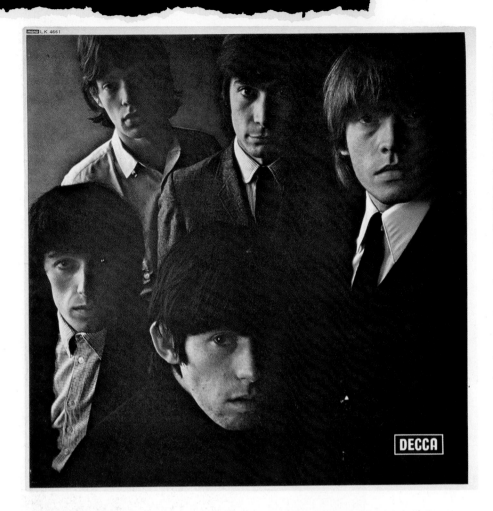

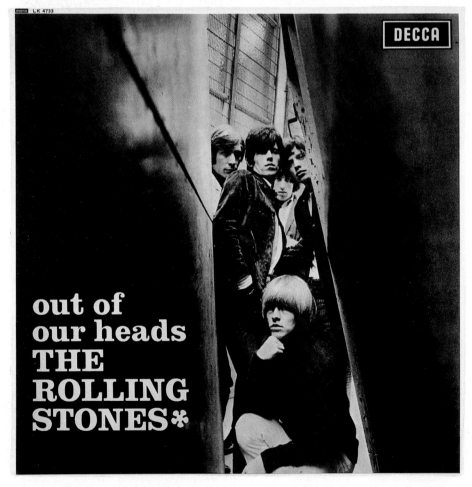

The Stones' second album, *The Rolling Stones No. 2* (top left), was released in the UK in January 1965, and previously in the US in October 1964 as *12 x 5*. In 1965 *Out Of Our Heads* was issued in the UK (bottom left), in the States (right, third from top), and as an export album (right, second from top). The Stones' fifth US album, *December's Children (And Everybody's)*, was issued in late 1965.

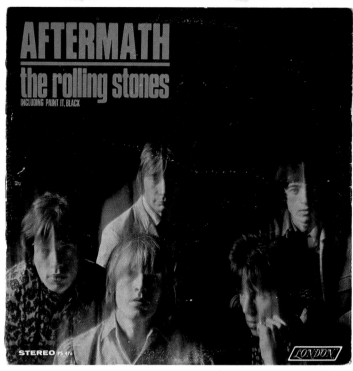

In July 1964, I was engineering a session for Jack Nitzsche at RCA in Hollywood; the song was "Yes sir, that's my baby". In walked the Rolling Stones and Andrew Oldham, who had stopped by to say hello to Jack, a friend they had met thru Phil Spector. In December of 1964, we did our first session together. Andrew had phoned me from England, and wanted to do a session en route to Australia. I was thrilled; since then, we have worked together thru "The Last Time"; "Satisfaction"; "Cloud"; "Breakdown" and a number of albums, in a way that has been rewarding both artistically and professionally, for working with the Stones is extremely exhilarating. They never go the easy route;—from the moment Mick and Keith run a song down to the rest of the group,—to Brian deciding on an acoustic or electric guitar, or something more bizarre,—to Bill sorting out a bass pattern,—to Charlie laying down the tempo;—to their friend Jack Nitzsche (always on the dates) or Road Manager Stu picking out chords on piano, organ, harpsichord or anything else that happens to be lying around. To some many hours later, at a final take,—it's all great. In this business of dubious standards, it's been great working with the Stones, who, contrary to the countless jibes of mediocre comedians all over the world, are real professionals, and a gas to work with.

Dave Hassinger, Engineer

SIDE ONE
MOTHERS LITTLE HELPER 2:40
STUPID GIRL 2:52
LADY JANE 3:06
UNDER MY THUMB 3:20
DONCHA BOTHER ME 2:35
GOIN' HOME 11:35

SIDE TWO
FLIGHT 505 3:25
HIGH AND DRY 3:06
OUT OF TIME 5:15
IT'S NOT EASY 2:52
I AM WAITING 3:10
TAKE IT OR LEAVE IT 2:47
THINK 3:10
WHAT TO DO 2:32

Vocals: Mick Jagger, Keith Richard
Guitars: Keith Richard, Brian Jones
Bass: Bill Wyman
Drums: Charlie Watts
Percussion: Charlie Watts, Jack Nitzsche, Mick Jagger
Marimbas, Bells:
Brian Jones, Charlie Watts, Bill Wyman
Dulcimer, Sitar: Brian Jones
Piano, Organ, Harpsichord:
Jack Nitzsche, Ian Stewart, Brian Jones, Bill Wyman
Lighting: Mick Jagger

Photography: Guy Webster, Jerrold Schatzberg
Cover Design: Sandy Beach

Songs by Mick Jagger and Keith Richard
Arranged by The Rolling Stones
Engineer: Dave Hassinger
Recorded at RCA Studios, Hollywood
Producer: Andrew Loog Oldham

DECCA Regd. Trade Mark

THE DECCA RECORD COMPANY LTD. LONDON
© 1966, The Decca Record Company Limited, London.

Laminated with 'Clarifoil' made by British Colanese Limited
Printed in England by Robert Stace.

Keeping track of the Stones' multitudinous releases in the UK and US was sport for only the thoroughly committed. Case in point, *Aftermath*, released in April 1966 in Britain (with fourteen tracks) was the Stones' fourth album (top left, signed back cover shown below it). The Stateside release in July 1966 (with eleven tracks) was their seventh (top right). *The Rolling Stones, Now!* was the third American release and contained songs from early LPs and 45s.

RIGHT An example of the Fan Club's official membership card, lapel button, complete with a black and white photograph of the boys.

cop in the place was all over Richards. 'Wait a minute!' yelled Andrew Oldham, ploughing into the middle of the human pile rolling about the stage, 'he didn't realize who it was!' Fortunately, after a couple more well-placed punches at the badly beaten Richards the police packed it in and (after threatening to arrest the entire band) allowed the boys to return to their hotel.

During the summer of 1966 the prophetic 'Paint It Black,' one of the Stones' most haunting and intriguing singles, flew to number one around the world. One day later the caustic, cautionary tune 'Mother's Little Helper' was also issued, becoming the first unmistakable anti-drug homily ever. As prolific as they were controversial, an unprecedented third single in as many months, 'Have You Seen Your Mother, Baby, Standing In The Shadow?' snuck out that September, driving home the unarguable reality of the world's insatiable hunger for Stones product. Tired of the same predictable graphic style used by the record companies on their sleeves the Stones decided to appear in full drag on the jacket for the latest single. Photographed in New York's Central Park by Jerry Schatzberg, the five young 'ladies' even adopted daring new names to go with this unexpected change of gender. Brian, the tartiest looking member of the group became Flossie, Mick was Sara, Bill now Penelope, Keith was Milly, and Charlie (still with moustache) became known for the occasion as Millicent.

Another Stones-related fantasy photo session took place that November with Brian Jones dressing up in full Nazi regalia with Anita Pallenberg for the cover of a German magazine. Wearing the prized Chivalry Cross around his neck (and crushing a doll beneath his jackboots) Jones predictably caught hell in the media, defending himself only with the offhand remark, 'I wear a Nazi uniform to show I'm anti-Nazi.'

The Stones entered the magic year of 1967 with the release (on 13 January) of 'Let's Spend The Night Together' (backed by the ethereal 'Ruby Tuesday'). Flying to New York to make yet another promotional appearance on the 'Ed Sullivan Show' the band met with the producers who (along with Sullivan) decided that if the band were going to perform the very suspect number then they would have to change the words to 'Let's Spend Some Time Together' in order to preserve the morals of the innocent nation. Almost immediately several American radio stations summarily banned the record, as did a few select record retailers.

When the big day arrived, the Stones took the stage leaving the entire nation wondering just what they would actually sing on the live broadcast. In the end they did a version that oscillated back and forth between the offending lyrics and Sullivan's sanitized version. Once again, the naughty Stones had deeply upset the super-straight showman.

By this time Mick and Marianne Faithfull were very much an item. To all the world they were the epitome of the jet-setting, super-hip rock 'n' roll couple. Travelling the globe together, attending the opera, gracing all the most exclusive galleries and restaurants, Mick and Marianne rivalled even Justin and Twiggy as the Swinging Sixties' swingingest pair. ⊃ 36

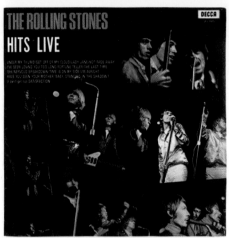

BELOW *Got LIVE If You Want It!* was released in 1966 Stateside and was the first Rolling Stones 'live' album — or was it? Two tracks, 'Fortune Teller' and 'I've Been Loving You Too Long' naughtily feature overdubbed screams.

MIDDLE Never released in Britain, the raucous LP was originally entitled *Hits LIVE*, but was later renamed *Have You Seen Your Mother LIVE!* (top) and was manufactured by Decca for export only.

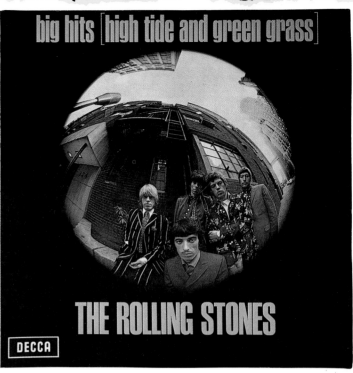

TOP *Big Hits (High Tide and Green Grass)*, released in Britain in November 1966 and in the US in April 1966, was the first of many Stones' 'greatest hits' compilations, once again with differing sleeves and tracks. *Big Hits* was also their first gatefold sleeve and included a four-page booklet of photos (bottom).

BOTTOM Interestingly, the US sleeve (above) used a photograph originally intended to adorn an LP entitled *Could You Walk On The Water?* Decca, predictably, refused to have anything to do with such a sacrilegious title. This would not be the last time Decca and the Stones were to seriously disagree.

Faithfull remembers: 'Whatever we did was reported in detail. We were the beautiful couple of the sixties, and for me it was very, very exciting. To be very young, very free, very rich and very careless. But it went too far, and when it got too much, they had to slap us down. That's when it really became a nightmare. . . It was really a reaction of society against what society itself had done, they had built us up too high and now they would tear us down.'

By February 1967 the Stones' amazing career was on track with the release of their classic album *Between The Buttons*. As the sixties wore on the top performers of the day became far more than simply popular entertainers. Important artists like John Lennon, Bob Dylan, Canadian poet Leonard Cohen, and

of course, the Stones were notable not only for what they sang but for what they had to say as well. Among the Rolling Stones, Mick was perhaps the most widely quoted member of the group, with Keith and then Brian running close behind as resident wisemen.

Questioned constantly on their views about everything from the Vietnam War to the thorny issue of the legalization of grass, the Stones soon realized that whatever they said would surely be reported around the world. As such, they, and indeed other big groups, seized the opportunity to comment upon what they perceived to be the graver inequities of modern society. Case in point, Brian Jones: 'Our generation is growing up with us and they believe in the same things we do. Nearly all of them think like us and are questioning some of the basic immoralities which are tolerated in present day society – the war in Vietnam, persecution of homosexuals, illegality of abortion and drug taking. All of these things are immoral. We are making our own statement, others are making more intellectual ones. We believe there can be no evolution without revolution. I realize there are other inequities; the ratio between affluence and reward for work done is all wrong. I know I earn too much, but I'm still young and there's something spiteful inside me which makes me want to hold on to what I've got.'

Philosophy aside, the Stones were continuing to do big ➪ 41

The Stones were not very big in the memorabilia stakes in the early 1960s, but what has survived is of great value. Jigsaw puzzles, bubblegum cards, photoramas, and the statutory books and magazines were all hot stuff for Stones-obsessed teens back then, causing parents everywhere to ante-up the petty cash or surrender to a non-stop barrage of adolescent pleading.

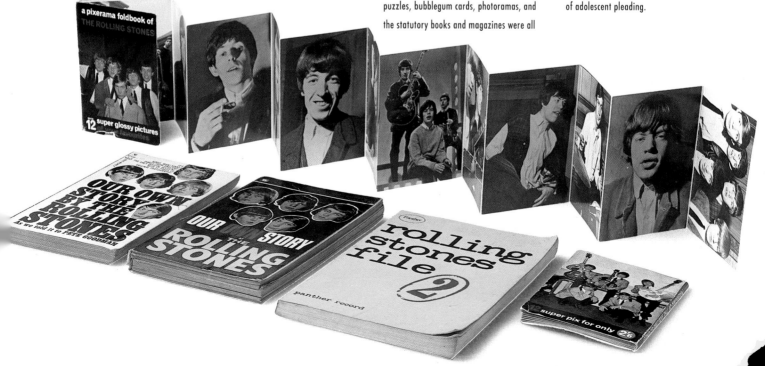

Between The Buttons (1967) became the Stones' sixth UK (top left) and eighth US (top right) album respectively. There were twelve distinctive tracks on each, but there were also significant differences. The American release included the new single 'Let's Spend The Night Together' along with 'Ruby Tuesday,' replacing Britain's 'Back Street Girl' and 'Please Go Home.' Both back covers highlighted Charlie Watts' original drawings (Decca back cover

left), along with his engaging, off-the-cuff rhymes. Mick Jagger's comment on the album, however, was something less than enthusiastic: ' "Back Street Girl" and "Connection" are really the only decent songs. The rest are more or less rubbish.'

BOTTOM The Stones' fan club similarly availed themselves of Charlie's artistic talents for their 1966 Christmas card (below). The inside message and postage details are also shown.

Their Satanic Majesties Request (1967) (inner and outer gatefolds shown above) was to many the Stones' less than satisfactory answer to the Beatles' stunning *Sgt. Pepper*. 'We were just so pissed off doing what we did and didn't want to go in the studio and cut another fucking rock album,' Jagger commented. 'So we just went in and did that.' *Majesties* was the world's first 3-D album cover, costing a massive £15,000 to produce. The jacket was shot by their good friend, the late Michael Cooper, who had also photographed the celebrated *Sgt. Pepper* cover. Interestingly, this was the first studio album not produced by Andrew Loog Oldham and heralded a parting of the ways between the group and their off-beat mentor.

RIGHT *Flowers* (1967) was a Decca compilation album, produced for export only, and was released in the US and several European countries. Legend has it there was a cryptic message on the front cover with each of the Stones faces on the top of a flower stem: all had leaves except for poor Brian's flower!

Sympathy for the Devil
No Expectations
Dear Doctor
Parachute Woman
Jig-Saw Puzzle

Street Fighting Man
Prodigal Son
Stray Cat Blues
Factory Girl
Salt of the Earth

Written by Mick Jagger and Keith Richard
Produced by Jimmy Miller
Recorded at Olympic Studios
Engineers Glyn Johns, Eddie and Gene
All selections Mirage Music Ltd
We are deeply indebted to Nicky Hopkins and to many friends

DECCA
High Trade Mark

Stereo SKL 4955

The Decca Record Company Limited
Decca House, 9 Albert Embankment, London, S.E.1.

© 1968 The Decca Record Company Limited, London

Sleeve printed in England by Robert Stace & Co. Ltd.

*Rolling Stones
Beggars Banquet*

R.S.V.P.

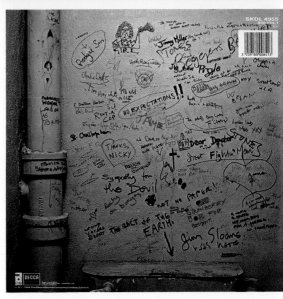

Beggars Banquet (1968) was the final album featuring Brian Jones. Decca refused the first sleeve design of a lavatory wall covered in graffiti (right). Jagger then wanted a brown paper sleeve with 'Unfit for children' stamped on it, but Decca still refused. The LP was eventually issued in November in a cream-coloured sleeve with a stunning inner photograph. The original sleeve was released some twenty years later. This album, by the way remains Keith Richards' favourite.

Jagger is mad over LP sleeve ban

THE BANNED STONES' LP COVER...

Mick Jagger protests against 'Dylan offensive' charge

IT is " We " against " Them-and-They " time again in the Rolling Stones' life, as they run head-on into another fracas with the " oldies." This time it looks as though the writing is on the wall " for the new album " Beggars the Establishment at recording com-find the new album

MICK Jagger is furious at a top-level decision to ban the sleeve design for their next album, " Beggars' Banquet," because it is alleged to be " offensive."

MICK JAGGER gets the custard pies flying as a finale to the Stones' "Beggar's Banquet " lunch last week. He gets a pie back and seems to like it, while on his left, LORD HARLECH, Welsh TV tycoon and once connected with Jackie Kennedy, seems to be enjoying it. Next, BRIAN JONES gets ready to blast off, and gets another pie in the eye, this time from publicist LES PERRIN, who got biggest coverage of the year for the stunt. He also

STONED AT LUNCH!
With pie-in-the-eye on the menu

ABOVE Newspaper headlines covering events surrounding the *Beggars Banquet* débâcle. RIGHT The 1968 TV film 'The Rock 'n' Roll Circus' was to feature stars such as John Lennon, Eric Clapton, and the Who. The show is still awaiting its premiere. BELOW is a thank-you letter from Mick Jagger to the Who.

business as the year rolled on. Now that Allen Klein had successfully renegotiated their contract with Decca the boys were at last making big bucks, allowing them both more time and a larger appetite for the good life, a pursuit the band took to heart. The Stones, however, continued to pay their dues. On 5 February the *News Of The World* reported that Mick Jagger had taken LSD while visiting the Moody Blues at their communal home in Roehampton (known as Roehampton Raves). In fact, the paper had mistakenly quoted from an interview Brian Jones had given the previous year in which he discussed his initiation into psychedelia. As a result, Jagger appeared on the popular Eamonn Andrews show announcing his intention to file suit against the paper.

On 12 February fifteen police officers mounted a surprise raid at Keith Richards' home in response to an anonymous tip indicating that the Stones were holding a 'drug orgy.' 'It just so happened that we had all taken acid and were in a completely freaked-out state when the police arrived,' says Richards. 'There was a big knock at the door. Everybody was just sort of gliding down slowly from the whole day of freaking about. The TV was on with the sound off and the record player was on. Strobe lights were flickering. Marianne had just decided that she wanted a bath and had wrapped herself up in a rug and was watching the box. 'Bang, bang, bang, there's this big knock at the door and I went to answer it. Oh, look, there's lots of little ladies and gentlemen outside. . .' ⇨

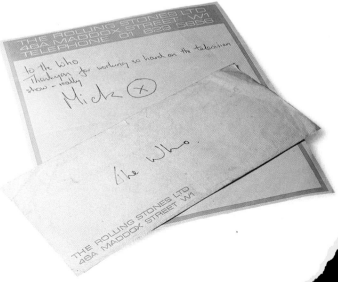

Sitting on the chesterfield (nude except for a big furry rug) Marianne Faithfull was far too stoned to actually fathom the seriousness of what was going on. She remembers: 'Through my acid haze, I remember being amazed at the number of policemen who were crowding into the room. Eighteen or nineteen of them, three of them policewomen who I guess had come to search me.'

By the time the police had succeeded in rampaging through Keith's home they had come up with only four amphetamine tablets in a jacket belonging to Marianne (which Jagger claimed was his and so was subsequently charged for possession of a dangerous drug). Richards was busted for allowing his estate, Redlands, to be used for the purpose of smoking cannabis resin.

The naked, tripped-out Marianne Faithfull (referred to as Miss X in the press and throughout the trial) was not charged.

On 10 May a similar raid was mounted at Brian Jones' flat in South Kensington, London, resulting in both Jones and his mate Prince Stanislaus Klossowski being hauled down to Chelsea Police Station and charged with possession of cannabis. After quite an extended interview Brian and his blue-blood pal made the required £250 bail and slipped out into the foggy London night like a couple of wounded hounds. 'The bust was the beginning of the end for poor Brian,' commented a close friend.

All this adversity, fortunately, didn't really stifle the Stones' creative forces. Brian laid down a soprano saxophone over-dub on the Beatles' 'Baby You're A Rich Man' at Olympic Studios just two days after the unhappy affair. A month later Mick and Keith joined with the Fab Four once again to add a few oohhhs and aaahhs to the background vocals on their class sixties' anthem 'All You Need Is Love.' Only days later a second Stones compilation album, the aptly named *Flowers*, was issued in America on London Records. Featuring three previously unreleased tracks ('Sittin' On A Fence,' 'My Girl,' and 'Ride On Baby') the gritty, blues-inspired album sold well, handy since it looked like the lads would require quite a bit of expensive legal representation over the next little while.

When Keith and Mick finally went to trial at Chichester Crown Court in West Sussex on 27 June 1967 the press pointed their reporting to some very abstract avenues of inquiry. 'Pop idol Mick Jagger went to court today in a lime-green jacket,' read one newspaper, 'a green and black tie, floral patterned white shirt and olive green pin-striped trousers to answer drug accusations.' Keith's fashion sense too came under scrutiny – 'Richards stood in the dock wearing a four-button Mod-style black suit and a Regency striped, high-necked shirt.' But wait! There were yet more startling revelations concerning the famous pair. 'After lunch Jagger wore a double-breasted green jacket, cream silk shirt and fancy grey tie and Richards had a black coat and orange tie. Following a break in testimony the accused pair returned to the courtroom wearing each other's jackets.' Definitely the apparel of confirmed reprobates to be sure.

As to the almost irrelevant issue of their eventual guilt or innocence very little was made. What a Rolling Stone had for lunch, however, was still bloody big news. 'For Jagger,' wrote the *Daily Mirror*, 'there was prawn cocktail, roast lamb and mint sauce, fresh strawberries and cream and two half-bottles of Beaujolais. Luncheon was delivered by Mr Arthur Collings and cost £2.60.' Stop the presses!

Without doubt the most bizarre culinary ingredient of this or any other trial centred on what the media termed the infamous Mars Bar incident. When the local constables entered the drawing room they were alleged to have found a Mars Bar protruding from an intimate portion of Marianne Faithfull's anatomy. Although no such occurrence was ever referred to during the trial, that didn't stop Fleet Street from running the story in banner headlines. 'It's enough to put you off candy forever,' quipped the wry John Lennon to a reporter at the time.

Hoopla aside, inside the court room it was all serious business as prosecutor Malcolm Morris hammered out in dour tones the sordid events of the night in question. Called as a witness for the prosecution, Police Sergeant John Challen led the legal attack against Mick, stating: 'I first went into the drawing room and then went upstairs to a bedroom. There I found a green jacket in the left-hand pocket of which I found a small phial containing four tablets. I took the jacket downstairs and Jagger admitted the jacket belonged to him. He said the tablets were also his and that his doctor prescribed them. I asked Jagger who his doctor was, and Jagger replied [it was] Dr Dixon-Firth. I asked what the tablets were for and Jagger replied, "to stay awake and work." '

ABOVE The now highly collectible mobile which was used for promotional purposes in British record shops.

OPPOSITE PAGE *Through The Past, Darkly (Big Hits Vol. 2)* (1969) was the Stones' second compilation album. Once again the band broke new ground by issuing the record in a unique gatefold hexagon-shaped sleeve.

The album was quite rightly dedicated to Brian Jones and contains an epitaph for the Stones' brilliant guitarist on the inner gatefold:

When this you see, remember me
and bear me in your mind.
Let all the world say what they may
speak of me as you find.

greetings **charliebillbrianmickkeith**

*Dear readers of the New Musical Express.
Jumping Jack Flash is really gassed that he made number one.
So are the Rolling Stones. Thankyou.
We are slaving over a hot album which is coming out next month. Until then.*

Mick Jagger
Bill Wyman
Keith Richard
Brian Jones

*Dearest readers of the Melody Maker.
Thankyou for making Jack Flash number one. We are pleased.
So is Jack Flash. We are slaving over a new album which should be out next month.
Have*
Mick Jagger
love Charlie
Bill Wyman
Keith Richard
Brian Jones

Called by the defence, Dr Firth confirmed that he had not prescribed the 'pep pills' to Jagger in writing but had done so verbally. To general disbelief Judge Block ordered the jury to dismiss the defence that the amphetamine was legitimately prescribed. 'I have ruled in law that these remarks cannot be regarded as a prescription by a duly authorized medical practitioner and it therefore follows that the defence open to Mr Jagger is not available to him. I therefore direct you [the jury] that there is no defence to this charge.' Deliberating for only five minutes the jury found Mick guilty. Accordingly, the hard-nosed Block refused bail and remanded the obviously shaken Jagger to immediate police custody.

The next morning it was Keith's turn on the hot seat with prosecutor Morris (bolstered by the previous day's easy win) diving in with both feet. 'In the room were eight men and one young woman. The settee in the drawing room was the main piece of furniture and there was a stone table. On the table was a tin marked "incense" and incense was what the tin contained. Also on the table was a briar pipe bowl which was taken away, carefully preserved, and the contents analyzed and found to contain traces of cannabis resin.

'On that same table a woman detective constable noticed some ash. This she carefully scraped off and put into a small transparent bag. Analysis showed that this, too, contained

cannabis resin. In one of the bedrooms on the first floor a Detective Sergeant found a pudding basin containing three cigarette ends and a quantity of what appeared to be cigarette ash. Analysis showed this to contain cannabis resin as well.'

Richards' defence, aptly handled by legal luminary Sir Michael Havers, centred on the fact that a hanger-on named Paul Schneiderman was the only person actually found with any cannabis on his person the evening of the raid. Richards' contention was that if any dope were indeed smoked that weekend it was without his knowledge and consent and, therefore, he should not be held culpable. Unfortunately, the jury didn't buy it and after deliberating for less than an hour found the famous defendant guilty as charged.

Richards was given one year in jail and a £500 fine. Jagger fared a little better with a three-month term and £100 in costs. Led out of the courtroom in handcuffs, Mick was carted off to Brixton Prison while Keith (and co-defendant Robert Fraser) were remanded to Wormwood Scrubs, one of the most notorious jails in Britain. Richards recalls the particulars of his new accommodation: 'They don't give you a knife and fork, they give you a spoon with very blunt edges so you can't do yourself in. They don't give you a belt in case you hang yourself. It's that bad in there. They give you a little piece of paper and a pencil. Both Robert and I, the first thing we did was sit down

and write: "Dear Mum, don't worry, I'm in here and someone's working to get me out, da-da-da." The first thing you automatically do when you wake up is drag the chair to the window and look to see what you can see out of the window. It's an automatic reaction. That one little square of sky, trying to reach it. It's amazing. I was going to have to make these little Christmas trees that go on cakes. And sewing up mailbags.'

As Richards bemoaned his sorry plight, Jagger too was coming to terms with life behind bars. 'I visited Mick in Brixton Prison the morning after his imprisonment,' remembers Marianne. 'He was terribly frightened and very, very upset. In fact, freaked out. Of course, I wasn't surprised. Although I wasn't in jail I knew how he felt, because it really was like the whole of the Establishment was out to get us. He sat with me and I held him and he wept in his frustration. He was really, really freaked out. But I think that was a great thing for him, to be able to let go like that, to rebut his whole attitude of staying cool no matter what. This was a real feeling, and he was showing it, crying, and why the hell shouldn't he?'

The fury set spinning by this unlikely turn of events was seemingly unparalleled in modern times. Day after day Fleet Street exhibited the Stones' dirty laundry and every last morsel of gossip and inference relating to Britain's fallen heroes. As the issue gained the impossible momentum of a full-fledged international incident even the normally staid *Times* published a pro-Stones editorial, concluding that Jagger 'probably received a more severe sentence than would have been thought proper for any purely anonymous young man.'

Following their release on bail (£7,000) Jagger and Richards filed the appropriate appeals, and on 31 July 1967 their cases were heard. Although Keith was unable to attend due to an unexpected case of chicken-pox, Mick turned up sporting a sombre dark business suit and thin black tie. Although Jagger's original conviction was upheld the judge ruled the original sentence 'excessive' and altered Jagger's sentence to one year's probation. Turning then to the case against Richards, the Chief Justice found that the evidence against him was both circumstantial and inconclusive and overturned the finding of the lower court. Intertwined in all this was the little-known fact that, upon sentencing Richards, Judge Block referred to him as 'scum' and 'filth' and 'people like you,' which didn't go down terribly well with either the Stones' defence or Block's colleagues, who later voted to turn him out of the Garrick Club in London over the incident.

The next legal hurdle to be overcome was the pending drugs charge against Brian Jones. Appearing at the Inner London Sessions on 30 October Jones looked very fragile as he mounted the steps to the witness box to hear the charges read against ▷

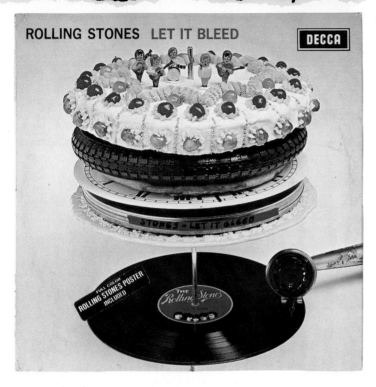

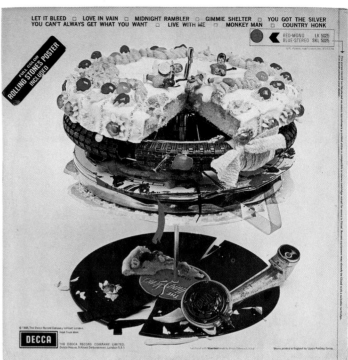

him. Entering a guilty plea to the offence of smoking cannabis, and yet another for allowing his residence to be used for unlawful purposes, the lonely Stone was then exonerated of two further charges of possession of cocaine and methedrine.

Assured by his solicitors that by pleading guilty to the two less serious charges he would be given probation, and perhaps a small fine, Jones was shattered when the judge solemnly pronounced his decision to commit the accused to Wormwood Scrubs for a nine-month term. Ordered to commence serving his time immediately Jones was shackled and led away. Fortunately, the sentence was reversed upon appeal, replaced instead by a £1,000 fine and three years' probation. Reeling internally from the non-stop pressures brought to bear by both the bust and his increasingly tentative role within the band, Jones suffered a severe nervous breakdown shortly after the conclusion of the case, only to be arrested again some five months later for possession of cannabis. On this occasion he received only a small fine and costs but was by now so overwhelmingly paranoid that, for a time, he was convinced that Mick and Keith were behind this legal savagery.

Under the strain of so many disruptions the Stones weren't able to concentrate properly on their music – a fact the innocent public weren't really aware of due to the stellar success of their still-high-flying 'Ruby Tuesday,' which shot to number one on 4 March. In an effort to try and cheer themselves up a bit that February, Keith, Brian, Anita, Tom Keylock (Richards' chauffeur) and another young lady, Deborah Dixon, left London by car to Marrakesh. By the time the party reached France Brian began complaining of breathing problems and was beginning to run a fever. Near Toulon Jones was hospitalized with pneumonia but urged the others to carry on to Morocco, promising to fly out to meet them upon his recovery.

Unfortunately, Keith and Anita soon became sexually entangled, blossoming into a full-fledged love affair by the time

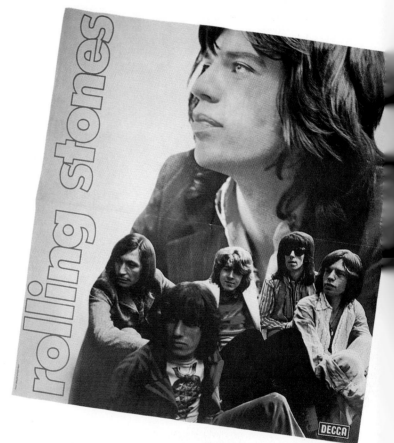

ABOVE *Let It Bleed*, first released in November 1969, originally had the working title *Sticky Fingers* but was later changed as a play on words with the Beatles' *Let It Be*. This album, incidentally, was guitarist Mick Taylor's first album as a fully-fledged Stone. Included with the album was the poster above showing the new Stones line-up.

OPPOSITE With the release of *'Get Yer Ya-Ya's Out!' The Rolling Stones In Concert* (1970, signed by Charlie), the last 'official' Stones album for Decca, Mick Jagger felt obliged to comment: 'If it weren't for bootleggers we probably wouldn't put out live albums. . . Our records will sound better and be cheaper.' Rare promotional copy and cassette also shown.

they reached Marbella, Spain. On 5 March, Anita reluctantly left Keith to meet up with Brian in France with the intention of travelling together back to Morocco in a few days. After a brief stopover in London, for a further medical check-up, Brian and Anita joined Mick (who had flown over) and Keith in Tangier. Driving together down to Marrakesh, a strong undercurrent of hostility emanated from both Anita and Keith towards Brian.

After a few sunny days spent sucking down the potent black hash and taking in the local culture, Brian took off with new-found chum and local eccentric Brion Gysin, to witness and record the magical Pipes of Pan as played by the master musicians of nearby Joujouka. On arriving back that evening Jones discovered that his entire entourage of friends had split, leaving him not only alone but almost completely broke. After a very rough night Brian flew on to Paris where he took refuge for a couple of days before jetting home to London. Refusing to believe that Anita was never to return Brian talked as if the split were only temporary, but deep down the truth was staring him in the face. 'I think the loss of Anita destroyed Brian,' says a friend. 'He was totally in love with her. It finished him. At that time, Brian had no direction. He said, "They took my music, they took my band, and now they've taken my love."'

Tired, tortured, and humiliated, Brian had to face the heartbreaking reality that, now that Anita had shifted her affections to Keith, nothing could ever again be right within the group. Throwing himself into an ever-widening cycle of self-destruction, Jones attempted to blot out the pain by mercilessly

dosing himself with not only dope and drink but acid, peyote, mushrooms, barbiturates, and just about anything that would help scatter his troubles for a little while. Despite their many problems, the Stones rallied for a three-week European tour on 25 March 1967, opening in Orebro, Sweden. Not surprisingly, the group were hounded by customs officials wherever they went. After a time, running the gauntlet through customs became almost as nerve-racking as the turbulent performances they gave. Throughout the manic, personally uneasy tour, Brian kept his distance from both Keith and Mick, too hurt to be friends but too proud of what the group had accomplished to want to pack it in.

In the winter of 1967, the Stones' seventh album in Great Britain and eleventh in the United States, *Their Satanic Majesties Request*, was released, capping off an exceedingly difficult year for all concerned. 'If it wasn't for the challenge of the music,' Brian later remarked, 'we couldn't have survived either as a group or as individuals.'

A new era for the Rolling Stones was ushered in in 1968. In February it was announced that American record producer Jimmy Miller would be taking over as the group's musical mentor, thereby allowing Jagger the luxury of distancing himself somewhat from the constant creative give-and-take required in the production of the Stones' work. 'Mick contacted me and said he liked the things I did with Traffic,' said Miller. 'He had been producing the Rolling Stones but he says he doesn't want to be on two sides of the control room window now. . . the ▷

'GET YER YA-YA'S OUT!'
The Rolling Stones in concert

'GET YER YA-YA'S OUT!'
The Rolling Stones in concert

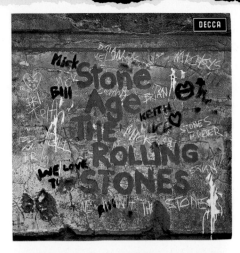

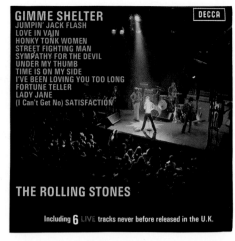

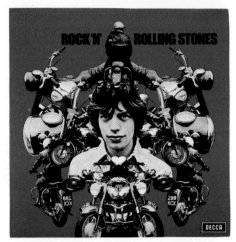

Stones are easy to work with. They know what they're after but it sometimes takes days to get it right. Mick Jagger sees just what he wants and won't settle for anything less.'

Beginning work that May on their new album, the group made a firm commitment to keep on track musically, never again allowing anything extraneous to come between them. And for a while anyway, it seemed to work. 'We're rehearsing because we've forgotten how to do it,' Mick explained at the time. 'We've forgotten how to put the plugs in the amplifier. We're just having a good time.' Recording again at Olympic Studios, the Stones found in the affable, big hearted Miller not only an ace producer but a friend and collaborator as well. Jo Jo Laine (Miller's one-time lover) recalls the subtle mix that led to their successful collaboration: 'In many ways Jimmy is just as much a character as any of the Stones combined. He used to tell

me that he and Brian got on particularly well, although he and Keith were probably the closest overall. Musically, of course, they were magic together. The way I see it, the Beatles had George Martin and the Stones had Jimmy Miller.'

Despite all the good vibrations raining down upon the group there were still a few tiny pockets of interpersonal dissent bubbling just below the surface. For a start, Bill Wyman felt left out when it came to raking in the lucrative writer's royalties from the Stones' many monster hits. After all, didn't they all contribute musically in the creation of the work?

Wyman recalls the controversy: 'I urged Charlie and Brian to join me in standing up for ourselves. I maintained that we had every right to earn something from the songs that Mick and Keith didn't bring into the studio complete, but which were co-operative band efforts. I didn't see why we should all pay equal session money for the studio rental, get equal record royalties – the Stones income has always been a five-way split – but absolutely nothing from songwriting and publishing of songs to which we'd genuinely contributed. Many other bands shared their publishing. I had raised the issue at meetings in the past with everyone present, but Brian's and Charlie's support fell by the wayside. I was on my own against Andrew, Mick and Keith who really slagged me off for being greedy. Yet where did the greed really lie?'

Wyman, of course, stood precious little chance of ever really altering the status quo. Ever since they first made it big, the hierarchy within the Stones had always been tilted towards Mick and Keith, with Brian coming in a consistent and largely ineffectual third.

Despite the political inequities within the group, though, the Stones continued to create much great music. On 25 May 1968 'Jumpin' Jack Flash' and 'Child Of The Moon' were released, entering the British charts at number twelve and surging forward all the way to number one. So chuffed were the band with the success of 'Jack' that they issued a 'thank you' to the fans in the *New Musical Express* in June: 'Dear readers of NME. 'Jumpin' Jack Flash' is really gassed that he made it to number 1. So are the Rolling Stones. Thank you. We are slaving over a hot new album which is coming out next month. Until then. . .'

The next month, on 26 July, a second single culled from their current sessions, 'Street Fighting Man' backed by 'No Expectations,' was issued in the States by London Records. All was going well for the band until Decca and London joined forces, opposing the graphic presented for the cover of the new album rumoured to be titled *Beggars Banquet*. The jacket, featuring a very dirty-looking bathroom wall littered with angry graffiti, was considered rather too down market for the public to bear – sending the Stones into their by now customary battle stance. 'We have tried to keep the cover within the bounds of good taste,' argued Jagger. 'I mean, we haven't shown the whole lavatory. That would have been rude. . . I don't think it's offensive. I even suggested that we put it out in a plain paper bag with 'Unfit For Children' and the title on the outside, if they felt that bad about it.'

Equally irritated about this artistic tempest in a teacup, Keith sounded off in the press: 'The job of the record company is to distribute. All they've got to do is put it in the shops, not dictate to people what they should or should not have.'

This was one controversy, however, that didn't go their way. Issued in Britain on 5 December, *Beggars Banquet* hit the streets adorned not with the Stones' nasty bathroom graffiti but, rather, a surprisingly plain, cream-coloured, pseudo invitation looking suspiciously like the Beatles' famous *White Album*.

To mark the grand occasion a luncheon was held in the Elizabethan Rooms at the Kensington Gore Hotel in London. Among the celebrated guests wined and dined by the Stones were Lord Harlech, band publicist Les Perrin, assorted trendy acquaintances and, of course, the ever present media (120 to be exact). Pop photographer Barrie Wentzell recalls the slightly off-

Determined to keep the dollars rolling in, Decca regularly churned out Stones reissues (opposite), much to the chagrin of the band (above). *Gimme Shelter* (1971) cashed in on the release of the documentary filmed at the Stones' disastrous Altamont concert in 1969.

centre event: 'The Stones were seated at a great, long table in front of us dressed in the most absurd Elizabethan costumes. Lunch, I believe, consisted of boar's head, cucumber and artichokes in Canary wine along with lots of fine claret and super-strong mead.'

After everyone was well satisfied, period clay pipes and snuff were distributed all around with Mick and the boys raising several elongated toasts to the good health of all. Jagger then doffed his top hat and made the following announcement: 'Right, have you all had enough to eat and drink? Thank you all for coming. I hope you've had a nice time and you've had your After Eights because we didn't invite you here to eat and drink and enjoy yourself, did we?' With that he opened a square, white cardboard box sitting next to him carefully lifting out a foam-filled pie which he then gleefully plunged into Brian's face. Instantly everyone joined in on the fun and a full-tilt Three Stooges pie fight ensued. 'Not quite the sort of party I'm accustomed to,' Lord Harlech quipped to a reporter afterwards. 'Still, I suppose I should have known something interesting would ensue. After all, the party was given by the Rolling Stones, wasn't it?'

Without doubt the biggest professional disappointment for the Stones in 1968 was the failure (in their eyes anyway) of ➪

their ambitious TV movie spectacular 'The Rock 'n' Roll Circus.' The concept behind the film was mind-boggling – the Stones would gather together the cream of rock's landed gentry to join with the band (in front of a live audience) for an evening of great music and over-the-top theatrics with an old-time circus theme. Among the superstar guests were John Lennon, Yoko Ono, Eric Clapton, Jethro Tull, the Who, Mitch Mitchell, Taj Mahal, Marianne Faithfull, and fashion model Donyale Luna.

Ironically, the only problem the Stones had was with their own performance which (according to Bill Wyman) didn't really measure up musically. 'The show was exhausting and exhilarating, but it was never shown. When Mick saw the rushes of the shoot he insisted that our appearance was below standard, since we'd gone on so late and so tired. The audience, too, lacked sparkle in the film for the same reason. He had a re-shoot costed, but this came in at £10,300, and nothing was done.' 'The Rock 'n' Roll Circus' gathers dust to this day – yet another costly indulgence.

The dawn of the new year (1969) beckoned in the darkest era yet for the Rolling Stones. On 8 June the Stones (minus Bill) met at Brian's new country estate, Cotchford Farm (former residence of *Winnie The Pooh* creator A. A. Milne), to try and diplomatically advise him that his services were no longer required by the group. Brian was predictably crushed but was so generally out of it at the time that he hardly said a word, later agreeing to issue a generic statement to the press citing a change in musical direction as the reason. 'The Rolling Stones' music is not to my taste any more,' he said. 'I want to play my own kind of music. Their music has progressed at a tangent to my own musical tastes. I have a desire to play my own brand of music rather than that of others, no matter how much I appreciate their musical concepts. We had a friendly meeting and agreed that an amicable termination, temporary or permanent, was the only answer. The only solution was to go our separate ways, but we shall still remain friends. I love those fellows.'

Always the master statesman Jagger, too, was anxious that the media understand that there were no hard feelings between the parties and that the split was both inevitable and amiable. 'The only solution to our problem was for Brian to leave us,' said Mick. 'He wants to play music which is more his own rather than always playing ours. We have decided that it is best for him to be free to follow his own inclinations. We have parted on the best of terms. We will continue to be friends and we're certainly going to meet socially in future. There's no question of us breaking up a friendship. Friendships like ours just don't break up like that.'

After the initial rush of media attention Brian felt interminably alone and defeated. The Rolling Stones, though, rolled right on, bringing in Mick Taylor on lead guitar. The quiet, affable Taylor fitted the bill admirably. Not only was he a great player but was just the kind of easygoing, non-confrontational junior partner Mick Jagger wanted, after so many years of having to deal with the unpredictable and volatile Jones. 'I was invited to do a session with the Rolling Stones,'

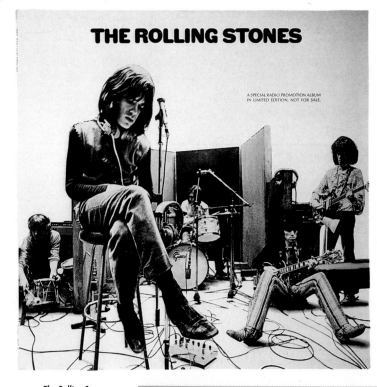

THE ROLLING STONES

A SPECIAL RADIO PROMOTION ALBUM
IN LIMITED EDITION, NOT FOR SALE.

ABOVE *The Rolling Stones Promotional Album* (1969) is now one of the rarest Stones albums ever produced. Only 400 were pressed, with 200 shipped Stateside and 200 reserved for the UK. Part of the back cover with a track listing is shown (right). **BOTTOM** ABKCO Records released *Songs of the Rolling Stones* in 1976. The album contained excerpts of some thirty Stones tracks for radio stations. *It's Here Luv!!!* features the Stones in tepid conversation with the highly forgettable Ed Rudy from INS Radio News. **OPPOSITE** On the Stones' departure from London Records in 1971, the label released a superb double LP compilation in the United States, *Hot Rocks 1964–1971*.

THIS ALBUM HAS BEEN PREPARED FOR RADIO STATIONS ONLY BY THE ROLLING STONES AS A PROGRAM AID. IT WAS FELT THAT MOST STATIONS HAVE IN THEIR LIBRARY BOTH VOLUMES OF THE ROLLING STONES' HITS LP'S (NPS-1 AND NPS-3) AND THAT ONE MORE LP, ASSEMBLED ESPECIALLY FOR RADIO STATIONS, COULD BE OF GREAT HELP IN PROGRAMMING. THIS LP, CONSISTING OF 14 ROLLING STONES SELECTIONS, SPANS THE COMPLETE RECORDED HISTORY OF THE ROLLING STONES BEGINNING WITH ONE OF THEIR EARLIEST RECORDINGS (ROUTE 66) AND ENDING WITH A BRAND NEW SELECTION WHICH WILL BE INCLUDED IN THE ROLLING STONES' NEXT LP (LOVE IN VAIN).
THIS LP, THEN, IN COMBINATION WITH THE TWO HITS LP'S CAN PROVIDE RADIO STATIONS WITH A COMPREHENSIVE HISTORY OF THE ROLLING STONES.
IF, FOR SOME REASON, YOU DO NOT HAVE BOTH ROLLING STONE HITS LP'S IN YOUR LIBRARY AND WOULD LIKE TO OBTAIN EITHER OR BOTH, WRITE TO "BROADCAST SERVICE"– LONDON RECORDS, INC., 539 W. 25th STREET, NEW YORK, N.Y. 10001, FOR DETAILS.

■ **SIDE ONE**
ROUTE 66*
(TROUPE-E. M. MORRIS & CO.–BMI–2:20)
PRODUCED BY ANDREW LOOG OLDHAM–1964
INCLUDED IN L.P. "THE ROLLING STONES" PS 375
WALKING THE DOG*
(THOMAS-EAST PUBLICATIONS–BMI–3:10)
PRODUCED BY ANDREW LOOG OLDHAM–1964
INCLUDED IN L.P. "THE ROLLING STONES" PS 375
AROUND AND AROUND*
(BERRY-ARC MUSIC CORP.–BMI–3:00)
PRODUCED BY ANDREW LOOG OLDHAM–1964
INCLUDED IN L.P. "12X5" PS 402
SUZIE Q*
(HAWKINS; LEWIS; BROADWATER-ARC MUSIC–BMI–1:59)
PRODUCED BY ANDREW LOOG OLDHAM–1965
INCLUDED IN L.P. "12X5" PS 402
EVERYBODY NEEDS SOMEBODY TO LOVE*
(RUSSELL; BURKE; WEXLER-KEETCH, CAESAR & DINO MUSIC–BMI–2:57)
PRODUCED BY ANDREW LOOG OLDHAM–1965
INCLUDED IN L.P. "THE ROLLING STONES NOW" PS 420
OFF THE HOOK*
(JAGGER; RICHARDS-IMMEDIATE MUSIC CORP.–BMI–2:35)
PRODUCED BY ANDREW LOOG OLDHAM–1965
INCLUDED IN L.P. "THE ROLLING STONES NOW" PS 420
I'M FREE*
(JAGGER; RICHARDS-GIDEON MUSIC, INC.–BMI–2:17)
PRODUCED BY ANDREW LOOG OLDHAM–1965
INCLUDED IN L.P. "DECEMBER'S CHILDREN" PS 451
SHE SAID YEAH*
(JACKSON; CHRISTY-VENICE MUSIC–BMI–1:30)
PRODUCED BY ANDREW LOOG OLDHAM–1965
INCLUDED IN L.P. "DECEMBER'S CHILDREN" PS 451

■ **SIDE TWO**
UNDER MY THUMB*
(JAGGER; RICHARD-GIDEON MUSIC, INC.–BMI–3:20)
PRODUCED BY ANDREW LOOG OLDHAM–1966
INCLUDED IN L.P. "AFTERMATH" PS 476
STUPID GIRL*
(JAGGER; RICHARD-GIDEON MUSIC, INC.–BMI–2:52)
PRODUCED BY ANDREW LOOG OLDHAM–1966
INCLUDED IN L.P. "AFTERMATH" PS 476
2000 MAN*
(JAGGER; RICHARD-GIDEON MUSIC INC.–BMI–3:05)
PRODUCED BY THE ROLLING STONES–1967
INCLUDED IN L.P. "THEIR SATANIC MAJESTIES REQUEST" NPS-2
SYMPATHY FOR THE DEVIL*
(JAGGER; RICHARD-GIDEON MUSIC INC.–BMI–6:14)
PRODUCED BY JIMMY MILLER–1968
INCLUDED IN L.P. "BEGGARS BANQUET" PS 539
PRODIGAL SON*
(REV. WILKINS-WYNWOOD MUSIC–BMI–2:47)
PRODUCED BY JIMMY MILLER–1968
INCLUDED IN L.P. "BEGGARS BANQUET" PS 539
LOVE IN VAIN*
(PAYNE-NOMA MUSIC INC.- NICE SONGS–BMI–4:20)
PRODUCED BY JIMMY MILLER–1969
TO BE INCLUDED IN THE L.P. "LET IT BLEED"

ALL SONGS ARRANGED BY THE ROLLING STONES
PHOTOGRAPHY BY ETHAN RUSSELL & ERIC HAYES
ART DIRECTIONS BY J. GOODCHILD & M. TATE
DESIGN & GRAPHICS BY VICTOR KAHN
*ELECTRONICALLY RE-RECORDED TO SIMULATE STEREO

MANUFACTURED BY NANKER PHELGE MUSIC LTD. □ AN ABKCO RECORD COMPANY □ DISTRI

SONGS OF
THE ROLLING STONES

1965
TALK ALBUM
IT'S HERE LUV!!!
STONES
THE ROLLING STONES
ED RUDY WITH NEW U.S. TOUR
NEWS DOCUMENTARY 4
VOLUME
GEAR & FAB!!

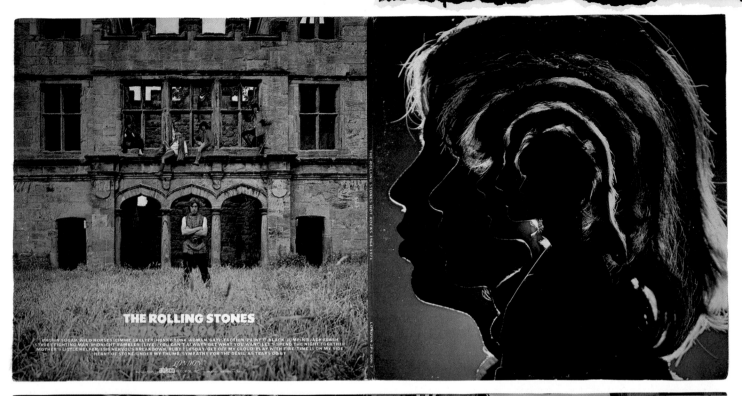

says Taylor. 'It puzzled me. I had never met Mick Jagger in my life and here he was phoning me. I went down and played on some tracks and thought little more about it. Then they asked me if I wanted to be a Stone. I was amazed. I said I'd love to be a Stone and that was that.'

After being sacked from the group, Brian, perhaps figuring it was now or never, began to straighten himself out. He cut back considerably on the illicit drugs, deeply paranoid that if he were ever busted again this time he might really be sent to the slammer. He also resumed old relationships, inviting long-time mate Alexis Korner and his family down to Cotchford Farm for quiet evenings spent sipping expensive wine and jamming on acoustic guitars. So pleasant were these homey interludes for Jones that he suggested joining Korner's group, New Church, an

offer the worldwise veteran graciously turned down, figuring that the superstar Stone would never be happy backing anyone after his glory days in the international limelight. 'He was probably more sane at that period than I'd known him for a very long time,' said Korner. 'He was in a calmer frame of mind; there were things he wanted to do musically and he loved the house. The villagers liked him, almost took it upon themselves to protect him from the world. He said to us that the house was where he would like to have his children.'

Finally in a position to settle back and enjoy the fruits of his vast success, Jones began making plans for a new group, even considering teaming up with John Lennon and Jimi Hendrix to form an all-star trio. When that little pipe dream didn't come to pass he didn't lose heart but rather forged ahead with ➪

The planned follow-up to *Hot Rocks* was to be titled *Necrophilia*, and was to have the tracks selected by the unpredictable Andrew Loog Oldham. A triple gatefold sleeve was designed by Fabio Nicoli using photography by the Stones' official photographer from the sixties, Gered Mankowitz. Only an extremely limited number had been produced when, rumour has it, Oldham and Allen Klein had a major disagreement over Oldham's eclectic track selection, which included controversial songs such as 'Andrews Blues' and 'Pay Your Dues' (the alternate version to 'Street Fighting Man'). Although *Necrophilia* was alloted a catalogue number (opposite), the project was mysteriously shelved and replaced by the more conservative double-album compilation *More Hot Rocks (big hits & fazed cookies)* released in 1972. The track listing for *More Hot Rocks* is shown above.

drummer Micky Waller (ex of the Jeff Beck Group) with the idea of getting together a English Credence Clearwater Revival-type group (one of Brian's all-time favourites).

Despite his new improved outlook, Brian missed being a Stone. Jim Carter-Fea, manager of the trendy Revolution Club in London, remembers running across Jones in those first post-Stones days and thinking how dejected and sad he looked. On one occasion Brian even drove him down to Olympic Studios (where the group were working), pulling slowly up to the curb, the two men sat outside in the car for several minutes before

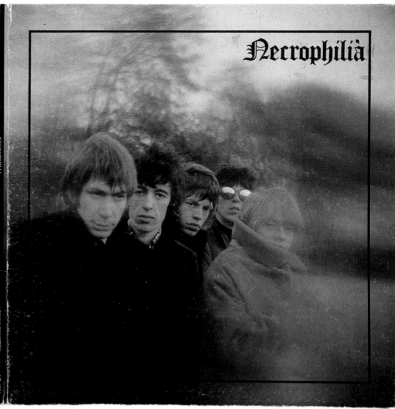

Brian revved up the motor and sped off. 'They're in there making music, and they don't want me,' whispered Jones. Carter-Fea could say nothing, there was nothing to say, for Brian Jones (and indeed the Rolling Stones themselves) it was the end of an era.

The pastoral sameness of life in the English countryside seemed to agree with Brian. Since buying Cotchford Farm he had personally overseen to the old estate's much-needed renovations, as well as taking a lot of care in furnishing the main house with a collection of exquisite antiques, tapestries, and period paintings. To aid in the work Brian hired a crew headed by a local contractor. Initially things went well but as time went by Jones could sense a brewing hostility from the workers. 'Some days they hide my motorcycle,' Brian confided to his friend Nicholas Fitzgerald. 'When I'm on the phone, the line will suddenly go dead. Then when I get the engineers in they say there's nothing wrong. They're always leaping up to answer the phone and then they tell me it was a wrong number. I just can't trust anybody. I know you think I'm paranoid. Maybe I am, but not about this. I know they're up to something.' ⇨ 56

ABOVE The Stones' UK singles. The band's initial 45 (released 24 June 1963) was Chuck Berry's 'Come On' backed by Willie Dixon's 'I Want To Be Loved.' Both tunes were recorded at Olympic Studios, London. 'I Want To Be Loved' represented the Stones' second take of Dixon's classic and features a much faster guitar track. Hovering in the charts for some fourteen weeks, the ambitious single ultimately rose only as high as number twenty-one. After Decca refused the Stones' second single, 'Poison Ivy' backed by 'Fortune Teller,' Lennon and McCartney graciously offered them 'I Wanna Be Your Man' backed by the semi-instrumental 'Stoned.' An early pressing mistakenly titled it 'Stones,' crediting composers Nanker, Phelge (known popularly as Messrs Jagger and Richards). The stirring, high-velocity single was released in November 1963.

The group's third venture in vinyl was the classic Buddy Holly hit 'Not Fade Away' backed by 'Little by Little' released on 3 February 1964. This time the Stones rocketed to number three on the charts. Happily, the next five releases went almost directly to number one with 'It's All Over Now' backed by 'Good Times, Bad Times' released in July 1964 followed by 'Little Red Rooster' backed by 'Off The Hook' issued on 1 November 1964; 'The Last Time' backed by 'Play With Fire' (1 February 1965); '(I Can't Get No) Satisfaction' backed by 'The Spider and the Fly' (1 August 1965) and 'Get Off Of My Cloud' and 'The Singer Not The Song' (1 October 1965).

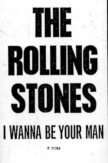

'19th Nervous Breakdown' backed by 'As Tears Go By' only climbed to number two (released 2 February 1966). 'Paint It Black' backed by 'Long Long While' (1 May 1966) did a bit better fortunately, once again reclaiming the coveted number one spot. Other high energy singles include 'Have You Seen Your Mother, Baby, Standing In The Shadow?' backed by 'Who's Driving Your Plane' (23 September 1966) and 'Street Fighting Man' with 'Surprise Surprise' (3 July 1971).

OPPOSITE The ever-rolling Stones sandwiched between two highly forgettable acts: The Orchids and songstress Adrienne Poster in this early newspaper ad. Decca also produced a concertina-style shop-counter display to promote five singles.

OPPOSITE BOTTOM Among the many curios produced by the official Rolling Stones Fan Club in the sixties was this set of 'unofficial' postage stamps.

RIGHT A highly prized original shop display from Decca Records dating from the early sixties.

DECCA RECORDS

TRUE HIGH FIDELITY

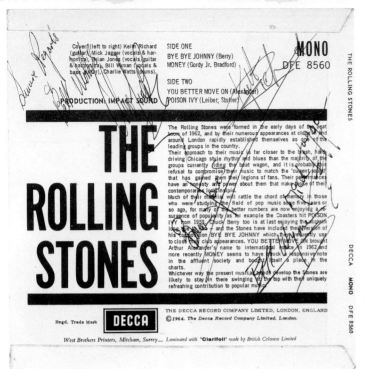

It seems Brian's fears were well founded. A. E. Hotchner's book on the Stones, *Blown Away*, chronicles the evil doings down on the farm. Ronni Money, a long-time associate of the group, remembers the prevalent mood at Jones' upmarket Elizabethan digs: 'All those months they'd been really sucking Brian dry. They'd all been living off him, faking bills, not doing their work, drinking his booze, all that stuff. People who suck off you don't like you, they hate you really, because that's what makes it easy for them to suck. Brian was foppish, he was rich, he lived luxuriously with beautiful young women, a chauffeur drove him about in a Rolls Royce, and these construction guys resented him for that, sneered at him.'

The culmination of this uneasy alliance between Jones and his new employees came late in the evening on 2 July 1969 when the contractor, his lady, and several of the crew showed up after work with their girlfriends for an unscheduled party. That afternoon Brian had dug out his saxophone and stood alone in his timber-lined cottage, playing in concord with the rustic bustle of rural Sussex. It would be his final concert.

Later in the evening, surrounded by the beer-drinking labourers, Brian sipped some wine and made small talk with his 'guests.' When everyone scattered out to the pool Brian changed into his trunks with the intention of taking a swim. Diving into the 80-degree waters of the floodlit pool Jones felt suddenly revitalized and before long was showing off on the diving board for the young ladies present. Standing on the side of the pool two unnamed (as of yet) workers began loudly taunting the blonde musician, obviously jealous over the attention he was receiving from their girlfriends. After a few minutes of what might still be regarded only as aggressive 'beer talk' the pair jumped in the water and began physically hassling Jones. An eye witness to the events of that long-ago sultry summer evening known only by the alias of 'Marty' remembers what happened next: 'I wasn't paying much attention at first, just that they were

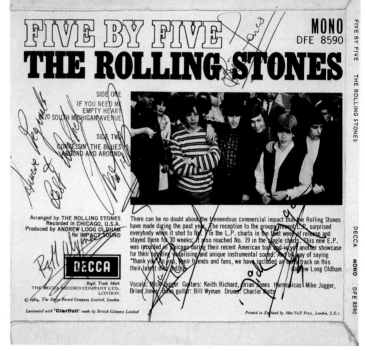

ABOVE The only examples of Rolling Stones EPs (7" extended plays) are three vinyls: 'The Rolling Stones' (17 January 1964, back cover shown, top left); 'Five By Five' (14 August 1964, – back cover shown); and the classic 'Got LIVE If You Want It!,' first taking flight on 11 June 1965. Also shown is the maxi 7" single containing 'Street Fighting Man,' released in 1971.

OPPOSITE A rare sampling of Decca's many export singles. Decca issued these with picture sleeves and without. Although all Decca UK singles had blue labels, some of these export singles were issued with a black label and would invariably carry a different B side (see the discography at the back of this book for variations). Note the dramatic cover for 'Street Fighting Man.' Although never banned in Europe, it was still somewhat different from the US issue, but nevertheless still depicted a violent scene.

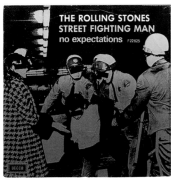

poking at Brian and roughing him up in the water, and a coupla the girls said, "Aw, let him alone will ya?" but that just made these lads pester him all the more. Then Brian tried to get out of the pool and they wouldn't let him, just kept pushing him back and pulling him under. . . These lads really got worked up at Brian the more he resisted. . . [They were] ducking him and then holding him under water and keeping him under and then letting him up for a coupla seconds and he was gasping and then down again. . . I could tell it was turning ugly as hell.'

By now things had spun way out of control with Brian struggling helplessly to reach the surface. Obviously frightened, one of the fellows holding Jones panicked and screamed for the other guy to let him up. Only seconds later someone yelled out, 'He's drowned.' Within seconds everyone ran for their cars, leaving Jones to sink slowly to the bottom of the pool. 'Sink like a Stone,' Marty grimly thought to himself. 'I always thought he was okay, but there were those he rubbed the wrong way, and it all just seemed to get out of hand that night.'

Over the next few days virtually everything of value was systematically stripped from Cotchford Farm. By the time anyone thought to lock the place up there was nothing left to steal. And Brian Jones lay in the morgue awaiting an autopsy at the hands of yet another faceless stranger. To all the world Brian was just a pretty-boy pop star who suffocated on his own hedonistic appetite for self destruction. The truth is Brian Jones was viciously and senselessly murdered by a couple of drunken labourers. The ultimate victim of the violent, ruthless and self-interested forces that moulded him, Brian Jones never found even a hint of justice or mercy. Not in his sweet short life, nor in his murky, murderous death.

The afternoon of 5 July 1969 was a little more humid than usual for the season, and a great deal more poignant. 300,000 people crammed into London's Hyde Park to commemorate the untimely death of Brian Jones with a free concert by the Stones. Mixed in among the crowd that afternoon were the élite of international pop as well as the hippie rabble of the day, all gathered to pay their final respects to this grown up Christopher Robin who, at twenty-six, had given the world perhaps more enduring music than any single artist of his time. Fronting the musical memorial were no less than five warm-up acts: Third Ear, Family, Alexis Korner's New Church, the Battered Ornaments, and King Crimson.

Walking on stage around five-thirty, the Stones silently took their places as the crowd surged forward for a better look. Quietening down the huge, sweltering mass that lay before them Jagger read out some lines from 'Adonais' by the Romantic poet, Percy Bysse Shelley:

➪ 60

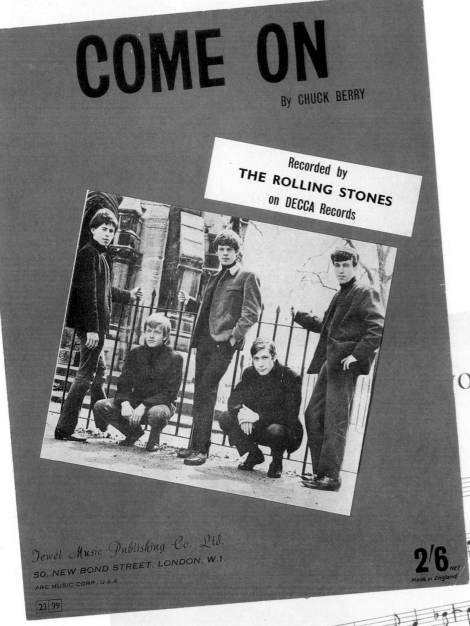

A selection of songsheets issued in
Britain from 1963 to 1969.

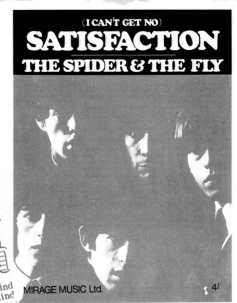

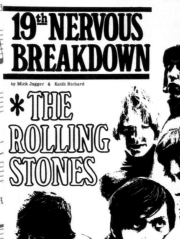

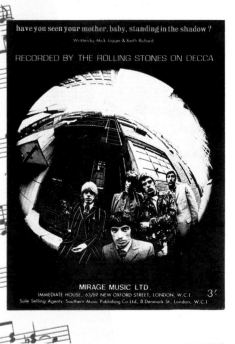

Peace, peace! he is not dead, he doth not sleep –
He hath awakened from the dream of life –
'Tis we, who lost in stormy visions, keep
With phantoms an unprofitable strife,
And in mad trance, strike with our spirit's knife
Invulnerable nothings. – We decay
Like corpses in a charnel; fear and grief
Convulse us and consume us day by day,
And cold hopes swarm like worms within our living clay.

The One remains, the many change and pass;
Heaven's light forever shines, Earth's shadows fly;
Life, like a dome of many-coloured glass,
Stains the white radiance of Eternity,
Until Death tramples it to fragments. – Die,
If thou wouldst be that which thou dost seek!

As the inevitable cameras flashed away Mick nodded to a waiting roadie who released 3,500 pure white butterflies into the sky as a final tribute to the Stones' fallen comrade. With that the band lurched into 'I'm Yours She's Mine,' not really in tune with each other, burdened as they were with their grief and blatantly rusty, not having played live for fourteen months.

The shaky one-hour performance sputtered on with 'Jumpin' Jack Flash,' followed by 'Mercy Mercy,' 'Down Home Girl,' 'Lovin' Cup,' 'Honky Tonk Women,' 'Midnight Rambler,' '(I Can't Get No) Satisfaction,' 'Street Fighting Man,' 'Sympathy For The Devil,' 'Love In Vain,' 'I'm Free,' 'Stray Cat Blues,' and 'No Expectations.'

Although the fans clearly loved the show, there were those that were less impressed. Ian Stewart found Jagger's overtly sexual gestures 'tacky,' while Stones insider Richard Hattrell termed the entire affair an 'opportunistic memorial,' commenting that Mick looked like a 'tart' prancing around the

American singles from the sixties. Happily for collectors, all US releases were issued in picture sleeves, the majority of which are now highly collectible. The group's first 45, 'I Wanna Be Your Man' backed by 'Stones,' was withdrawn at the last moment and was replaced with 'Not Fade Away' and 'I Wanna Be Your Man,' (March 1964). Of course, as with the group's albums, there were significant differences between the US and UK releases

(and there were more releases in America than in Britain).

Without doubt the rarest and most desirable picture sleeve of all has to be 'Street Fighting Man.' The grim graphic depicting demonstrators being beaten by police was just a little too hot for retailers to handle. Immediately withdrawn from the stores, the single now sells for a cool $6,000 among well-heeled aficionados.

feel for them, feel near to them. He was born on 28 February 1943 and I was born on 25 February 1943; he was with Mick and Keith and I was with John and Paul, so there was a sort of understanding between the two of us. Our positions were similar, and I often met him in times of trouble. There was nothing the matter with him that a little extra love wouldn't have cured. I don't think he had enough love or understanding. He was very nice, sincere and sensitive, and we must remember that's what he was.'

'I used to know him quite well,' the Who's Pete Townshend remembered. 'The Stones have always been a group I really dug. Dug all the dodgy aspects of them as well, and Brian Jones has always been what I've regarded as one of the dodgy aspects. The way he fitted in and the way he didn't fit was one of the strong dynamics of the group. When he stopped playing with them I thought that dynamic was going to be missing, but it still seems to be there. The Stones have managed by some miracle to have replaced him. Not with Mick Taylor, I mean, he's like a musician, but they've kind of filled the hole. Perhaps the fact that he's dead has made that dynamic kind of permanent.'

Back to the business at hand. The Stones' next musical coup, the sexually ambiguous single 'Honky Tonk Women,' shot to number one on both sides of the Atlantic by early August, thus paving the way for the successful release of their stirring compilation *Through The Past, Darkly (Big Hits Vol. 2)*, released in America on 12 September. Pete Bennett remembers the trials of getting the Stones' new single on the air: 'When the guys sent me the tape of 'Honky Tonk Women' I knew I had a problem. There were other times the Stones sent me songs too long for the radio stations so I had to call up and tell them to cut it down. Usually they didn't give a damn, that is until I reminded them that if they didn't edit the songs the radio wouldn't play them. It happened with 'Let's Spend The Night Together,' 'Lady Jane,' and 'Paint It Black.'

stage in his white Michael Fish 'dress,' his face painted with rouge, mascara, and even lipstick.

Jagger's reaction to Jones' passing was, on the surface anyway, quite touching: 'I am wordless, sad and shocked,' he said. 'Something has gone. We were like a pack, a family, we Stones. I just say my prayers for him. I hope he becomes blessed. I hope he is finding peace; I really want him to. I wasn't ever really close to him.'

While Jones was being laid to rest on 10 July in his home town of Cheltenham, the troubled musician's celebrated colleagues were eulogizing their departed brother. 'When we met I liked him quite a lot,' said George Harrison. 'He was a good fellow, you know. I got to know him very well, and I felt very close to him; you know how it is with some people, you

⊳ 66

A collection of foreign single sleeves. The great thing about overseas 45s was that they were issued in picture sleeves generally unique to each particular country.

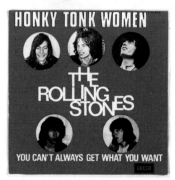

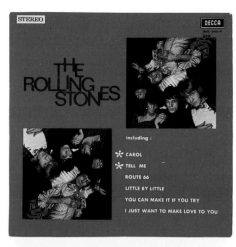

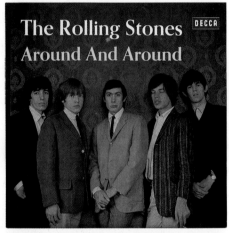

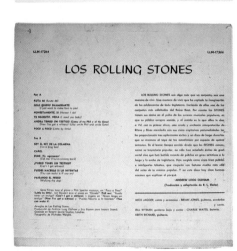

A selection of rare foreign albums. The Japanese generally came up with some great cover photos. Teldec (Decca in Germany) also managed to produce some fairly original graphics.

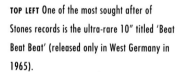

'In 1969 the stations were very cautious about lyrics. There were complaints about sex and drug references. Unfortunately, there were big problems with the lyrics of 'Honky Tonk Women.' I called Jagger about this at his home in London. "Listen, Mick," I said, "what about the line, *I laid a divorcee in New York City*, it's too controversial." "The hell with that," he said. "You just get it out, and I'll talk to London Records." '

'When I finally received the acetate for 'Honky Tonk Women' I called WMCA and told them I was coming in with the new Rolling Stones single. If it came out that WMCA, the number one station, banned the song then nobody would touch it, exclusive or not. But if they played it then everybody else would figure that the FCC had okay'd it. They put the record on and when the problem lyric came on in the second verse the programme director looked at the disc jockey who looked at the music director who just looked up at the ceiling.

' "We can't possibly play this record," the programme director said, "the lyrics are really offensive." "What lyric?" "It said, *I laid a divorcee in New York City*." "No it doesn't," I bluffed, "it said, *I played a divorcee*."

'Anyway, they called in two of their corporate attorneys and played the record again. And again the verdict was that there was no way they were going to play this record on the air. But the lawyers gave me an out. "If you can prove that it really says *played a divorcee* then we can play it," one said. "If you can come up with the lead sheets with those lyrics then we'll play it."

'Fortunately, the Stones sent me a lead sheet along with the tape of 'Honky Tonk Women.' If I didn't pull this thing off not only would they not play the record but my own credibility would be shot as well. 'Back in the office I checked the ten typewriters we had. One was close to the type on the lead sheet. Not exactly, but close enough. I photocopied the sheet, and where it said *laid a divorcee* I whited that out and typed in *played a divorcee*. Two hours later I was back at WMCA with my

TOP LEFT One of the most sought after of Stones records is the ultra-rare 10" titled 'Beat Beat Beat' (released only in West Germany in 1965).

ABOVE The Japanese version of *Let It Bleed* was issued with a magnificent five-page pull-out comprising the lyrics to the songs and a photograph of each member of the band.

handiwork. They agreed to play the record and it went on to become a number one single.'

That October the band flew to Los Angeles to prepare for their upcoming tour of the States and finish mixing their new album *Let It Bleed*. On 7 November the Stones officially began their sixth US stint, playing the State University at Fort Collins, Colorado. The next several shows went smoothly enough, culminating in a grand free concert on 6 December 1969 at Altamont Speedway in Livermore, California. Supporting the Stones that fateful afternoon were Jefferson Airplane, Crosby, Stills, Nash and Young, the Flying Burrito Brothers, and the riveting, salsa-inspired Santana.

Being so close to San Francisco, the open air show was jam-packed with over 500,000 enthusiastic fans. Vocal advocates of the new left, the Stones shunned the security force normally used at such events in favour of the San Francisco arm of the Hell's Angels. Although the mass of incense-burning hippies generally tolerated the redneck bikers, they didn't really like them and, unfortunately, the feeling was mutual. By ⇨74

The Stones have long been associated with works by other artists. Gene Pitney's 1964 hit 'That Girl Belongs to Yesterday' was penned by Jagger and Richards. Mick performed 'Da Doo Run Run' on *Hard-up Heroes* (1974) and contributed to the *Tonite Lets All Make Love In London* soundtrack. The Stones collaborated with Alexis Korner on the album *Get Off My Cloud* and with The Andrew Oldham Orchestra on various records. *Baroque N' Stones* (1966) was an 'interesting' compilation of early Stones tunes performed by The New Renaissance Society. The Who's 1967 cover of 'The Last Time' (bottom left) was recorded in support of Mick and Keith who were well on their way to a paid vacation courtesy of Her Majesty for various drug offences.

Songs Recorded by **THE ROLLING STONES**

I'M MOVIN' ON • WALKING THE DOG
IF YOU NEED ME • MERCY MERCY
UNDER THE BOARDWALK
HITCH HIKE

CARLIN MUSIC CORP. 17, Savile Row, London, W.1.   6/-

THE **ROLLING STONES** SONG BOOK

EXCLUSIVE NEW PHOTOS AND SIX HIT SONGS   5/-

A Flagrant Misuse Of The English Language

In Other Words

8 New Song Hits by THE ROLLING STONES
Written by MICK JAGGER & KEITH RICHARD

MIRAGE MUSIC LTD.
138/147, IVOR COURT, GLOUCESTER PLACE, LONDON, N.W.1.
Sole Selling Agents: Southern Music Publishing Co. Ltd., 8, Denmark Street, London, W.C.2.   7/6

THE ROLLING STONES
SONG ALBUM

© Copyright
SOUTHE...
For Switzer...
For Belgium...
For Scandina...

JEWEL MUSIC PUBLISHING CO LTD
50 New Bond Street London W 1
Copyright MCMLXV by Arc Music Corp.

...mbH Vienna.

...ved in England

THE **ROLLING STONES**
SOUVENIR SONG BOOK
$1.50

IT'S ALL OVER NOW / LITTLE BY LITTLE / NOT FADE
AWAY / NOW I'VE GOT A WITNESS / STONED / TELL ME

big hits [high tide & green grass]
RECORDED BY THE ROLLING STONES ON DECCA

MIRAGE MUSIC LTD.
IMMEDIATE HOUSE, 63/69 NEW OXFORD STREET, LONDON, W.C.1.
Sole Selling Agents: Southern Music Publishing Co. Ltd., 8 Denmark St., London, W.C.1.
7/6

Made in E...

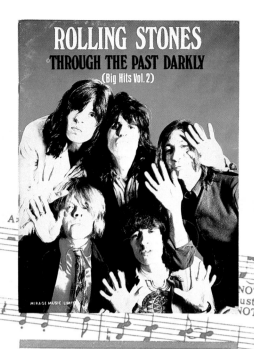

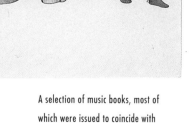

A selection of music books, most of which were issued to coincide with the release of the Stones albums.

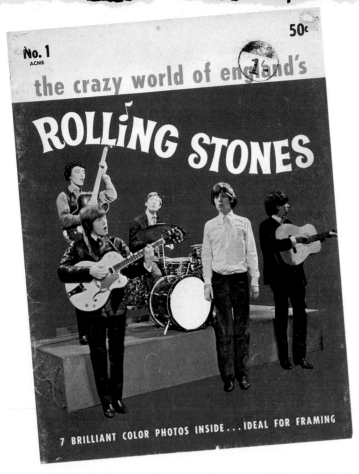

Pop oriented magazines and books were big business for ambitious publishers both then as now, especially if one or all of the Rolling Stones appeared on the cover. Here are a few tasty examples from both America and the United Kingdom.

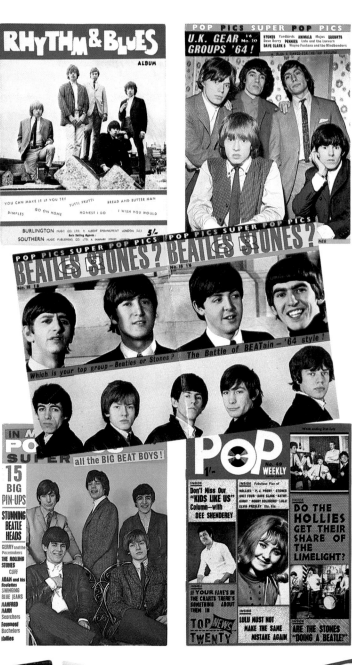

THE ROLLING STONES

Roll Over Beethoven

J. Habig

THE ROLLING STONES

WHO ARE THE STONES?

LIMITED EDITION INTERVIEW PICTURE DISC

BAK 2109 · SIDE 1

Although they've been around since the Second World War, picture discs became immensely popular worldwide in the seventies and eighties. Here, then, for your delectation are a selection of suitably collectible discs mixing together both official releases from the seventies and eighties (left column), and bootlegs. The top left record was the first official Rolling Stones picture disc, produced in France.

BELOW The bootleg picture disc of 'Cocksucker Blues' contains two different versions of the bawdy song (an 'indecent' tune understandably never officially released).

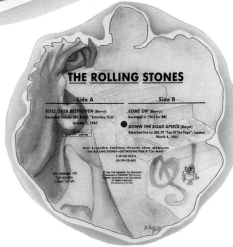

THE ROLLING STONES

Side A | Side B

ROLL OVER BEETHOVEN (Berry)
Recorded live for BBC Radio "Saturday Club",
October 5, 1963

COME ON (Berry)
Recorded in 1963 for BBC

DOWN THE ROAD APIECE (Raye)
Recorded live for BBC-TV "Top Of The Pops", London,
March 4, 1965

Great Live Recordings

DOCUMENT

The Rolling Stones live in 1965

Side One (Other Side)   3:43   Side Two (This Side)   3:03
Satisfaction (Jagger/Richards)   Cry To Me (Russell)

Both tracks were recorded in London, Sept. 23, 1965

Other Rolling Stones Releases
On Document Records:
DR 007 CD - Rolling Stones - Live in London '63-'65
DR 012 CD - Rolling Stones - Rough, Dirty & Irresistible
DR 014 Shape Disc - Rolling Stones – Live at Camden Theatre

DR 702
Document Records

Limited Edition — Only 1000 Copies worldwide!

Especially made for The International Music Meeting 1989
March 11-12, Kongresshalle Berlin, West Germany

Graphics: IRMA
Foto: Ullstein - Alexander Enger

Document Records is a Trade Mark of Disc de Luxe, s.à.r.l., Luxembourg

These rare and very collectible bootleg picture discs, produced in the early eighties, contain Stones material originally recorded in the sixties.

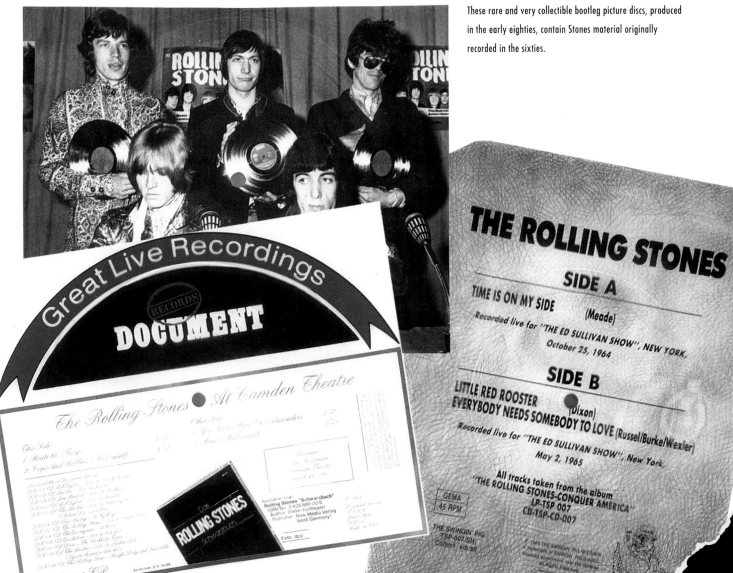

Great Live Recordings

DOCUMENT

The Rolling Stones ● At Camden Theatre

THE ROLLING STONES

SIDE A

TIME IS ON MY SIDE   (Meade)

Recorded live for "THE ED SULLIVAN SHOW", NEW YORK,
October 25, 1964

SIDE B

LITTLE RED ROOSTER   (Dixon)
EVERYBODY NEEDS SOMEBODY TO LOVE (Russel/Burke/Wexler)

Recorded live for "THE ED SULLIVAN SHOW", New York,
May 2, 1965

All tracks taken from the album
"THE ROLLING STONES-CONQUER AMERICA"
LP-TSP 007
CD-TSP-CD-007

GEMA   45 RPM

THE SWINGIN' PIG
TSP-007/SH
Collect 'em all

RELEASED TODAY
the new ROLLING STONES ellpee/14

THEIR SATANIC MAJESTIES REQUEST

THE ROLLING STONES NEW LP

JUST LISTEN TO THE
BEGGAR'S BANQUET

THE ROLLING STONES

DECCA LK 4786
produced by andrew loog oldham

early afternoon several fans had complained to the organizers that the Angels were manhandling scores of innocently stoned kids, and otherwise throwing their ample weight around. Adding to the tension was the unhappy fact that so many spaced-out people in such a restricted area created impossibly long lines for everything, from hot dogs and soda to dope.

By the time Jefferson Airplane took the stage small pockets of insane brutality were beginning to break out all over the teeming humanity gathered to pay obeisance to the Stones, sending waves of incomprehensible terror rippling through the sweltering, tripped-out crowd.

To make matters worse, the few medics in attendance were unable to cope effectively with the numerous casualties carried into their tent by concerned fans. Altamont was rapidly becoming the great disaster predicted by everyone's parents as the inevitable wages of the uninhibited hippie lifestyle.

It is well known that the ultimate transgression to a biker is for anyone to mess with his bike which, unfortunately, also occurred. It was the unmistakable beginning of the end. 'I ain't no cop,' remembered Angel Sonny Barger. 'I ain't gonna police nothing. I just want to sit there on the front of the stage, drink beer and have a good time, like we was told. But when they started kickin' our bikes, man, that started it. I ain't no peace creep, man. Ain't nobody gonna get my bike. Anybody that tries that is gonna get got. And they got got!'

Finally mounting the makeshift stage, and joining about a hundred or so people already lining the cluttered perimeter, the Stones kicked off the set with a shaky rendition of 'Jumpin' Jack Flash.' A naked young woman, while attempting to climb on to the stage, was immediately tackled by no less than five burly Angels. 'I'm sure it doesn't require all of you to take care of this,' Jagger pleaded into the mike as the poor girl was thrown back into the crowd and then savagely beaten with pool cues. The Angels retreated leering violently at Jagger, one of them even mimicking the androgynous Stone's mincing dance steps as the crowd tittered nervously.

Cascading into 'Sympathy For The Devil,' Mick shouted out the disturbing lyrics even as a young black man, Meredith Hunter, was being stabbed to death in a frantic tumble with the Stones' stormtroopers near the front of the stage. Witnesses later insisted that the poor guy was guilty of nothing more than being in the company of a pretty young white girl, something the redneck bikers didn't appreciate. Others claim that Hunter had suddenly lurched towards the stage, thus attracting the attention of the Angels who chased him down and then stabbed him in the back after seeing him pull a pistol from beneath his jacket. After the bikers had finished him off they reportedly walked away, returning to their posts at the front of the stage as if nothing had happened. Shocked fans turned him over to find what several later described as a 'big hole' in his back spewing

blood. Several kids picked him up and slowly made their way through the thoroughly freaked-out crowd to the Red Cross tent behind the stage.

Jagger appealed for a doctor as the music ground to a spluttering halt. 'Brothers and sisters, be cool now,' he entreated the audience. 'That means everybody just cool it. Is there anybody there who's been hurt? We always have something very funny happen when we start that number.'

Hoping vainly that another dose of high-voltage rock 'n' roll might somehow soothe the savage vibes hovering ominously over the darkened raceway the Stones once again began to play only to be drowned out by a hail of jeers raining from all quarters. Reacting to an Angel mercilessly beating up on a kid Keith Richards stopped playing mid-riff shouting 'Either those cats cool it, man, or we don't play. . . If you don't cool it, you ain't gonna hear no music!' The rest of the Stones stood frozen as several burly Angels slowly circled the band with murderous intent. 'Fuck you!' mouthed Richards to the biggest and ugliest. Amazingly, the beered-up barbarians responded by backing off from the band, allowing the concert to resume. By the time the Stones mimed their final goodbyes that evening four people lay dead, another 700 were treated for bad trips and over ninety-eight went to hospital for injuries ranging from head lacerations to broken bones.

The media fallout was, of course, swift and brutal:

SWINGING SIXTIES MEET WITH FOUL PLAY screamed one headline. MURDER GREETS THE STONES IN FRISCO proclaimed another. Ian Stewart remembers the inevitable controversy: 'The Altamont catastrophe took place in December 1969, as the sixties came to an end. As far as I was concerned, Altamont was the death knell to all those things we thought would last forever. I personally felt the sixties had been an extravagant stage show and I was a spectator. Altamont brought down the curtain to no applause.'

The Stones ushered in the new decade by announcing a European tour commencing in The Hague on 8 May 1970. That summer the group's seven-year agreement with Decca Records expired, but before being formally released from their contract, they were compelled to deliver one more tune. Ever willing to oblige, they boys dashed off a little ditty entitled 'Cocksucker Blues' for the occasion. The stout hearts at Decca, however, were not impressed with the song's 'obscene' lyrics and summarily refused to release the scatological tune.

That September the Stones' fifteenth album in the US and eleventh in the UK, 'Get Yer Ya Ya's Out!', hit the streets and within days sailed directly to the top of the charts. By the end of October the band was once again hard at work at Olympic Studios, laying down tracks for yet another new album. If nothing else, the boys had inherited an inbred work ethic from their staunchly middle-class families, and it was paying off.

PERFORMANCE AND TOUR DATES 1962-1970

1962

JULY
12	Marquee Jazz Club, London
	Ealing Jazz Club, London

AUGUST
	Ealing Jazz Club, London

SEPTEMBER
	Ealing Jazz Club, London
	Ealing Jazz Club, London
	Ealing Jazz Club, London
	Marquee Jazz Club, London

OCTOBER
5	Woodstock Hotel, North Cheam, Surrey
	Ealing Jazz Club, London
	Ealing Jazz Club, London
	Marquee Jazz Club, London

NOVEMBER
	Ealing Jazz Club, London
	Flamingo Jazz Club, London
	Red Lion Pub, Sutton, Surrey
	Ealing Jazz Club, London
	Flamingo Jazz Club, London
30	Piccadilly Jazz Club, London

DECEMBER
4	Ealing Jazz Club, London
	Red Lion Pub, Sutton, Surrey
12	Sidcup Art College, Sidcup, Kent
15	Youth Club, CHurch Hall, Putney, London
21	Piccadilly Jazz Club, London
22	Ealing Jazz Club, London

1963

JANUARY
5	Ealing Jazz Club, London
7	Flamingo Jazz Club, London
9	Red Lion Pub, Sutton, Surrey
10	Marquee Jazz Club, London
11	Ricky Tick Club, Star and Garter Pub, Windsor, Berkshire
14	Flamingo Jazz Club, London
17	Marquee Jazz Club, London
19	Ealing Jazz Club, London
21	Flamingo Jazz Club, London
23	Red Lion Pub, Sutton, Surrey
25	Ricky Tick Club, Star and Garter Pub, Windsor, Berkshire
26	Ealing Jazz Club, London
28	Flamingo Jazz Club, London
31	Marquee Jazz Club, London

FEBRUARY
1	Ricky Tick Club, Star and Garter Pub, Windsor, Berkshire
2	Ealing Jazz Club, London
5	Ealing Jazz Club, London
6	Red Lion Pub, Sutton, Surrey
7	Haringey Jazz Club, Manor House Pub, London
8	Ricky Tick Club, Star and Garter Pub, Windsor, Berkshire
9	Ealing Jazz Club, London
12	Ealing Jazz Club, London
14	Haringey Jazz Club, Manor House Pub, London
16	Ealing Jazz Club, London
19	Ealing Jazz Club, London
20	Red Lion Pub, London
22	Ricky Tick Club, Star and Garter Pub, Windsor, Berkshire
23	Ealing Jazz Club, London
24	Station Hotel, Richmond, Surrey
28	Haringey Jazz Club, Manor House Pub, London

MARCH
2	Ealing Jazz Club, London
3	Studio 51, Ken Colyer Club, London
	Station Hotel, Richmond, Surrey
6	Red Lion Pub, Sutton, Surrey
7	Haringey Jazz Club, Manor House Pub, London
8	Ricky Tick Club, Star and Garter Pub, Windsor, Berkshire
9	Wooden Bridge Hotel, Guildford, Surrey
10	Studio 51, Ken Colyer Club, London
	Station Hotel, Richmond, Surrey
14	Haringey Jazz Club, Manor House Pub, London
15	Ricky Tick Club, Star and Garter Pub,Windsor, Berkshire
17	Studio 51, Ken Colyer Club, London
	Station Hotel, Richmond, Surrey
20	Red Lion Pub, Sutton, Surrey
22	Ricky Tick Club, Star and Garter Pub, Windsor, Berkshire
24	Studio 51, Ken Colyer Club, London
	Station Hotel, Richmond, Surrey
29	Ricky Tick Club, Star and Garter Pub, Windsor, Berkshire
30	Wooden Bridge Hotel, Guildford, Surrey
31	Studio 51, Ken Colyer Club, London
	Station Hotel, Richmond, Surrey

APRIL
3	Red Lion Pub, Sutton, Surrey
7	Studio 51, Ken Colyer Club, London
	Station Hotel, Richmond, Surrey
13	Antelope Hotel, Poole, Dorset
14	Studio 51, Ken Colyer Club, London
	Crawdaddy Club, Station Hotel, Richmond, Surrey
19	Wooden Bridge Hotel, Guildford, Surrey
21	Crawdaddy Club, Station Hotel, Richmond, Surrey
24	Eel Pie Island, Twickenham, Surrey
26	Ricky Tick Club, Star and Garter Pub, Windsor, Berkshire
28	Studio 51, Colyer Club, London
	Crawdaddy Club, Station Hotel, Richmond, Surrey

MAY
1	Eel Pie Island, Twickenham, Surrey
3	Ricky Tick Club, Star and Garter Pub, Windsor, Berkshire
4	News of the World Charity Gala, Battersea Park, London
5	Studio 51, Ken Colyer Club, London
	Crawdaddy Club, Station Hotel, Richmond, Surrey
8	Eel Pie Island, Twickenham, Surrey
12	Studio 51, Ken Colyer Club, London
	Crawdaddy Club, Station Hotel, Richmond, Surrey
15	Eel Pie Island, Twickenham, Surrey
17	Wooden Bridge Hotel, Guildford, Surrey
19	Studio 51, Ken Colyer Club, London
	Crawdaddy Club, Station Hotel, Richmond, Surrey
22	Eel Pie Island, Twickenham, Surrey
24	Ricky Tick Club, Star and Garter Pub, Windsor, Berkshire
26	Studio 51, Ken Colyer Club, London
	Crawdaddy Club, Station Hotel, Richmond Surrey
29	Eel Pie Island, Twickenham, Surrey
31	Ricky Tick Club, Star and Garter Pub, Windsor, Berkshire

JUNE
2	Studio 51, Ken Colyer Club, London
	Crawdaddy Club, Station Hotel, Richmond, Surrey
3	Studio 51, Ken Colyer Club, London
5	Eel Pie Island, Twickenham, Middlesex
7	Wooden Bridge Hotel, Guildford, Surrey
9	Studio 51, Ken Colyer Club, London
	Crawdaddy Club, Station Hotel, Richmond, Surrey
10	Studio 51, Ken Colyer Club, London
12	Eel Pie Island, Twickenham, Middlesex
14	Ricky Tick Club, Star and Garter Pub, Windsor, Berkshire
16	Studio 51, Ken Colyer Club, London
	Crawdaddy Club , Station Hotel, Richmond Surrey
17	Studio 51, Ken Colyer Club, London
19	Eel Pie Island, Twickenham, Middlesex
20	Scene Club, London

	21	Ricky Tick Club, Star and Garter Pub, Windsor, Berkshire
	22	Wooden Bridge Hotel, Guildford, Surrey
	23	Studio 51, Ken Colyer Club, London
	24	Studio 51, Ken Colyer Club, London
	26	Eel Pie Island, Twickenham, Middlesex
	27	Scene Club, London
	28	Ricky Tick Club, Star and Garter Pub, Windsor, Berkshire
	30	Studio 51, Ken Colyer Club, London
		Crawdaddy Club, Athletic Ground, Richmond, Surrey
JULY	1	Studio 51, Ken Colyer Club, London
	3	Eel Pie Island, Twickenham, Middlesex
	4	Scene Club, London
	5	Ricky Tick Club, Star and Garter Pub, Windsor, Berkshire
	6	Kings Lynn
	8	Studio 51, Ken Colyer Club, London
	10	Eel Pie Island, Twickenham, Middlesex
	11	Scene Club, London
	12	Twickenham Design College,
		Eel Pie Island, Twickenham, Middlesex
	13	Alcove Club, Middlesborough, Yorkshire
	14	Studio 51, Ken Colyer Club, London
		Crawdaddy Club, Athletic Ground, Richmond, Surrey
	15	Studio 51, Ken Colyer Club, London
	17	Eel Pie Island, Twickenham, Middlesex
	19	Deb Dance, Hastings, Sussex
	20	Corn Exchange, Wisbech, Cambridgeshire
	21	Studio 51. Ken Colyer Club, London
		Crawdaddy Club, Athletic Ground, Richmond, Surrey
	22	Studio 51, Ken Colyer Club, London
	24	Eel Pie Island, Twickenham, Middlesex
	26	Ricky Tick Club, Star and Garter Pub, Windsor, Berkshire
	27	California Ballroom, Dunstable, Bedfordshire
	28	Studio 51, Ken Colyer Club, London
		Crawdaddy Club, Athletic Ground, Richmond, Surrey
	29	Studio 51, Ken Colyer Club, London
	30	Ricky Tick Club, Thames Hotel, Windsor, Berkshire
	31	Eel Pie Island, Twickenham, Middlesex
AUGUST	2	Wooden Bridge Hotel, Guildford, Surrey
	3	St. Leonard's Hall, Horsham, Sussex
	4	Studio 51, Ken Colyer Club, London
		Crawdaddy Club , Athletic Ground, Richmond, Surrey
	5	Botwell House, Hayes, Middlesex
	6	Ricky Tick Club, Thames Hotel, Windsor, Berkshir
	7	Eel Pie Island, Twickenham, Middlesex
	9	California Ballroom, Dunstable, Bedfordshire
	10	Plaza Theatre, Handsworth, Birmingham, Warwickshire
		Plaza Theatre, Oldhill, Birmingham, Warwickshire
	11	Studio 51, Ken Colyer Club, London
		3rd Richmond Jazz Festival, Athletic Grounds, Richmond, Surrey
	12	Studio 51, Ken Colyer Club, London
	13	Town Hall, High Wycombe, Buckinghamshire
	14	Eel Pie Island, Twickenham, Middlesex
	15	Dreamland Ballroom, Margate, Kent
	16	Winter Gardens, Banbury, Oxfordshire
	17	Memorial Hall, Northwich, Cheshire
	18	Studio 51, Ken Colyer Club, London
		Crawdaddy Club, Athletic Ground, Richmond, Surrey
	19	Atlanta Ballroom, Woking, Surrey
	20	Ricky Tick Club, Thames Hotel, Windsor, Berkshire
	21	Eel Pie Island, Twickenham, Middlesex
	23	Worplesdon Village Hall, Guildford, Surrey
	25	Studio 51, Ken Colyer Club, London
		Crawdaddy Club, Athletic Ground, Richmond, Surrey
	26	Studio 51, Ken Colyer Club, London
	27	Ricky Tick Club, Thames Hotel, Windsor, Berkshire
	28	Eel Pie Island, Twickenham, Middlesex
	30	Oasis Club, Manchester, Lancashire
	31	Royal Lido Ballroom, Prestatyn, Wales

SEPTEMBER	1	Studio 51, Ken Colyer Club, London
		Crawdaddy Club, Athletic Ground, Richmond, Surrey
	2	Studio 51, Ken Colyer Club, London
	3	Ricky Tick Club, Thames Hotel, Windsor, Berkshire
	4	Eel Pie Island, Twickenham, Middlesex
	5	Strand Palace Theatre, Walmer, Kent
	6	Grand Hotel Ballroom, Lowestoft, Suffolk
	7	Kings Hall, Aberystwyth, Wales
	9	Studio 51, Ken Colyer Club, London
	10	Ricky Tick Club, Thames Hotel, Windsor, Berkshire
	11	Eel Pie Island, Twickenham, Middlesex
	12	Cellar Club, Kingston-upon-Thames, Surrey
	13	California Ballroom, Dunstable, Bedfordshire
	14	Ritz Ballroom, Kings Heath, Birmingham, Warwickshire
		Plaza Theatre, Oldhill, Birmingham, Warwickshire
	15	Great Pop Prom, Royal Albert Hall, London
		Crawdaddy Club, Athletic Ground, Richmond, Surrey
	16	Studio 51, Ken Colyer Club, London
	17	British Legion Hall, Barrow-on-the-Hill, London
	18	Eel Pie Island, Twickenham, Middlesex
	19	St John's Hall, Watford, Hertfordshire
	20	Savoy Ballroom, Southsea, Hampshire
	21	Corn Exchange, Peterborough, Northamptonshire
	22	Studio 51, Ken Colyer Club, London
		Crawdaddy Club, Athletic Ground, Richmond, Surrey

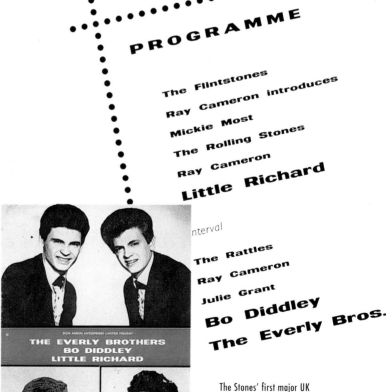

PROGRAMME

The Flintstones
Ray Cameron introduces
Mickie Most
The Rolling Stones
Ray Cameron
Little Richard

Interval

The Rattles
Ray Cameron
Julie Grant
Bo Diddley
The Everly Bros.

DON ARDEN ENTERPRISES LIMITED PRESENT
THE EVERLY BROTHERS
BO DIDDLEY
LITTLE RICHARD

The Stones' first major UK tour (programme and billing above) commenced on 29 September 1963 and was headlined by the Everly Brothers, Bo Diddley, and the wonderful Little Richard.

23	Studio 51, Ken Colyer Club, London	
24	Ricky Tick Club, Thames Hotel, Windsor, Berkshire	
25	Eel Pie Island, Twickenham, Middlesex	
27	Floral Hall, Morecambe, Lancashire	
28	Assembly Hall, Walthamstow, London	
29	New Victoria Theatre, London	
30	Ballroom, Cambridge, Cambridgeshire	

OCTOBER

1	Odeon Theatre, Streatham, London
2	Regal Theatre, Edmonton, London
3	Odeon Theatre, Southend, Essex
4	Odeon Theatre, Guildford, Surrey
5	Gaumont Theatre, Watford
6	Capitol Theatre, Cardiff, Wales
8	Odeon Theatre, Cheltenham, Gloucestershire
9	Gaumont Theatre, Worcester, Worcestershire
10	Gaumont Theatre, Wolverhampton, Staffordshire
11	Gaumont Theatre, Derby, Derbyshire
12	Gaumont Theatre, Doncaster, Yorkshire
13	Odeon Theatre, Liverpool, Lancashire
15	Majestic Ballroom, Kingston-upon-Hull, Yorkshire
16	Odeon Theatre, Manchester, Lancashire
17	Odeon Theatre, Glasgow, Scotland
18	Odeon Theatre, Newcastle-upon-Tyne, Northumberlan
19	Gaumont Theatre, Bradford, Yorkshire
20	Gaumont Theatre, Hanley, Staffordshire
22	Gaumont Theatre, Sheffield, Yorkshire
23	Odeon Theatre, Nottingham, Nottinghamshire
24	Odeon Theatre, Birmingham, Warwickshire
25	Gaumont Theatre, Taunton, Somerset
26	Gaumont Theatre, Bournemouth, Hampshire
27	Gaumont Theatre, Salisbury, Wiltshire
29	Gaumont Theatre, Southampton, Hampshire
30	Odeon Theatre, St. Albans, Hertfordshire
31	Odeon Theatre, Lewisham, London

NOVEMBER

1	Odeon Theatre, Rochester, Kent
2	Gaumont Theatre, Ipswich, Suffolk
3	Odeon Theatre, Hammersmith, London
4	Top Rank Ballroom, Preston, Lancashire
5	Cavern Club, Liverpool, Lancashire
6	Queens Hall, Leeds, Yorkshire
8	Club a Go-Go, Newcastle-upon-Tyne, Northumberland
9	Club a Go-Go, Whitley Bay, Northumberland
10	Town Hall, Crewe, Cheshire
11	Pavilion Ballroom, Bath, Somerset
12	Town Hall, High Wycombe, Buckinghamshire
13	City Hall, Sheffield, Yorkshire
15	Co-op Ballroom Nuneaton, Warwickshire (2 shows)
16	Matrix Ballroom, Coventry, Warwickshire
19	State Ballroom, Kilburn, London
20	Chiswick Polytechnic Dance, Athletic Club, Richmond, Surrey
21	McIlroys Ballroom, Swindon, Wiltshire
22	Town Hall, Greenwich, London
23	The Baths, Leyton, London
	Chez Don Club, Dalston, London
24	Studio 51, Ken Colyer Club, London
	Majestic Ballroom, Luton, Bedfordshire
25	Ballroom, Warrington, Lancashire
26	Ballroom, Altrincham, Cheshire
27	Ballroom, Wigan, Lancashire
	Memorial Hall, Northwick, Cheshire
28	Amble, Northumberland
30	Kings Hall, Stoke-on-Trent, Staffordshire

DECEMBER

1	Oasis Club, Manchester, Lancashire
2	Assembly Rooms, Tamworth, Staffordshire
3	Floral Hall, Southportk Lancashire
4	The Baths, Doncaster, Yorkshire

5	Theatre, Worcester, Worcestershire
6	Odeon Theatre, Romford, Essex
7	Fairfield Halls, Croydon, Surrey
8	Olympia Ballroom, Reading, Berkshire
	Gaumont Theatre, Watford, Herfordshire
10	Chester, Cheshire
11	Bradford Arts Ball, King and Queens Hall, Bradford, Yorkshire
12	Locarno Ballroom, Liverpool, Lancashire
13	Ballroom, Hereford, Herefordshire
14	The Baths, Epsom, Surrey
15	Civic Hall, Guildford, Surrey
17	Town Hall, High Wycombe, Buckinghamshire
18	Corn Exchange, Bristol, Gloucestershire
20	Lido Ballroom, Winchester, Hampshire
21	Kayser Bondor Ballroom, Baldock, Hertfordshire
22	St. Mary's Hall, Putney, London
24	Town Hall, Leek, Staffordshire
26	Selby's Restaurant, London
27	Town Hall, Reading, Berkshire
28	Club Noreik, Tottenham, London
30	Studio 51, Ken Colyer Club, London
31	Drill Hall, Lincoln, Lincolnshire

1964

JANUARY

3	Glenlyn Ballroom, Forest Hill, London
4	Town Hall, Oxford, Oxfordshire
5	Olympia Ballroom, Reading, Berkshire
6	Granada Theatre, Harrow-on-the-Hill, London
7	Adelphi Theatre, Slough, Buckinghamshire
8	Granada Theatre, Maidstone, Kent
9	Granada Theatre, Kettering, Northamptonshire
10	Granada Theatre, Walthamstow
11	The Baths, Epsom, Surrey
12	Granada Theatre, Tooting, London
13	Barrowlands Ballroom, Glasgow, Scotland
14	Granada Theatre, Mansfield, Northamptonshire
15	Granada Theatre, Bedford, Bedfordshire
16	McIlroys Ballroom, Swindon, Wiltshire
17	City Hall, Salisbury, Wiltshire
18	Pier Ballroom, Hastings, Sussex
19	The Theatre, Coventry, Warwickshire
20	Granada Theatre, Woolwich, London
21	Granada Theatre, Aylesbury, Buckinghamshire
22	Granada Theatre, Shrewsbury, Shropshire
23	Pavilion, Lowestoft, Suffolk,
24	The Palais, Wimbledon, London
25	California Ballroom, Dunstable, Bedfordshire
26	De Montfort Hall, Leicester, Leicestershire
27	Colston Hall, Bristol, Gloucestershire
31	Public Hall, Preston, Lancashire

FEBRUARY

1	Valentine Charity Pop Show, Royal Albert Hall, London
2	Country Club, Hampstead, London
5	Ballroom, Willenhall, Staffordshire
8	Regal Theatre, Edmonton, London
	Club Noreik, Tottenham, London
9	De Montfort Hall, Leicester, Leicestershire
10	Odeon Theatre, Cheltenham, loucestershire
11	Granada Theatre, Rugby, Warwickshire
12	Odeon Theatre, Guildford, Surrey
13	Granada Theatre, Kingston-upon-Thames, Surrey
14	Gaumont Theatre, Watford, Hertfordshire
15	Odeon Theatre, Rochester, Kent
16	The Guildhall, Portsmouth, Hampshire
17	Granada Theatre, Greenford, Middlesex
18	Rank Theatre, Colchester, Essex
19	Rank Theatre, Stockton-on-Tees, Durham
20	Rank Theatre, Sunderland, Durham
21	Gaumont Theatre, Hanley, Staffordshire

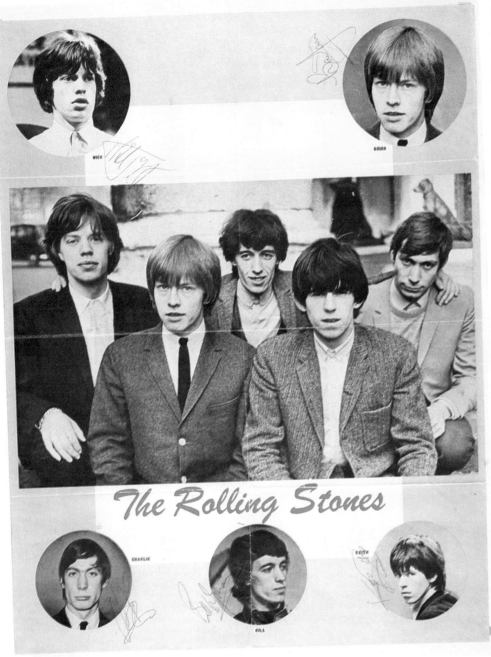

ROBERT STIGWOOD
ASSOCIATES LTD.
presents

ALL STARS '64

SOUVENIR PROGRAMME 2/-

A much sought-after signed promo poster of the boys dating from 1964 (right), and two collectible early tour posters (above).

	22	Winter Gardens, Bournemouth, Hampshire		25	Town Hall, Birmingham, Warwickshire
	23	Hippodrome Theatre, Birmingham, Warwickshire		26	Town Hall, Kidderminster, Worcestershire
	24	Odeon Theatre, Southend, Essex		27	Ex-Serviceman's Club, Windsor, Berkshire
	25	Odeon Theatre, Romford, Essex		28	Wilton Hall, Bletchley, Buckinghamshire
	26	Rialto Theatre, York, Yorkshire			Club Noreik, Tottenham, London
	27	City Hall, Sheffield, Yorkshire		30	Ricky Tick Club, Plaza Ballroom, Guildford, Surrey
	28	Sophia Gardens, Cardiff, Wales			Olympia Ballroom, Reading, Berkshire
	29	Hippodrome, Brighton, Sussex		31	West Cliff Hall, Ramsgate, Kent.
MARCH	1	Empire Theatre, Liverpool, Lancashire	**APRIL**	1	Locarno Ballroom, Stevenage, Hertfordshire
	2	Albert Hall, Nottingham, Nottinghamshire		3	The Palais, Wimbledon, London
	3	Opera House, Blackpool, Lancashire		4	Leas Cliff Hall, Folkestone, Kent
	4	Gaumont Theatre, Bradford, Yorkshire		5	Gaumont Theatre, Ipswich, Suffolk
	5	Odeon Theatre, Blackburn, Lancashire		6	Royal Hotel Ballroom, Lowestoft, Suffolk
	6	Gaumont Theatre, Wolverhampton, Staffordshire		8	Mod Ball, Empire Pool, Wembley
	7	Winter Gardens, Morecambe, Lancashire		9	McIlroy's Ballroom, Swindon, Wiltshire
	15	Invicta Ballroom, Chatham, Kent		10	The Baths, Leyton, London
	17	Assembly Hall, Tunbridge Wells, Kent		11	Pier Ballroom, Hastings, Sussex
	18	City Hall, Salisbury, Wiltshire		12	Fairfield Halls, Croydon, Surrey
	21	Whitehall, East Grinstead, Sussex		16	Cubi-Club, Rochdale, Lancashire
	22	Pavilion, Ryde, Isle of Wight, Hampshire		17	Locarno Ballroom, Coventry, Warwickshire
	23	Guildhall, Southampton, Hampshire		18	Royalty Theatre, Chester, Cheshire

	22	Carlton Ballroom, Slough, Buckinghamshire
	24	Gaumont Theatre, Norwich, Norfolk
	25	Odeon Theatre, Luton, Bedfordshire
	26	NME Poll-Winners Concert, Empire Pool, Wembley, Middlesex
	27	Pop Prom, Royal Albert Hall, London
	28	Public hall, Wallington, Surrey
	30	Majestic Ballroom, Birkenhead, Cheshire
MAY	1	Imperial Ballroom, Nelson, Lancashire
	2	Spa Royal Hall, Bridlington, Yorkshire
	3	Palace Theatre, Manchester, Lancashire
	7	Savoy Ballroom, Southsea, Hampshire
	8	Town Hall, Hove, Sussex
	9	Savoy Ballroom, Catford, London
	10	Colston Hall, Bristol, Gloucestershire
	11	Winter Gardens, Bournemouth, Hampshire
	13	City Hall, Newcastle-upon-Tyne, Northumberland
	14	St. Georges Hall, Bradford, Yorkshire
	15	Trentham Gardens, Stoke-on-Trent, Staffordshire
	16	Regal Theatre, Edmonton, London
	17	Odeon Theatre, Folkestone, Kent
	18	Chantinghall Hotel, Hamilton, Lanarkshire, Scotland
	19	Capitol Theatre, Aberdeen, Scotland
	20	Caird Hall, Dundee, Scotland
	21	Regal Theatre, Edinburgh, Scotland
	23	The University, Leicester Leicestershire
	24	The Theatre, Coventry, Warwickshire
	25	Granada Theatre, East Ham, London
	26	Town Hall, Birmingham, Warwickshire
	27	Danilo Theatre, Cannock, Staffordshire
	28	Essoldo Theatre, Stockport, Cheshire
	29	City Hall, Sheffield, Yorkshire
	30	Adelphi Theatre, Slough, Buckinghamshire
	31	Pop Hit Parade, Empire Pool, Wembley, Middlesex (2 shows)
JUNE	5	Swing Auditorium, San Bernardino, California
	6	State Fair, San Antonio, Texas (2 shows)
	7	State Fair, San Antonio, Texas (afternoon) (2 shows)
	12	Ballroom, Excelsior Fair, Minneapolis, Minnesota
	13	Music Hall, Omaha, Nebraska
	14	Olympia Stadium, Detroit, Michigan
	17	Westview Park, Pittsburgh, Pennsylvania
	19	State Farm Arena, Harrisburg, Pennsylvania
	20	Carnegie Hall, New York (afternoon)
		Carnegie Hall, New York (evening)
	22	Magdalen College, Oxford, Oxfordshire
	26	Alexandra Palace, London
JULY	11	Spa Royal Hall, Bridlington, Yorkshire
	12	Queens Hall, Leeds, Yorkshire
	18	Beat City Club, London
	19	Hippodrome, Brighton, Sussex
	24	Empress Ballroom, Blackpool, Lancashire
	25	Imperial Ballroom, Nelson, Cheshire
	26	De Montfort Hall, Leicester, Leicestershire
	31	Ulster Hall, Belfast, Northern Ireland
		Flamingo Ballroom, Ballymena, Northern Ireland
AUGUST	1	Pier Ballroom Hastings, Sussex
	2	Longleat House, Warminster, Wiltshire
	8	Kurhaus, Scheveningen, The Hague, Holland
	9	New Elizabethan Ballroom, Belle Vue, Manchester, Lancashire
	10	Tower Ballroom, New Brighton, Cheshire
	11	Winter Gardens, Blackpool, Lancashire
	13	Palace Ballroom Douglas, Isle of Man
	14	Palais, Wimbledon, London
	18	St Georges Hall, New Theatre Ballroom, Guernsey, Channel Islands
	19	St Georges Hall, New Theatre Ballroom, Guernsey, Channel Islands
	20	St Georges Hall, New Theatre Ballroom, Guernsey, Channel Islands

The Rolling Stones Show

Rare tour programmes from various UK tours in the sixties. Tickets are also very collectible and can fetch big bucks at auction.

OPPOSITE PAGE BELOW An action-packed poster advertising the TAMI Show at the Civic Auditorium, Santa Monica, California, held on 28 and 29 October 1964.

THE ROLLING STONES

This advance ticket, price 8/6d., admits the purchaser to the Tower Ballroom, New Brighton, on Monday, 10th August, 1964, starting at 7-30 p.m. prompt and finishing at 11-30 p.m. for The Cavern presentation produced by Bob Wooler, starring on stage the Rolling Stones plus the 12 finalists in the Rael-Brook/Cavern Club 1964 Beat Group contest. Licensed bars have been applied for and refreshments will be available. No special late transport will be laid on, so you are advised to check on times of last trains and buses, etc. The Rolling Stones will be on stage at about 10 p.m. for approximately 50 minutes. Please come along early and tell your friends all about this great show!

Nº 4417

GAUMONT :: DONCASTER
ROBERT STIGWOOD ASSOCIATES LTD.
(in Association with Eric Easton Ltd.) present
THE ROLLING STONES TOUR
1st Performance 6-15 p.m.
THURSDAY
SEPTEMBER 24
STALLS 10/6
BLOCK
8 A 2
No ticket exchanged nor money refunded
THIS PORTION TO BE RETAINED

ALBERT A. BONICI and ANDY LOTHIAN, JNR.
present
Star Parade
MARK PETERS AND THE SILHOUETTES
PETER AND GORDON
THE ROLLING STONES
FREDDIE AND THE DREAMERS
MILLIE AND THE FIVE EMBERS
DAVE BERRY AND THE CRUISERS
SOUVENIR PROGRAMME 2/6

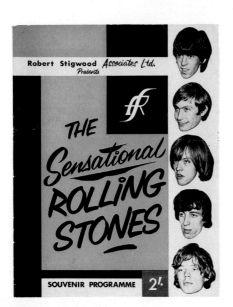

Robert Stigwood Associates Ltd. Presents
THE Sensational ROLLING STONES
SOUVENIR PROGRAMME 2/-

	21	Springfield Hall, St Helier, Jersey, Channel Islands
	22	Springfield Hall, St Helier, Jersey, Channel Islands
	23	Gaumont Theatre, Bournemouth, Hampshire
	24	Gaumont Theatre, Weymouth, Dorset
	25	Odeon Theatre, Weston-super-Mare, Somerset
	26	Odeon Theatre, Exeter, Devon
	27	ABC Theatre, Plymouth, Devon
	28	Gaumont Theatre, Taunton, Somerset
	29	Town Hall, Torquay, Devon
	30	Gaumont Theatre, Bournemouth, Hampshire
SEPTEMBER	5	Astoria Theatre, Finsbury Park, London
	6	Odeon Theatre, Leicester, Leicestershire
	8	Odeon Theatre, Colchester, Essex
	9	Odeon Theatre, Luton, Bedfordshire
	10	Odeon Theatre, Cheltenham, Gloucestershire
	11	Capitol Theatre, Cardiff, Wales
	13	Empire Theatre, Liverpool, Lancashire
	14	ABC Theatre, Chester, Cheshire
	15	Odeon Theatre, Manchester, Lancashire
	16	ABC Theatre, Wigan, Lancashire
	17	ABC Theatre, Carlisle, Cumberland
	18	Odeon Theatre, Newcastle-upon-Tyne, Northumberland
	19	Usher Hall, Edinburgh, Scotland
	20	ABC Theatre, Stockton-on-Tees, Durham
	21	ABC Theatre, Kingston-upon-Hull, Yorkshire
	22	ABC Theatre, Lincoln, Lincolnshire
	24	Gaumont Theatre, Doncaster, Yorkshire
	25	Gaumont Theatre, Hanley, Staffordshire
	26	Odeon Theatre, Bradford, Yorkshire
	27	Hippodrome Theatre, Birmingham, Warwickshire
	29	Odeon Theatre, Guildford, Surrey
OCTOBER	1	Colston Hall, Bristol, Gloucestershire
	2	Odeon Theatre, Exeter, Devon
	3	Regal Theatre, Edmonton, London
	4	Gaumont Theatre, Southampton, Hampshire
	5	Gaumont Theatre, Wolverhampton, Staffordshire
	6	Gaumont Theatre, Watford, Hertfordshire
	8	Odeon Theatre, Lewisham, London
	9	Gaumont Theatre, Ipswich, Suffolk
	10	Odeon Theatre, Southend, Essex
	11	Hippodrome, Brighton, Sussex
	20	Olympia Theatre, Paris, France
	24	Academy of Music, New York (2 shows)
	26	Memorial Auditorium, Sacramento, California
	28	Tami Show, Civic Auditorium, Santa Monica, California
	29	Tami Show, Civic Auditorium, Santa Monica, California
	31	Swing Auditorium, San Bernardino, California
NOVEMBER	1	Civic Auditorium, Long Beach Arena, California (afternoon)
		Balboa Park Bowl, San Diego, California (evening)
	3	Public Hall, Cleveland, Ohio
	4	Loews Theatre, Providence, Rhode Island
	11	Auditorium, Milwaukee, Wisconsin
	12	Coliseum, Fort Wayne, Indiana
	13	Hara Arena, Dayton, Ohio
	14	Memorial Auditorium, Louisville, Kentucky
	15	Arie Crown Theatre, McCormick Place, Chicago, Illinois
	20	Glad Rag Ball, Empire Pool, Wembley, Middlesex
DECEMBER	4	Fairfield Halls, Croydon, Surrey

1965

JANUARY	6	ABC Theatre, Belfast, Northern Ireland
	7	Adelphi Theatre, Dublin, Eire
	8	Savoy Theatre, Cork, Eire
	10	Commodore Theatre, Hammersmith, London
	22	Manufacturers Auditorium, Agricultural Hall, Sydney, Australia
	25	City Hall, Brisbane, Australia

	26	City Hall, Brisbane, Australia
	27	Manufacturers Auditorium, Agricultural Hall, Sydney, Australia
	28	Palais Theatre, St Kilda, Melbourne, Australia (2 shows)
	29	Palais Theatre, St Kilda, Melbourne, Australia
FEBRUARY	1	Theatre Royal, Christchurch, New Zealand (2 shows)
	2	Civic Theatre, Invercargill, New Zealand (2 shows)
	3.	Town Hall, Dunedin, New Zealand (2 shows)
	6	Town Hall, Auckland, New Zealand (2 shows)
	8	Local venue, Wellington, New Zealand (2 shows)
	10	Palais Theatre, St Kilda, Melbourne, Australia (2 shows)
	12	Centennial Hall, Adelaide, Australia
	13	Capitol Theatre, Perth, Australia (afternoon)
		Capitol Theatre, Perth, Australia (evening) (2 shows)
	16	Badminton Stadium, Singapore (2 shows)
MARCH	5	Regal Theatre, Edmonton, London (2 shows)
	6	Empire Theatre, Liverpool, Lancashire (2 shows)
	7	Palace Theatre, Manchester, Lancashire (2 shows)
	8	Futurist Theatre, Scarborough, Yorkshire (2 shows)
	9	Odeon Theatre, Sunderland, Durham (2 shows)
	10	ABC Theatre, Huddersfield, Yorkshire (2 shows)
	11	City Hall, Sheffield, Yorkshire (2 shows)
	12	Trocadero Theatre, Leicester, Leicestershire (2 shows)
	13	Granada Theatre, Rugby, Warwickshire (2 shows)
	14	Odeon Theatre, Rochester, Kent (2 shows)
	15	Odeon Theatre, Guildford, Surrey (2 shows)
	16	Granada Theatre, Greenford, Middlesex (2 shows)
	17	Odeon Theatre, Southend, Essex (2 shows)

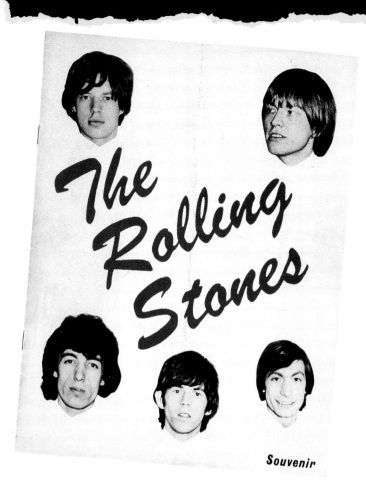

The Rolling Stones

Souvenir

	18	ABC Theatre, Romford, Essex (2 shows)
	26	Fyns Forum, Odense, Denmark (2 shows)
	28	Koncert Sal, Tivoli Gardens, Copenhagen, Denmark (2 shows)
	30	Koncert Sal, Tivoli Gardens, Copenhagen, Denmark (2 shows)
	31	Masshallen, Gothenberg, Sweden (2 shows)
APRIL	1	Kungliga Tennishallen, Stockholm, Sweden (2 shows)
	2	Kungliga Tennishallen, Stockholm, Sweden
	3	Open-air venue, Helsinki, Finland
	11	NME Poll-Winners Concert, Empire Pool, Wembley, Middlesex
	16	Olympia Theatre, Paris, France
	17	Olympia Theatre, Paris, France
	18	Olympia Theatre, Paris, France
	23	Maurice Richard Arena, Montreal, Canada
	24	YMCA Auditorium, Ottawa, Canada
	25	Maple Leaf Gardens, Toronto, Canada
	26	Treasure Island Gardens, London, Canada
	29	Palace Theatre, Albany, New York (2 shows)
	30	Auditorium, Worcester, Massachusetts
MAY	1	Academy of Music, New York (afternoon)
		Convention Hall, Philadelphia, Pennsylvania (evening)
	4	Georgia Southern College Auditorium, Statesboro, Georgia
	6	Jack Russell Stadium, Clearwater, Florida
	7	Legion Field Stadium, Birmingham, Alabama
	8	Coliseum, Jacksonville, Florida
	9	Arie Crown Theatre, McCormick Place, Chicago, Illinois
	14	New Civic Auditorium, San Francisco, California
	15	Swing Auditorium, San Bernardino, California
	16	Civic Auditorium, Long Beach, California (afternoon)
	17	Community Concourse, Convention Hall, San Diego, California
	21	Civic Auditorium, San Jose, California
	22	Convention Hall, Ratcliffe Stadium,Fresno,California (afternoon)
		Municipal auditorium, Sacramento, California (evening)
	29	Academy of Music, New York (2 shows)
JUNE	15	Odeon Theatre, Glasgow, Scotland (2 shows)
	16	Usher Hall, Edinburgh, Scotland (2 shows)
	17	Capitol Theatre, Aberdeen, Scotland (2 shows)
	18	Caird Hall, Dundee, Scotland (2 shows)
	24	Messhallen, Oslo, Norway
	25	Yyteri Beach, Pori, Finland
	26	A Hall, Copenhagen, Denmark (2 shows)
	29	Baltiska Hallen, Malmo, Sweden (2 shows)
JULYy	16	Odeon Theatre, Exeter, Devon (2 shows)
	17	The Guildhall, Portsmouth, Hampshire (2 shows)

	18	Gaumont Theatre, Bournemouth, Hampshire (2 shows)
	25	ABC Theatre, Great Yarmouth, Norfolk (2 shows)
	26	Local venue, Leicester, Leicestershire
AUGUST	8	Odeon Theatre, Blackpool, Lancashire
	1	London Palladium, London (2 shows)
	22	Futurist Theatre, Scarborough, Yorkshire (2 shows)
SEPTEMBER	3	Adelphi Theatre, Dublin, Eire (2 shows)
	4	ABC Theatre, Belfast, Northern Ireland (2 shows)
	8	Palace Ballroom, Douglas, Isle of Man
	11	Munsterland Halle, Munster, West Germany (2 shows)
	12	Gruga Halle, Essen, West Germany (2 shows)
	13	Ernst Merck Halle, Hamburg, West Germany (2 shows)
	14	Circus-krone-Bau, Munich, West Germany (2 shows)
	15	Waldbuhne Halle, West Berlin, West Germany
	17	Wiener Stadthalle, Vienna, Austria
	24	Astoria Theatre, Finsbury Park, London (2 shows)
	25	Gaumont Theatre, Southampton, Hampshire (2 shows)
	26	Colston Hall, Bristol, Gloucestershire (2 shows)
	27	Odeon Theatre, Cheltenham, Gloucestershire (2 shows)
	28	Capitol Theatre, Cardiff, Wales (2 shows)
	28	Capitol Theatre, Cardiff, Wales (2 shows)
	29	Granada Theatre, Shrewsbury, Shropshire (2 shows)
	30	Gaumont Theatre, Hanley, Staffordshire (2 shows)
OCTOBER	1	ABC Theatre, Chester, Cheshire (2 shows)
	2	ABC Theatre, Wigan, Lancashire (2 shows)
	3	Odeon Theatre, Manchester, Lancashire (2 shows)
	4	Gaudomt Theatre, Bradford, Yorkshire (2 shows)
	5	ABC Theatre, Carlisle, Cumberland (2 shows)
	6	Odeon Theatre, Glasgow, Scotland (2 shows)
	7	City Hall, Newcastle, Northumberland (2 shows)
	8	ABC Theatre, Stockton-on-Tees, Durham (2 shows)
	9	Odeon Theatre, Leeds, Yorkshire (2 shows)
	10	Empire Theatre, Liverpool, Lancashire (2 shows)
	11	Gaumont Theatre, Sheffield, Yorkshire (2 shows)
	12	Gaumont Theatre, Doncaster, Yorkshire (2 shows)
	13	De Montfort Hall, Leicester, Leicestershire (2 shows)
	15	Regal Theatre, Cambridge, Cambridgeshire (2 shows)
	16	ABC Theatre, Northampton, Northamptonshire (2 shows)
	17	Granada Theatre, Tooting, London (2 shows)
	29	Forum, Montreal, Canada
	30	Barton Hall, Cornell University, Ithaca, New York (afternoon)
		War Memorial Hall, Syracuse, New York (evening)
	31	Maple Leaf Gardens, Toronto, Canada.
NOVEMBER	1	Memorial Auditorium, Rochester, New York
	3	Auditorium, Providence, Rhode Island
	4	Arena, Newhaven, Connecticut (2 shows)
	5	The Gardens, Boston, Massachusetts
	6	Academy of Music, New York (afternoon
		Convention Hall, Philadelphia, Pennsylvania (evening)
	7	Mosque Theatre, Newark, New Jersey (2 shows)
	10	Reynolds Coliseum, Raleigh, North Carolina
	12	Memorial Auditorium, Greensboro, North Carolina
	13	Coliseum, Washington, DC (afternoon)
		Civic Centre, Baltimore, Maryland (evening)
	14	Civic Coliseum (Auditorium), Knoxville, Tennessee
	15	Coliseum, Charlotte, North Carolina
	16	Municipal Auditorium, Nashville, Tennessee
	17	Mid South Coliseum, Memphis, Tennessee
	20	State Fair Youth Centre, Shreveport, Louisiana
	21	Will Rogers Stadium, Fort Worth, Texas (afternoon)
		Memorial Auditorium, Dallas, Texas (evening)
	23	Assembly Center, Tulsa, Oklahoma
	24	Civic Center (Arena), Pittsburgh, Pennsylvania
	25	Arena (Auditorium), Milwaukee, Wisconsin
	26	Cobo Hall, Detroit, Michigan

Stylish colour programme to accompany the
Stones on tour in 1965.

	27	Hara Arena, Dayton, Ohio (afternoon)
		The Gardens, Cincinnati, Ohio (evening)
	28	Arie Crown Theatre, McCormick Place, Chicago, Illinois (2 shows)
	29	Coliseum, Denver, Colorado
	30	Veterans Memorial Coliseum, Phoenix, Arizona
DECEMBER	1	Agrodrome, Vancouver, Canada
	2	Coliseum, Seattle, Washington
	3	Memorial Auditorium, Sacramento, California
	4	Civic Auditorium, San Jose, California (2 shows)
	5	Convention Hall, San Diego, California (afternoon)
		Sports Arena, Los Angeles, California (evening)(last night)

1966

FEBRUARY	18	Commemorative Auditorium, Showgrounds, Sydney, Australia (2 shows)
	19	Commemorative Auditorium, Showgrounds, Sydney, Australia (2 shows)
	21	City Hall, Brisbane, Australia (2 shows)
	22	Centennial Hall, Adelaide, Australia
	23	Palais Theatre, St. Kilda, Melbourne, Australia (2 shows)
	24	Palais Theatre, St. Kilda, Melbourne, Australia (2 shows)
	25	Palais Theatre, St. Kilda, Melbourne, Australia (2 shows)
	28	Town Hall, Wellington, New Zealand (2 shows)
MARCH	1	Civic Theatre, Auckland, New Zealand
	2	Capitol Theatre, Perth, Australia (last night)
	26	Braband Hall, Den Bosche, The Hague, Holland
	27	Palais des Sports, Brussels, Belgium
	29	Olympia Theatre, Paris, France (2 shows)
	30	Salle Vallier, Marseilles, France
	31	Palais d'Hiver, Lyon, France (2 shows)
APRIL	3	Kungliga Tennishallen, Stockholm, Sweden (2 shows)
	5	K. B. Hallen, Copenhagen, Denmark (2 shows)
MAY	1	NME Poll-Winners Concert, Empire Pool, Wembley, Middlesex
JUNE	24	Manning Bowl, Lynn, Massachusetts
	25	Local venue, Cleveland, Ohio (afternoon)
		Civic Arena, Pittsburgh, Pennsylvania (evening)
	26	Coliseum, Washington DC (afternoon)
		Local venue, Baltimore, Maryland (evening)
	27	Dillon Stadium, Hartford, Connecticut
	28	Local venue, Buffalo, New York
	29	Maple Leaf Gardens, Toronto, Canada
	30	Forum, Montreal, Canada
JULY	1	Local venue, Atlantic City, New Jersey
	2	Forest Hills Tennis Stadium, Queens, New York
	3	Asbury Park, New Jersey
	4	Local venue, Virginia Beach, Virginia
	6	War Memorial Auditorium, Syracuse, New York
	8	Cobo Hall, Detroit, Michigan
	9	State Fairgrounds Coliseum, Indianapolis, Indiana
	10	Arie Crown Theatre, McCormick Palace, Chicago, Illinois
	11	Sam Houston Coliseum, Houston, Texas
	12	Kiel Convention Hall, St. Louis, Missouri
	14	Local venue, Winnipeg, Canada
	15	Civic Auditorium, Omaha, Nebraska
	19	PNE Forum, Vancouver, Canada
	20	Local venue, Seattle, Washington
	21	Memorial Coliseum, Portland, Oregon
	22	Local venue, Sacramento, California
	23	Lagoon, Davis County, Salt Lake City, Utah (afternoon)
		Local venue, Phoenix, Arizona (evening)
	24	Local venue, Bakersfield, California (2 shows)
	25	Hollywood Bowl, Los Angeles, California
	26	Local venue, San Francisco, California
	28	International Sports Centre, Honolulu, Hawaii

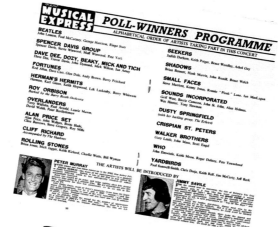

Programme for the Stones' second Australian tour, February-March 1966 (top left), and for the 1966 tour of the US (bottom).
Also shown is the programme and billing for the New Musical Express Poll Winners All-Star Concert held at Wembley, England, on 1 May 1966.

SEPTEMBER	23	Royal Albert Hall, London (2 shows)
	24	Odeon Theatre, Leeds, Yorkshire (2 shows)
	25	Empire Theatre, Liverpool, Lancashire (2 shows)
	28	Apollo Theatre, Ardwick, Manchester, Lancashire (2 shows)
	29	ABC Theatre, Stockton-on-Tees, Durham (2 shows)
	30	Odeon Theatre, Glasgow, Scotland (2 shows)
OCTOBER	1	City Hall, Newcastle-upon-Tyne, Northumberland (2 shows)
	2	Gaumont Theatre, Ipswich, Suffolk (2 shows)
	6	Odeon Theatre, Birmingham, Staffordshire (2 shows)
	7	Colston Hall, Bristol, Gloucestershire (2 shows)
	8	Capitol Theatre, Cardiff, Wales (2 shows)
	9	Gaumont Theatre, Southampton, Hampshire (2 shows)

1967

MARCH	25	Indoor Hall, Malmo, Sweden (2 shows)
	27	Indoor Hall, Orebro, Sweden (2 shows)
	29	Stadthalle, Bremen, West Germany (2 shows)
	30	Sporthalle, Cologne, West Germany (2 shows)
	31	Westfallenhalle, Dortmund, West Germany
APRIL	1	Ernst Merck Halle, Hamburg, West Germany (2 shows)
	2	Stadthalle, Vienna, Austria (2 shows)
	5	Palazzo dello Sport, Bologna, Italy (2 shows)
	6	Palazzo dello Sport, Rome, Italy (2 shows)
	8	Palazzo dello Sport, Milan, Italy 2 shows)
	9	Palazzo dello Sport, Genoa, Italy (2 shows)
	11	Olympia Theatre, Paris, France (2 shows)
	13	Sala Kongresowej, Palace of Culture, Warsaw, Poland (2 shows)
	14	Hallen Stadium, Zurich, Switzerland
	15	Hautreust Hall, The Hague, Holland
	17	Panathinaikos Football Stadium, Athens, Greece

1968

| MAY | 12 | NME Poll-Winners Concert, Empire Pool, Wembley, Middlesex |

1969

JUNE	25	Coliseum, Rome, Italy
	26	Coliseum, Rome, Italy
JULY	5	Free concert, Hyde Park, London
NOVEMBER	7	State University, Fort Collins, Colorado
	8	Forum, Los Angeles, California (2 shows)
	9	Coliseum, Oakland, California
	10	Sports Arena, San Diego, California

Programme for the Stones' 1966 British tour (top left) accompanied by the flyer for the 28 September shows at the ABC Theatre, Ardwick, Manchester (top right).
RIGHT A booklet produced following the Brian Jones' memorial concert held at Hyde Park, London, on 5 July 1969. At the concert Mick Jagger recited some lines by Shelley.

11	Coliseum, Phoenix, Arizona
13	Moody Coliseum, Dallas, Texas
14	University Coliseum, Auburn, Alabama
15	Assembly Hall, University of Illinois, Champagne, Illinois (2 shows)
16	International Amphitheatre, Chicago, Illinois
20	Forum, Los Angeles, California
24	Olympia Stadium, Detroit, Michigan (2 shows)
25	Spectrum, Philadelphia, Pennsylvania
26	Civic Centre, Baltimore, Maryland
27	Madison Square Gardens, New York
28	Madison Square Gardens, New York (2 shows)
29	The Gardens, Boston, Massachusetts (2 shows)
30	Festival, International , West Palm Beach, Florida

DECEMBER

6	Free Concert, Altamont Speedway, Livermore, California
14	Saville Theatre, London (2 shows)
21	Lyceum Theatre, London (2 shows)

1970
SEPTEMBER

2	Olympic Stadium, Helsinki, Finland
4	Royal Tennishallen, Stockholm, Sweden
9	Tennis Stadium, Aarhus, Denmark
12	Forum, Copenhagen, Denmark
14	Ernst-Merck-Halle, Hamburg, Germany
16	Deutschlandhalle, West Berlin, Germany
18	Building Number 11, Cologne, Germany
20	Killesberg, Stuttgart, Germany
22-3	L'Olympia, Paris, France
27	Stadthalle, Vienna, Austria
29	Palazzo dello Sport, Rome, Italy

OCTOBER

1	Palazzo dello Sport, Milan, Italy
3	Palais des Sports, Lyons, France
5	Festhalle, Frankfurt, Germany
7	Grugahalle, Essen, Germany
9	Rai Halle, Amsterdam, Holland

A bootleg picture disc of the
Stones' ill-fated free concert at
Altamont Speedway,
Livermore, California, 6
December 1969 (left).
BELOW The press kit for the
historic film *Gimme Shelter*,
shot at Altamont.

With the coming of 1971, the Rolling Stones' great international success had created a rather sticky problem. Stay in Great Britain and pay out the majority of their earnings in tax, or move to the sunny South of France, thus becoming rock's very first tax exiles. Ultimately, the latter alternative was chosen. To rustle up a little ready cash and say so long to their adoring fans, a farewell tour of England was announced on 6 February. One month later the five musicians hit the road, opening their sell-out tour at Newcastle City Hall.

Decca, now acting very much the spurned lover, were determined to cash in on their former clients while they still could. The easy answer was to lift from the vaults whatever material was left and put it out as a so-called 'lost' LP. The result, *Stone Age*, was released throughout Europe on 23 April. The Stones, though, were not amused. Taking out a paid ad in the British music press they hit back: '[The album] is, in our opinion, below the standard we try to maintain, both in content and cover design.' Predictably, like their previous musical offerings, *Stone Age* hovered at the top of the charts for quite a few weeks.

Free agents at last, the band formed their own label called, appropriately enough, Rolling Stones Records, with distribution in the States handled by Atlantic Records, and by the Kinney Group elsewhere. Jagger explained: 'By signing this contract we are guaranteeing to produce six new albums over the next four years; this includes *Sticky Fingers*. There may also be some solo albums projecting the Rolling Stones individually over this period as well.'

By now comfortably settled into their new lives as self-imposed exiles, the Stones were allowed to spend no more than ninety days a year in Britain or else risk their money-saving status. Of course, the new living arrangements weren't exactly hard to take. Jagger leased a manor house in Mougins, Picasso's old hometown. Bill Wyman, meanwhile, took a place at La Bastide Saint-Antoine, Charlie Watts a cosy cottage at Cevennes, Mick Taylor a house in Grasse, and Keith Richards a rambling villa in Villefranche-sur-Mer, which served as the group's unofficial headquarters while abroad.

One of those who did not receive an invitation to accompany the band to France was Marianne Faithfull. Plagued by a savage heroin addiction and weary of her upside-down life with Jagger and the Stones, Faithfull parted company with Mick before the band left home for the Continent. Jagger's new love was Bianca Perez Morena de Macias, a high-society socialite who had previously been linked romantically with actor Michael Caine and heavy-weight record producer Eddie Barclay. From the moment she met Mick at a post-show party at the Georges V Hotel in Paris on 23 September, the two were inseparable. Stones' chum, designer Thea Porter, recalls her early   ⇨

Ron, Mick, and Keith on stage during their eleven-week American tour, in East Rutherford, New Jersey, on 5 November 1981.

associations with the Nicaraguan-born beauty: 'There were people who had known her in Paris, where she had been one of the many rootless foreign girls without means who were seen in nightclubs, fantastically well dressed. They poured scorn on the idea that she was the daughter of a diplomat or a rich plantation owner, as she variously claimed. And since she had been around for at least seven years, they were amused when she told journalists she was twenty-one.'

Professionally, the Stones were doing wonderfully. On 23 April their new album, *Sticky Fingers*, was released, sporting ten new air-tight tunes and a trendy cover by Pop Art guru Andy Warhol. The real news, though, was Mick and Bianca's great romance. After it was announced on 2 May that he had given her a £4,000 diamond bracelet for her birthday the media took flight, convinced that Jagger and Perez would soon be tying the knot, an allegation Bianca hotly refuted: 'There's not going to be a wedding this week, next week, or ever. Mick and I are very happy together. We don't need to get married. Why should we?'

The world's media, hurling themselves across the water to St Tropez, arrived to find the glitterati of pop poised for the sacred occasion on the slight stone steps of the seventeenth-century St Anne Chapel. There to witness the all-star nuptials were designer Ossie Clark, film director Donald Cammell, record execs Marshall Chess and Ahmet Ertegun, Nicky Hopkins, Kenny Jones, Bobby Keys, Ronnie Lane, Lord Lichfield, Paul and Linda McCartney, Jimmy Miller, Ringo and Maureen Starr, Stephen Stills, Doris Troy, Roger Vadim, and Ronnie Wood.

As the couple exchanged rings a section from Bach's 'Wedding March' was played and, at the request of the bride, a medley of themes from the film *Love Story*. Afterwards, a reception was held at the swank Câfé des Arts in town, ending in a superstar jam. The next day headlines around the globe proclaimed the triumphant news.

The next afternoon Mick and Bianca left for Cannes by yacht, stopping at a château accessible only by sea. That July it was announced they were expecting their first child together, and on 21 October 1971 a daughter they named Jade was born at the Belvedere Nursing Home in Paris. Mick would later comment only that he was 'overjoyed' and that the new mum was 'tired but happy.'

Interestingly, it wasn't only the Jaggers that were welcoming their offspring into this world. On 17 April 1972 Keith Richards and Anita Pallenberg had a daughter the couple called Dandelion (later changing her name to the more socially acceptable Angela). Although never exactly regarded as the fatherly type, Keith was smitten with the baby girl and showered her with great care and attention. Keith and Anita's first child together, a boy named Marlon, had been born three years earlier while the band were still based in Britain.

Of course, life as a Rolling Stone was nothing if not unendingly hectic and stressful, a dynamic which inevitably influenced all of the band's outlook on family life. Richards' problems, though, were greatly exacerbated by his (and Anita's) continuing drug use. Keith, of course, always had the  ⇨92

TOP LEFT Mick Jagger and Bianca Perez Morena de Macias strolling together in St Tropez, France, on 5 November 1971; **TOP MIDDLE** Mick and Bianca at their wedding in St Anne Chapel, St Tropez, 5 December 1971; **TOP RIGHT** Jagger on his way into court for yet another hearing for his divorce from Bianca (London, 9 July 1979); **BOTTOM LEFT** Mick and Bianca; **BOTTOM MIDDLE** Keith as he was in the middle seventies; **BOTTOM RIGHT** Mick joins actor Tom Conti backstage in New York for Conti's last night as the star of *Whose Life is it Anyway?*, 28 October 1979.

TOP LEFT Mick's parents leaving his New York apartment in November 1981. They were in town to catch the Stones at Madison Square Garden; **TOP RIGHT** Mick on stage (1981); **RIGHT** The Stones with promo man extraordinaire Pete Bennett (1972).

option of taking off on the road to tour or record. His missus, however, was more or less shackled to home and hearth – a reality which caused Anita to question her life with Richards.

'Keith and I tried to get clean of our heroin addiction before we left England. We both took cures, but twenty-four hours after we occupied the villa we were back injecting ourselves because a cure's no good when you live in the middle of pushers and users. . . The following year I gave birth to a daughter. . . It should have been a good time but it was difficult having children and belonging to Keith's world. . . He'd go off to perform and I'd have to stay there by myself still stuck on heroin, but now I'd have to look after my own supply since Keith was not around to provide for the two of us. Being on heroin the way I was, I had the kids to take care of but I couldn't do a good job of it. I was

more interested in getting my supply than I was in looking after them. People started to condemn me as a bad person, neglecting my kids, only interested in feeding my habit. Instead of getting them dinner I'd go out and wander around and meet people and spend the night in the park looking for flying saucers. . . While Keith was away, I'd be starting to get off heroin, really trying, but then he'd return and he'd get me on it just as bad as before.'

By 10 January 1972 the Rolling Stones were hard at work in LA preparing for their seventh upcoming North American tour as well as forging ahead with yet another new LP. By the end of April, Britain's *New Musical Express* was giving away a special seven-inch flexi single to promote the record to be called *Exile On Main St*. The provocative double album finally hit the streets on 26 May, boasting eighteen well-defined tracks and a striking

TOP LEFT The boys at East Rutherford, New Jersey, 1981; TOP RIGHT Jagger in full flight; RIGHT Mick at thirty and (far right) in Paris to announce the Stones' ten-nation European tour (April 1982).

black and white montage cover by film director Robert Frank. Produced by Jimmy Miller, *Exile* contained two classic blues tracks, 'Shake Your Hips' and 'Stop Breaking Down,' as well as a Mick Taylor/Jagger/Richards' composition entitled 'Ventilator Blues.' Entering the UK charts at number two (later sliding easily to the top spot) the record also soared to number one in America where it sold in phone book digits.

On 3 June the ever rolling Stones commenced their latest tour, opening at the Pacific Coliseum in Vancouver to an expectant crowd of more than 17,000. The next evening the band played nearby Seattle, moving south to Frisco's famous Winterland on 6 June. A week later the Stones and their ever-present entourage had moved on to Tucson, Arizona, where the crowd got a little out of control, forcing police to tear gas some

three hundred potential gate-crashers. In Montreal, a month later, the group's equipment van was blown up by terrorists, and the next night (18 July) Mick and Keith were arrested in connection with an alleged assault on a local photographer while playing Boston Garden. 'All in a night's work,' commented Richards to reporters. 'Welcome to a day in the life of the Rolling Stones.'

As the Stones cut their randy way across America that summer, film-maker Robert Frank was hard at work directing a documentary on the upside-down tour. Entitled *Cocksucker Blues*, the two-hour piece was scheduled to open at New York's Plaza Theatre, but was pulled from the bill at the last moment due to worry over some explicit scenes that had found their way into the final cut. 'The whole thing was daft,' Ian Stewart ⇨

commented. 'There was this one bit that seemed to upset a few people concerning a nude young lady we had for lunch one afternoon on the airplane. To be honest it was all staged for the cameras. After all, this was the Rolling Stones on tour here, mate. We had to make things at least a little bit naughty.'

Naughtier still was word from Nice on 2 December that warrants had been issued against Keith and Anita on drug charges. Outraged that the entire band was under suspicion for the alleged actions of Richards, Jagger struck out with a little pointed PR of his own: 'Charlie Watts, Bill Wyman, Mick Taylor, and myself deny categorically that we have been charged by the French police with the buying and use of heroin. It has never been suggested that we used or bought heroin. The four of us were not released on 'provisional liberty' because we had never been arrested on any charge. . . At no time did we hold drug parties in our homes.'

Eventually, several local 'hippie types' were arrested in connection with the investigation. One of the culprits stated he was a cook employed by Keith Richards, while the others were described in the papers as simply 'Stones fans.' Inevitably, the group's legal woes caused a sold-out Japanese tour to be cancelled after visa problems stemming from the French bust. 'The only time you hear about me is when the warrants are out,' complained Richards. 'What I resent is that they tried to drag my old lady into it, which I find particularly distasteful.'

Disaster seemed to dog the Stones during this period, culminating in Jagger's in-laws being threatened by a massive earthquake which hit their home in Managua on 23 December 1972. Three days later Mick and Bianca flew from London to Nicaragua to mount a search for her missing parents. Arriving in

ABOVE Keith Richards in 1982 (photograph by Gered Mankowitz);
BELOW Mick, Jerry, and Andy Warhol enjoying a bit of a late-night gossip.

ABOVE Ian Stewart at the piano in 1982 (photograph Gered Mankowitz);
BELOW RIGHT Enjoying a stroll on the beach.

Bianca's ravaged hometown on 28 December, the Jaggers delivered 2,000 syringes to help check the outbreak of typhoid in the area, now without not only telephone service, water and electricity, but dangerously low on medical supplies as well. After three days Bianca finally found her parents. Meanwhile, back in Britain, headlines screamed that the couple were themselves lost after false reports that the two had been killed in the frenzied aftermath of the tumultuous quake.

Committed to the cause of marshalling further aid for the shattered country, Mick convinced the rest of the band that a hands-on approach was needed if they hoped to make a dent against the catastrophic calamity. Towards that end, it was decided the Stones would play a benefit to assist the many thousands of victims left homeless by the terrifying quake. On 18 January 1973 a concert was held at the Los Angeles Forum headlined by the Rolling Stones. Raising over $500,000 from the roaring one-night stand the boys felt good about having the chance to finally give something back after so many years of working on their own behalf. Jagger and Co's good works, however, didn't stop there. On 9 May 1973 Mick and Bianca presented a cheque to the US senate for £350,000, ear-marked for the Pan-American Development Fund. ↪100

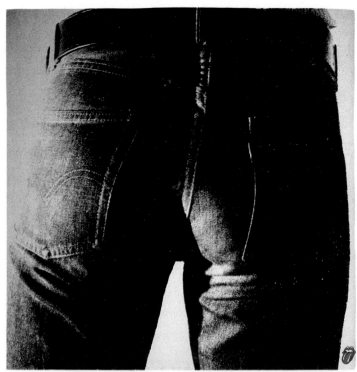

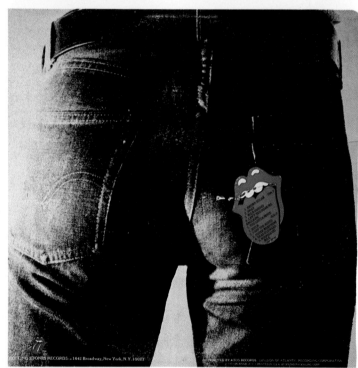

Sticky Fingers (April 1971) was the Stones' first album on their very own label. The cover design by Pop Art guru Andy Warhol was deemed unacceptable in Spain (for reasons of propriety) and was duly replaced with an alternate jacket illustrating a dismembered hand protruding from a can of treacle (opposite bottom).

Sticky Fingers went on to become the number one selling record in both Britain and America, lodging itself securely at the top of the charts for an astounding twenty-five-week stay. **BOTTOM LEFT** shows the UK release; **RIGHT** The US promotional release.

TOP LEFT *Sticky Fingers* inner sleeve;
TOP RIGHT Promotional poster;
RIGHT The music book;
BOTTOM LEFT The Spanish version of
Sticky Fingers; BOTTOM RIGHT *An
Interview Disc with Mick Jagger by
Tom Donahue* (April 1971) issued for
'promotional purposes only.' This was
the very first piece of vinyl issued on
Rolling Stones Records.

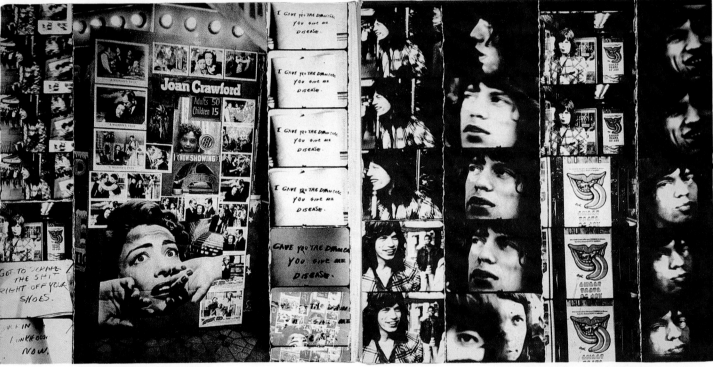

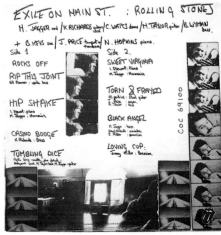

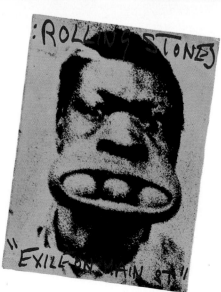

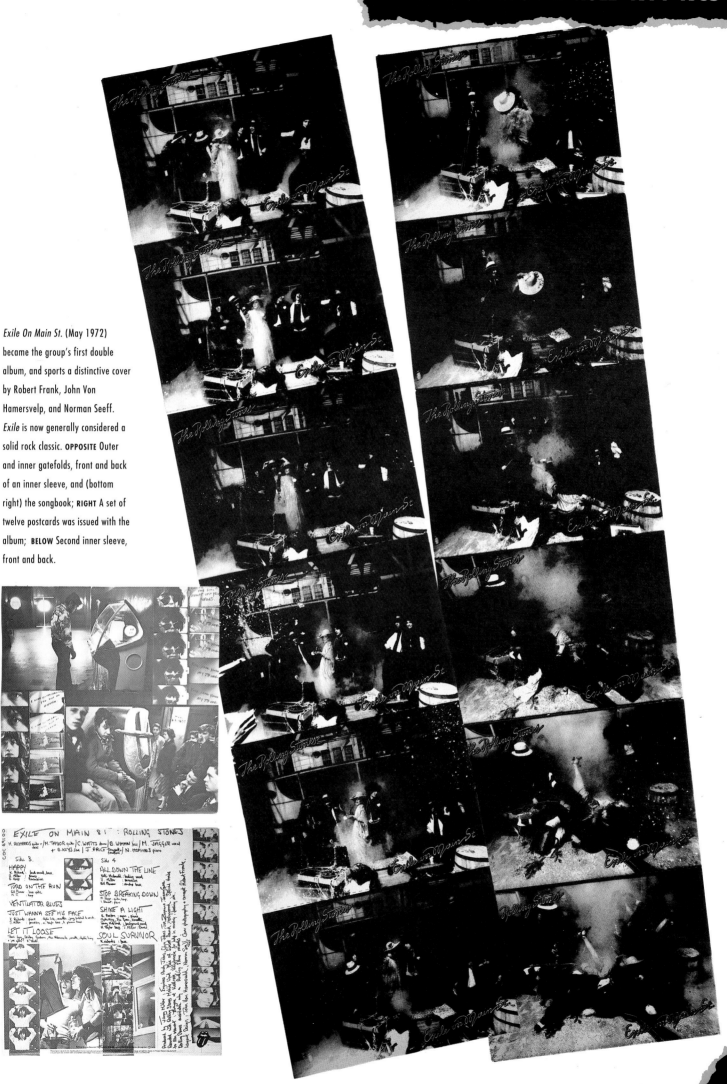

Exile On Main St. (May 1972)
became the group's first double
album, and sports a distinctive cover
by Robert Frank, John Von
Hamersvelp, and Norman Seeff.
Exile is now generally considered a
solid rock classic. **OPPOSITE** Outer
and inner gatefolds, front and back
of an inner sleeve, and (bottom
right) the songbook; **RIGHT** A set of
twelve postcards was issued with the
album; **BELOW** Second inner sleeve,
front and back.

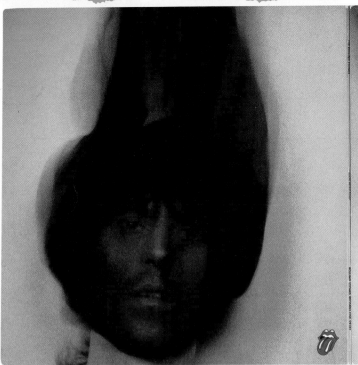

The Rolling Stones

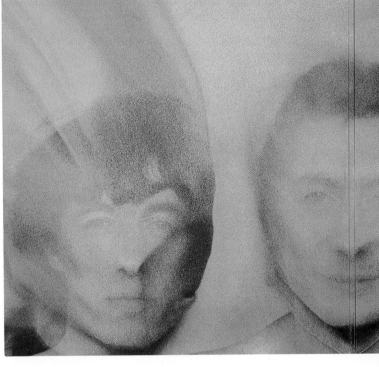

Throughout these trying and exciting times the career-conscious Stones continued to issue a great deal of new product. Back in May 1972 the group's saucy, gospel-inspired rock 'n' roller, 'Tumbling Dice,' went out climbing only as high as number ten in America. This was followed by 'Happy' (backed by 'All Down The Line') that July, the first Stones single with Richards on lead vocal.

Towards the end of the year yet another anthology was issued in the States under the unlikely title of *More Hot Rocks (big hits and fazed cookies)*. London Records had released the preceding compilation, *Hot Rocks 1964–1971*, in the US in 1971 on the Stones' departure from the label. All things considered, 1972 was not really too bad a year.

A bumper crop of new Stones' music was harvested in 1973,

It's Only Rock 'n Roll (October 1974) boasted several superstar guests including keyboard wiz Billy Preston, Linda Hopkins, and slide guitar maestro Ry Cooder. David Bowie was also rumoured to have sung back-up vocals on the title track. This, by the way, was Mick Taylor's last album with the Stones.
RIGHT The Argentine release (signed by Ron Wood who was not yet with the Stones); BELOW Promo photograph for the single 'It's Only Rock 'n Roll' signed by Mick Taylor; BELOW RIGHT Made In The Shade (June 1975) was hastily released to coincide with the group's American tour.

OPPOSITE Goat's Head Soup (31 August 1973) was released to coincide with the Stones' upcoming European tour and included such tunes as 'Starfucker' (later retitled 'Star Star' for obvious reasons), 'Dancing with Mr. D.', and the plaintive 'Angie.' Commenting on the subject of groupies which the controversial 'Starfucker' alludes to, Jagger told reporters: 'If girls can do that, I can certainly write about it. This does not mean I'm an anti-feminist.' Curiously, the inner sleeve was printed with this cryptic warning: 'Since 1969 the Rolling Stones only on Rolling Stones Records. This is a new record – beware of packaging.'

Rolling Stones

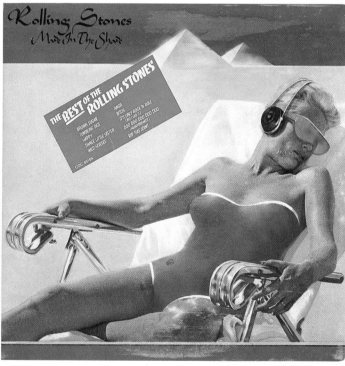

kicking off with the single 'Sad Day' backed by 'You Can't Always Get What You Want' on 29 April. Following this came the haunting hard-luck ballad 'Angie,' backed with 'Silver Train,' from the Stones' forthcoming LP Goat's Head Soup. Recorded in Jamaica, 'Angie' did well, reaching number two in Great Britain and the top ten in the US.

As for the devilish-sounding new album, all concerned were psyched for yet another roaring Rolling Stones success. Jagger recalls the inner workings of the band's new opus: 'I felt close to this album and really put all I had into it. . . But whatever you do it's always wrong. If you do it rocky, people say, "oh it's just the same old rock 'n' roll," and if you do ballads, they say it's too pretty.' As had happened so many, many times before,

Goat's Head Soup became the number one record of the day.

Although the year 1974 was unusually quiet for the Stones, a few interesting events did take place. Foremost among them was the advent of bassist Bill Wyman's first solo LP, Monkey Grip, on 10 May. A personal milestone for the naturally reserved Wyman, the record didn't really ignite with the public and soon died a death, only to be resurrected in cut-out bins across Britain and America. Today, naturally, it is quite a collector's item.

That summer saw the release of the band's first album in eleven months, the sloppy It's Only Rock 'n Roll. Recorded in Munich, the Stones enlisted the aid of Billy Preston on keyboards. 'Billy was great,' remembered Ian Stewart later. 'He has a real feel for our music and was ever the gentleman. Perhaps I should have been jealous, but I never was.'

Unquestionably the most gripping news of 1974 was Mick Taylor's rather surprising decision to leave the band to play with former Cream bassman Jack Bruce. Jagger first heard the news from Taylor at a garden party at the home of music biz impresario Robert Stigwood. Taylor explains: 'I'd worked with them for so long that I didn't think I could go much farther without some different musicians. So when this chance with Jack came up, well, I wanted to go with him. I'd known for several months that he wanted to put together a new band. We'd played a lot together and really hit it off. It was all purely musical. There was no personal animosity in the split. There was no row, no quibbling or squabbling.'

As the inevitable media frenzy reached its peak, rumours began to circulate that Taylor bailed out due to certain financial

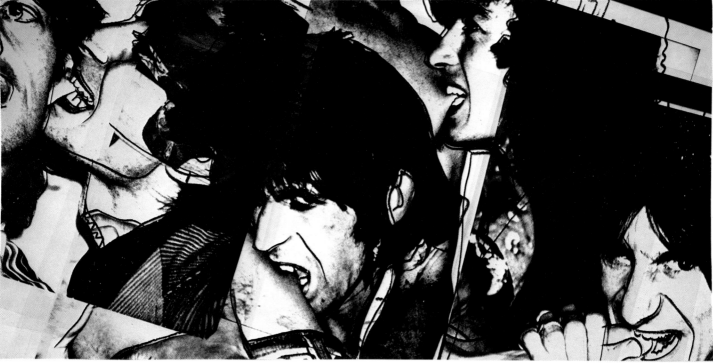

OPPOSITE *Black And Blue* (April 1976) featured not only special guests Harvey Mander and Wayne Perkins, but also new Stone, Ron Wood. The promotional poster for the album showed a scantily clad, bruised and bound young woman which predictably ignited the passions of ardent feminists on both sides of the Atlantic. Jagger, however, kept his cool, commenting: 'We had a lot of trouble with that poster you know. A lot of bright girls just take it with a pinch of salt, but there are a lot of women who are disgraceful and if you have the misfortune to have an affair with one of those, well, it's a personal thing.'

ABOVE *Love You Live* (September 1977) saw the Stones teaming up once again with Andy Warhol for the group's their third 'official' live album. The LP was dedicated to the only recently departed Keith Harwood, the Stones' long-time and talented engineer ('Those whom the gods love grow young'). It was rumoured that Mick personally flew the tapes over to America for Richards's approval as he was undergoing drug rehabilitation in Cherry Hill, New Jersey.

inequities within the band – a suggestion Taylor refused to even entertain. 'I'm very disturbed by those rumours. . . It had absolutely nothing to do with those things. I think the rumours were started by an interview I did in a trade paper, but the things I said were taken out of context. And I never wanted the things I said written, reported, or repeated. Whatever I felt about credits on songs, they had nothing to do with my decision to leave. If Mick or Keith ever want to do solo albums, I'd like to work with them. I don't want my friendship with the Rolling Stones jeopardized, or anything I may do with them later.'

Hard at work recording their new album (to be called *Black And Blue*), the band was besieged by the media regarding Taylor's replacement. Before the dust had settled (and before former Faces guitarist Ron Wood came on board that ⇨107

OPPOSITE A montage of Andy Warhol photographs from the *Love You Live* photo session, and the official *Love You Live* promotional chattering teeth. OPPOSITE BELOW The lurid inner sleeves.

RIGHT A set of *Love You Live* promotional stickers handed out at the album's launch party. MIDDLE RIGHT The Mexican cover of *Love You Live*. BOTTOM *Time Waits For No One: Anthology 1971–1977* (May 1978, UK only). It seems that whenever the Stones changed labels or distributors they issued a live or compilation LP. This soggy collection, unfortunately, falls into the latter category.

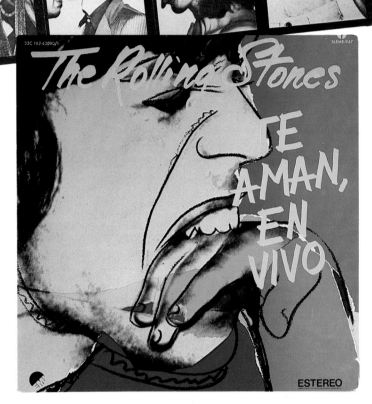

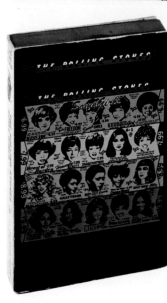

Some Girls (June 1978), the Stones' first album for EMI, was undeniably one of the group's better LPs for some time and contained the humorous, homosexually inclined 'When the Whip Comes Down,' of which Mick has jokingly said: 'I don't know why I wrote it. Maybe I came out of the closet.' The cover design became an issue when Raquel Welch, unhappy over her inclusion on the freaky collage-style cover, tried unsuccessfully to alter the infamous graphic. Lucille Ball, however, wielded a little more clout and eventually succeeded in persuading them to obscure the 'offensive' design.

TOP Two variations of the inner sleeve to
Some Girls; ABOVE RIGHT the music book
produced for the album.

ABOVE LEFT are the front and back labels of
an ultra-rare studio acetate from the
recording sessions of the impressive LP.

April) practically every able-bodied musician in Britain was
rumoured to be up for the job. That May the Stones and
'Woody' (as he was affectionately known) played together
publicly for the first time on a decorated flat-bed truck rolling
slowly down Fifth Avenue in New York (staged to promote
their upcoming tour). The unprecedented series of gigs was to
last three months, traversing the States and South America.

Holed up in a rented mansion with the band in Montauk,
Long Island, Wood worked frantically to master the Stone's
extended set of thirty-four powerhouse tunes. During a
rehearsal Jagger accidentally stuck his hand through a plate glass
window and gave himself a nasty wound requiring twenty
stitches. 'It was a bit messy,' mused Mick later, 'but I won't need
a cast or anything.'

The fifty-eight date tour opened on 1 June 1975 (Ron
Wood's twenty-eighth birthday) at the Louisiana State
University in Baton Rouge. As the Stones whipped their way
through twenty-two rapid fire tunes, Wood laid low any
lingering doubts over his ability to keep pace with his more
seasoned colleagues, trading searing licks with Keith with
perhaps even greater intensity than his distinguished predecessor.

'I loved Mick Taylor for his beauty,' Bill Wyman commented
at the time. 'He was technically really great. But he was shy,
maybe like Charlie and me. Mick wasn't so funky but he led us
into other things. Ron is a bit like Keith; he takes us back. He's
not such a fantastic musician, perhaps, but he's more fun, got
more personality.'

To help promote the tour yet another 'greatest hits' ⟳113

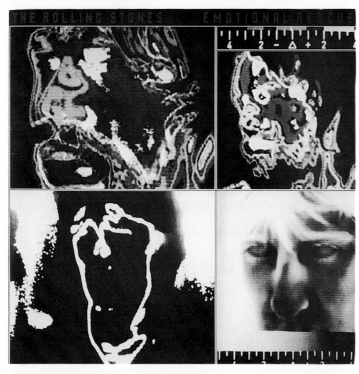

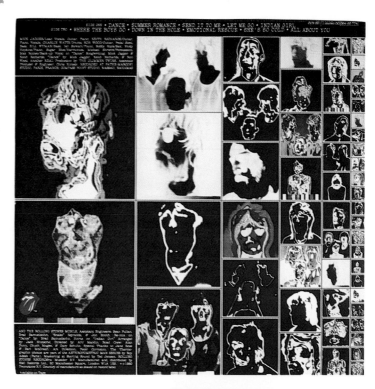

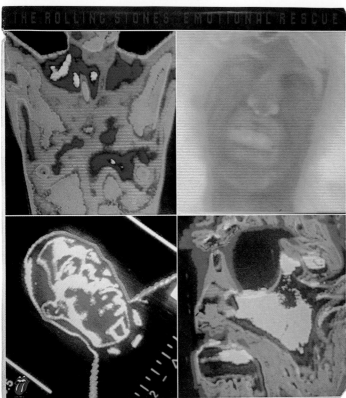

Emotional Rescue (June 1980) was the Stones' twenty-eighth UK LP, and twenty-seventh in the US. Rumour has it that Keith broke his own endurance record during sessions for the album, working nine gruelling days without sleep.

Yet again the Stones break new ground using thermographics for the cover images (top), the free poster (middle left), the three promo posters (right), and the music book (below).

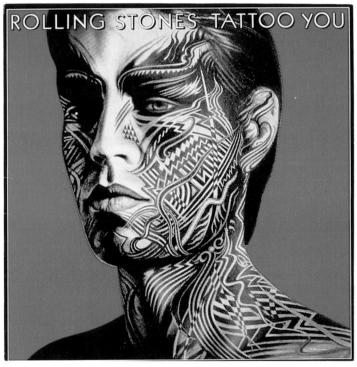

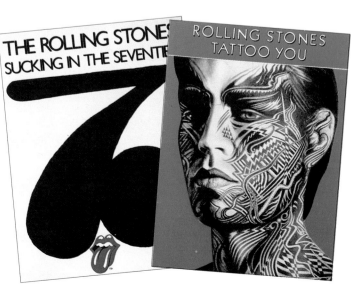

TOP *Sucking In The Seventies* (May 1981) was another compilation boasting two relative rarities: 'If I Was A Dancer (Dance Pt. 2),' and a live version of 'When The Whip Comes Down' (top row).

ABOVE In October 1981 the successful *Tattoo You* was released. Of the forty recorded songs, only eleven appeared on the album. One wonders what happened to the remaining twenty-nine?

ABOVE During the Stones' 1982 European tour, EMI released *Still Life (American Concert 1981)*, the Stones' fourth live LP (inner and outer gatefolds). Included were two classic rockers, 'Twenty Flight Rock' and 'Going To A Go Go.' **RIGHT** *Still Life*

was also issued as a picture disc, the band's first to be released on both continents (back and front shown, right). **BELOW** is the American tour poster, and the inner sleeve (bottom right).

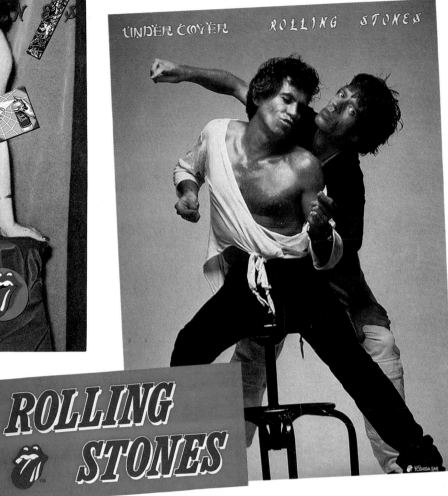

ROLLING STONES

Undercover (November 1983) got the Stones into more trouble with a limited edition sleeve featuring removable stickers (Japanese poster, top left, and four promo posters).
BELOW RIGHT *Rewind (1971-1984)* was the Stones' uneven 1984 compilation.

UNDERCOVER

UNDERCOVER OF THE NIGHT / SHE WAS HOT / TIE YOU UP (THE PAIN OF LOVE) / WANNA HOLD YOU / FEEL ON BABY / TOO MUCH BLOOD / PRETTY BEAT UP / TOO TOUGH / ALL THE WAY DOWN / IT MUST BE HELL

AVAILABLE ON 7" and 12"
12" EXTENDED CHEEKY MIX
features 6 min 22 secs Dub Version of
"Undercover .." unavailable elsewhere.

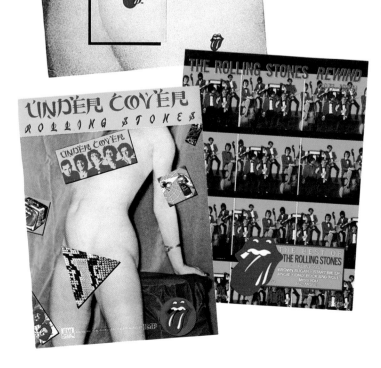

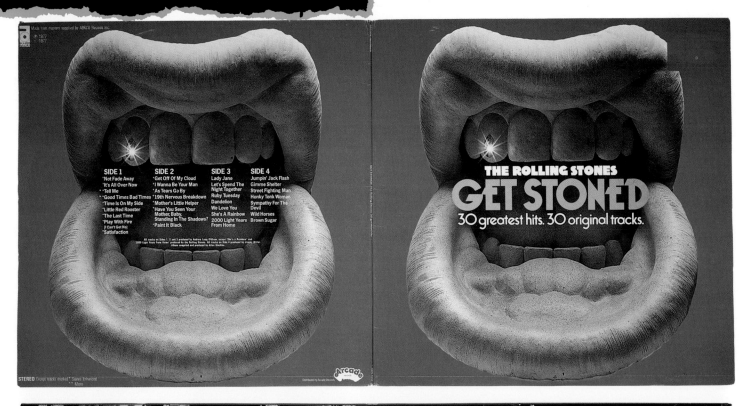

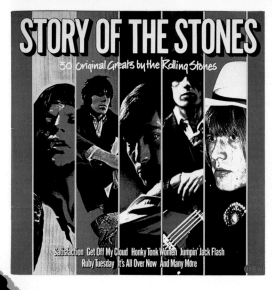

ABOVE It had to happen, the Stones on budget TV-advertised labels Arcade and K-tel. Is nothing sacred? *Get Stoned: 30 Greatest Hits, 30 Original Tracks* was released on the Arcade label in 1977 (outer and inner gatefolds shown).

LEFT *Story of the Stones* (1982) was issued by K-tel. A much sought-after rarity is the radio show album *In the Beginning* released in 1980 and featuring one track by the Stones.

From the BBC to Westwood One, radio shows featuring Stones music and interviews were big business around the world. Master tapes were transferred to vinyl and then sent to radio stations clearly marked 'Not for Sale' or 'Promotional Use Only.' But the smell of the almighty dollar soon let them loose on the ever eager public. Not many were pressed so they are now very collectible. A small selection are shown here.

package was released on 13 June. Entitled *Made In The Shade*, the slick ten-song LP climbed only as high as number eight in the UK and number six in America. Although the band's manic, crowd-pleasing tours were still big news, musically speaking the seventies were not the best time for the Stones. While they continued to rake in millions at every carefully thought out step, their new material seemed somehow lacking compositionally.

As with so many of the sixties rock giants, would the Rolling Stones too be forced to acknowledge that their best work had been done in the past?

Ron Wood officially became a Rolling Stone forever and always on 28 February 1976. Two weeks later the band went back out on the road to resume their world domination of the touring circuit. In one of the wackier quotes from that ➪

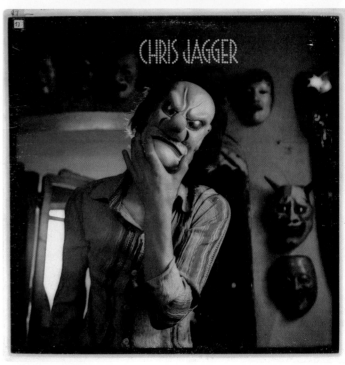

TOP Kracker became the first and only band to record on Rolling Stones Records. Their only release, *Kracker Brand* (1973), did nothing and they almost immediately disappeared from view. **ABOVE AND LEFT** The Stones waited until 1978 to release another artist on their label. With Jagger's help, Peter Tosh's *Bush Doctor* (1978) was more successful. By the early seventies the Stones were being asked to play on other people's records (as individuals), including LPs by Peter Frampton, Carly Simon, Leslie West (*The Great Fatsby*), Dr John, and even Jagger's own little brother Chris. Ian Stewart, a sought-after musician in his own right, appeared on Guido Toffoletti's blues-oriented *No Compromise* album (1985).

long-ago, turbulent time, Ron Wood reportedly asked Pete Townshend: 'You got Eric Clapton off of drugs, can't you help me get off the road?' The off-hand remark soon became a running gag throughout the tour.

On 28 March 1976, Anita Pallenberg gave birth to a tiny son Tara, named after the couples' late friend, Guinness heir Tara Browne. Keith was thrilled, but tragically, just ten weeks later, the child passed away of an unspecified flu virus in a Swiss

hospital. So dedicated was Richards to the group he decided that news of his infant son's passing could potentially overshadow the tour and the heartbroken guitarist ordered a tight media ban on the sad happening. 'At the time I lost Tara,' says Anita, 'I went through a very heavy nervous breakdown. For about three months I was very upset.'

As Keith and Anita commenced the long, slow process of coming to terms with their loss, the Jagger family, too, was in

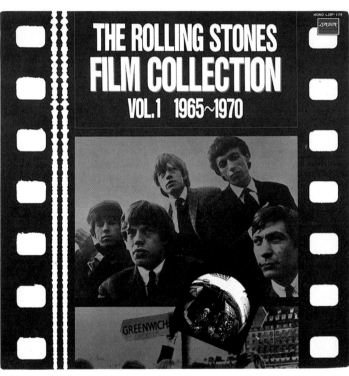

TOP LEFT The release of the film *Jumpin' Jack Flash* in 1986 gave the Stones a movie title to their credit; **TOP RIGHT** The Japanese LP *Walkin' Thru The Sleepy City* (1982) comprises Jagger/Richards tunes as performed by other artists in the sixties, including Marianne Faithfull and the vivacious Lulu. **ABOVE** The Japanese were still the only country coming up with even roughly original repackaging, as with *The Rolling Stones Film Collection Vols.1 & 2* (1983), two albums of Stones compositions used in various movies.

crisis. For months, tabloids on both sides of the Atlantic had been reporting rumours that Mick and Bianca's marriage was coming apart, a reality both hotly denied right up to the bitter, inevitable end. 'I never really fall in love for a long time with anybody,' Bianca has been quoted as saying. 'I'm afraid to. I have a deep fear of doing that.' Mick, too, seemed pretty nonchalant about the whole affair, telling Britain's *Woman's Own*: 'I got married for something to do. I thought it was a good idea. I've never been madly, deeply in love. I wouldn't know what it feels like. I'm not really an emotional person.'

For the moment, however, there were far more imperative concerns facing the Stones as a result of Keith Richards' arrest on 27 February 1977, at Toronto's swanky Harbour Castle Hilton, for possession of heroin for resale. Richards was bailed later the same evening.

In spite of such weighty legal matters, the ever-rolling wheels of commerce kept right on turning. On 16 February 1977, a spokesman for the group announced that the Rolling Stones had signed a six-album distribution deal with EMI for all territories other than North America. Originally, rumour had it that the band was about to go with Polydor. But word of the ⇨121

As the Stones' appeal became universal, the album covers rarely changed design from country to country. The only time they did was, generally, on the issue of various compilations – a selection of which are shown on these two pages.

In Britain and America, however, Decca and London appeared to be still living on the past, which was by now wearing a bit thin. The record-buying public was getting bone-tired of the same old tunes repackaged in indifferent, sloppy covers.

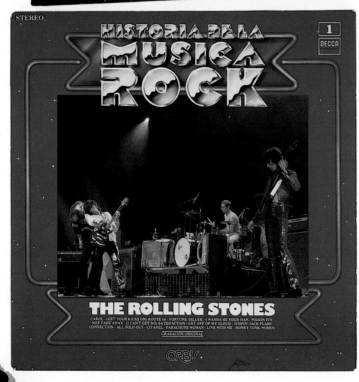

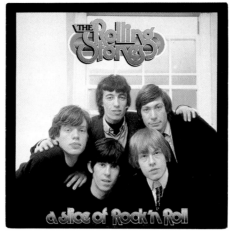

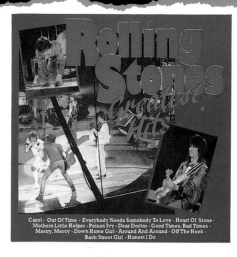

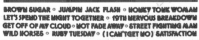

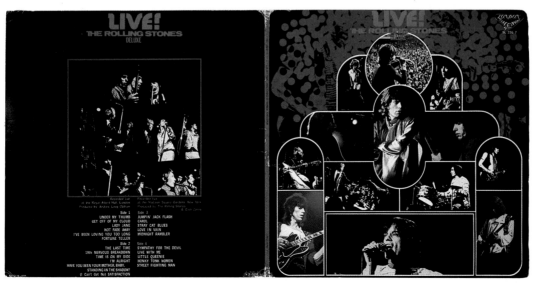

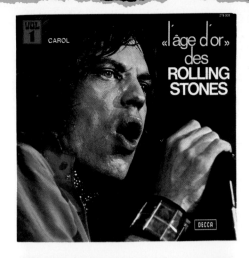

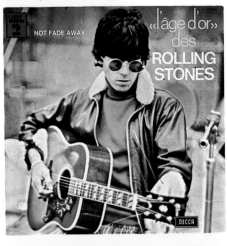

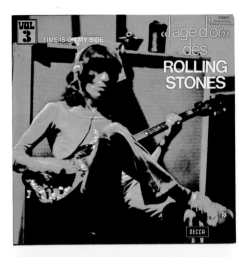

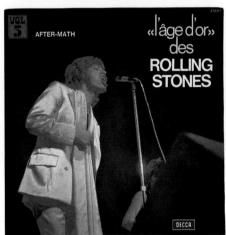

The French get it right yet again with these distinctive and engaging covers. Reproduced on these two pages is a very rare nineteen-album set entitled *"L'Age D'Or" des Rolling Stones*, released by Decca in France.

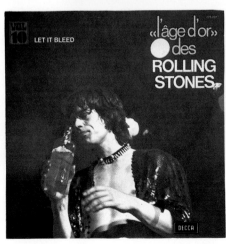

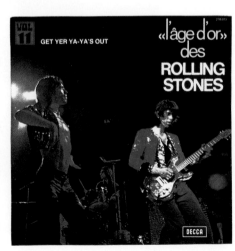

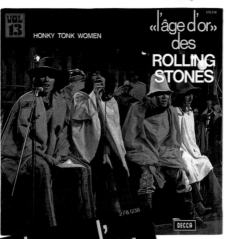

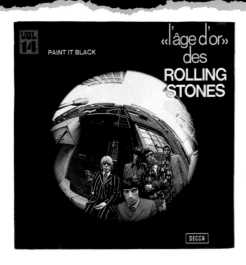

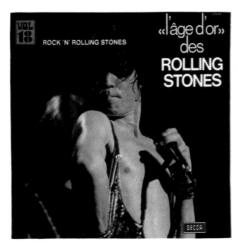

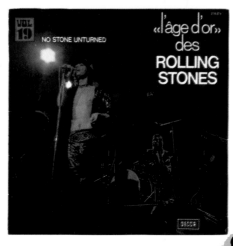

OPPOSITE AND LEFT The Stones on CD at last! In 1986 London/ABCKO released all their Stones albums (from 1964 to 1971) in the US and Europe. In the UK, however, Decca have (as of yet) not released the early Stones LPs on CD. ABCKO later reissued the mono albums in something called 'Remastered Digital Stereo,' a gimmick which didn't really do the Stones' early 'primitive' sound any good at all.

BELOW A display poster depicting the entire Stones catalogue on CD, up to and including *Still Life* (1982).

pending deal was apparently leaked by company officials at the Cannes Film Festival, which displeased the media-conscious Stones to the point that they respectfully withdrew.

By mid-autumn, the ever-intriguing Mick and Bianca soap opera was now in full swing. On 19 October the foreign press reported that Jagger was keeping company with leggy Texas-born supermodel Jerry Hall. Meanwhile, Mrs Jagger was spotted partying with tennis pro Bjorn Borg at trendy Studio 54 in Manhattan at New Year 1978. That May, Bianca officially filed for divorce in London while her husband was away rehearsing for an upcoming tour of the US. In a newspaper story entitled DIVORCE? IT'S NEWS TO ME Jagger attempted to duck the issue saying, 'Nothing has been handed to me. I saw Bianca a few days ago. We had a party for our daughter.'

On 15 September 1977 the Stones' ragged double album *Love You Live*, was released, incorporating the best of the band recorded in Paris (during the 1976 tour) with one side dedicated to the Stones' sweltering gigs at the El Mocambo Club in Toronto on 4 and 5 March 1977. Among the ultra-rare tunes were Willie Dixon's 'Little Red Rooster,' Chuck Berry's 'Around and Around,' Bo Diddley's 'Crackin' Up,' and Muddy Water's 'Mannish Boy.'

'Miss You,' one of the Stones' most infectiously danceable tracks, hit the streets in mid-May of 1978, prompting several hard-core critics to charge that Jagger and Richards had sold out to the current flourishing disco craze. Mick, however, pointed out that the song had been written long before the world ▷126

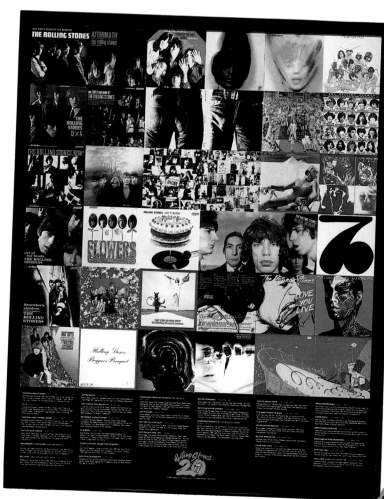

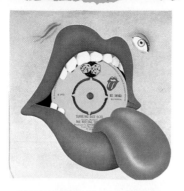

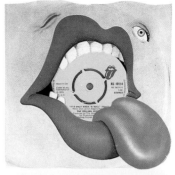

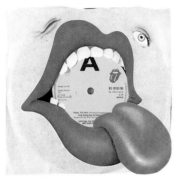

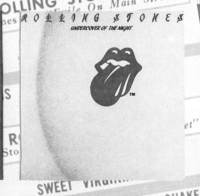

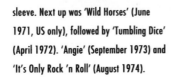

The first single on Rolling Stones Records was 'Brown Sugar' backed by 'Bitch' (April 1971). The UK issue had a bonus track, 'Let It Rock,' and was their first UK release in a picture sleeve. Next up was 'Wild Horses' (June 1971, US only), followed by 'Tumbling Dice' (April 1972). 'Angie' (September 1973) and 'It's Only Rock 'n Roll' (August 1974).

The US fared better with the extra 45s 'Happy' (July 1972), 'Doo Doo Doo Doo Doo (Heart Breaker)' (December 1973), and 'Ain't Too Proud To Beg' (October 1974). Then came 'Fool To Cry' (May 1976), and, now with EMI, 'Miss You' (June 1978). The next US single, 'Beast Of Burden' (August 1978) caused controversy as the sleeve depicted a lion sitting on a

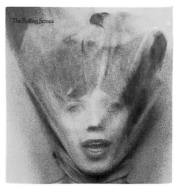

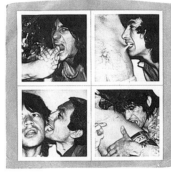

young lady in repose. The image was mistaken for one of bestiality and the cover (now very rare) was withdrawn. 'Respectable' was next out (September 1978), then 'Shattered'

(1979, US only), 'Emotional Rescue' (July 1980), and 'She's So Cold' (October 1980). 'Start Me Up' and 'Waiting On A Friend' were out in 1981. Three live 45s appeared in

1982: 'Going to A Go Go,' 'Time Is On My Side,' and 'Let's Spend The Night Together' (promo only), plus 'Hang Fire' (US only). After 'Undercover Of The Night' (November 1983),

the last single for EMI was 'She Was Hot' (February 1984). 'Brown Sugar' was re-released (July 1984) as their farewell. Background: collectable juke box labels.

123

Decca issued their Stones singles in a limited-edition box set (left) for the UK only. If you were lucky enough to get one, it came with a free poster and badge (right). Unfortunately, you did not get the original B-sides.

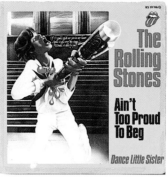

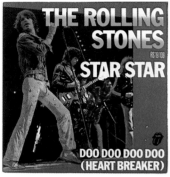

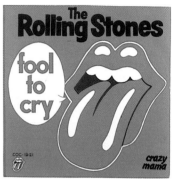

ABOVE Poland issued records in a flexi-postcard/picture disc form. The more liberated countries (Germany/Holland) also released banned records such as 'Star Star' (originally 'Starfucker').

LEFT The first Soviet Stones EP, released in 1975.

OPPOSITE BELOW Generally, when a Stones' single was issued in a foreign country it had a different sleeve, although the record inside was usually the same.

was blessed with John Travolta and the warbly Bee Gees. One interesting feature of the track was the searing extended harmonica solo by virtuoso player Sugar Blue. 'They was it, man,' he told reporters. 'Those boys can really play their asses off. I love 'em all.'

On 9 June the controversial *Some Girls* album was released. Interestingly, this time the problem wasn't with the Stones' slash and burn music, but rather with the record's colourful cover art. Freely making use of several famous female faces (including Marilyn Monroe, Lucille Ball, Raquel Welch, Brigitte Bardot, Jayne Mansfield and Farrah Fawcett, among others), the Stones inflamed the sensibilities of Miss Ball and Miss Welch, who threatened legal action against both Atlantic Records and the Stones. To try and calm the waters, it was decided that in the

US the offending photos would be blackened, while in England new covers would be produced. Naturally, the original pressing soon became a hot collector's item, commanding relatively big bucks from that day to this. A single taken from the album, 'Beast Of Burden' backed by 'When The Whip Comes Down,' was issued in the US at the end of August.

But the really big news was Keith's upcoming trial in Toronto on the heroin charge of two years before. In October 1978 the case was finally heard, with Richards pleading guilty to a lesser charge after long, drawn-out negotiations between his attorneys and the prosecution. Richards' lawyer, Austin Cooper, pleaded for probation: 'In 1969 he started with heroin and it got to the state where he was taking such quantities of the drug and getting no euphoria from it. He was doing such powerful amounts – as

The French released these rare, distinctive and engaging singles, issued not as a box set (as Decca had done) but as a numbered (1–25) set. ' "L'Age D'Or" Des Rolling Stones' Generously, the French offered a different picture sleeve for each memorable tune.

much as two and a half grams a day – just to feel normal. He tells of three unsuccessful attempts to cure the addiction but the fourth is now working. He should not be dealt with as a special person, but I ask your Honour to understand him as a creative, tortured person, as a major contributor to an art form. He turned to heroin to prop up a sagging existence. I ask you to understand the whole man. He has fought a tremendous personal battle to rid himself of this terrible problem.'

Apparently swayed by Cooper's persuasive arguments, Judge Lloyd Graburn handed down a one-year suspended sentence. After hearing from a young, blind female Stones fan, Judge Graburn ordered Richards to perform a concert for the Canadian National Institute for the Blind within the next six months. In addition, Keith was also ordered to continue

treatment to combat his addiction, and keep the local probation department informed of his progress.

Mick and Bianca Jagger, meanwhile, were deeply entwined in a wrenching no-win divorce that gathered banner headlines around the globe. Now defended by attorney-to-the-stars Marvin Mitchelson, Bianca's list of demands from her estranged husband seemed to grow by the hour. One publication estimated her intended 'essential' monthly expenses to amount to over $13,000 per month. Mitchelson took the offensive: 'Bianca is furious because Mick has the financial squeeze on her, closing her bank accounts and returning her bills unpaid. Mrs Jagger filed for divorce in London last May, but she never served Jagger because she hoped for a reconciliation, especially since they have a little daughter. Of course, it becomes ⇨146

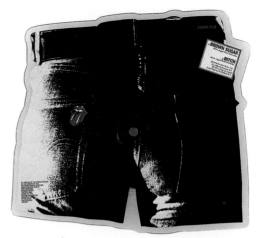

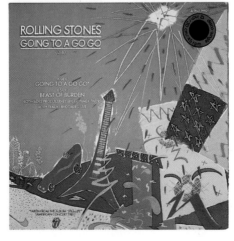

12" singles really happened for the Stones in 1978 with the release of 'Miss You' backed by 'Far Away Eyes' (their first single for EMI) in pink vinyl. Their initial 12" single, however, was the (now extremely rare) promotional release of 'Hot Stuff' backed by 'Crazy Mama' taken from their *Black and Blue* LP, and pressed on black and blue vinyl (1976).

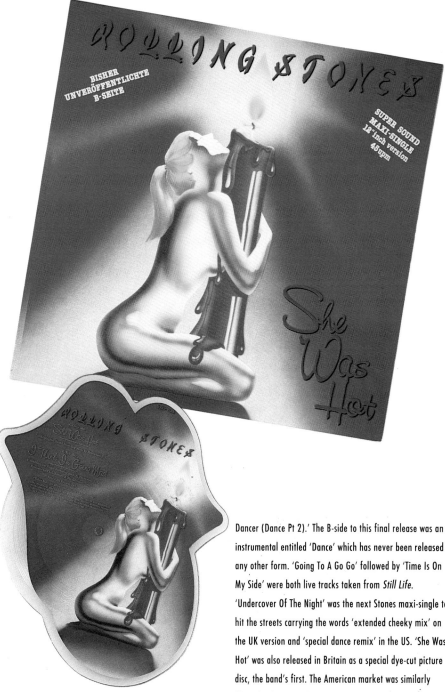

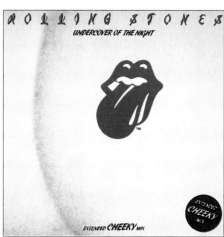

Next came a 'disco oldie' from Atlantic Records, 'Miss You' backed by 'Hot Stuff.' The next official 12" was 'Going To A

Go Go,' but there were a few promotional issues in between, including 'Start Me Up,' 'Emotional Rescue,' and 'If I Was A

Dancer (Dance Pt 2).' The B-side to this final release was an instrumental entitled 'Dance' which has never been released in any other form. 'Going To A Go Go' followed by 'Time Is On My Side' were both live tracks taken from *Still Life*. 'Undercover Of The Night' was the next Stones maxi-single to hit the streets carrying the words 'extended cheeky mix' on the UK version and 'special dance remix' in the US. 'She Was Hot' was also released in Britain as a special dye-cut picture disc, the band's first. The American market was similarly blessed with a special 12" issue of 'Too Much Blood' which boasted three different versions of the same song. The Stones' last issue for EMI, incidentally, was a picture disc of 'Brown Sugar' (1984), based on the cover design for *Sticky Fingers*.

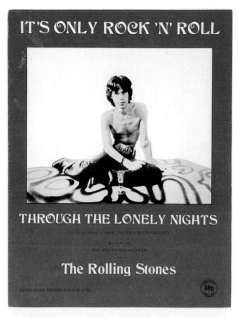

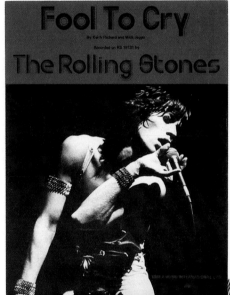

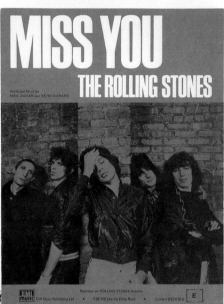

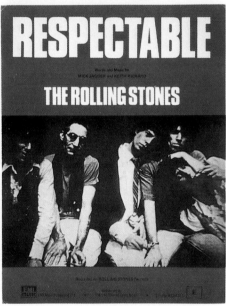

Songsheets and music books have always been a major part of the music publishing world and are a significant source of income for the artists. Here are a few prime examples.

OPPOSITE The first Stones calendar appeared in 1984 and publication continues to this day.

THE FIRST OFFICIAL

Rolling Stones

CALENDAR 1985

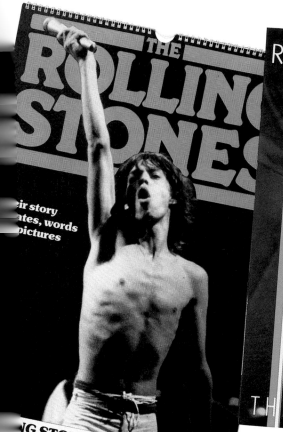

their story
dates, words
pictures

NG STONES CALENDAR 1984

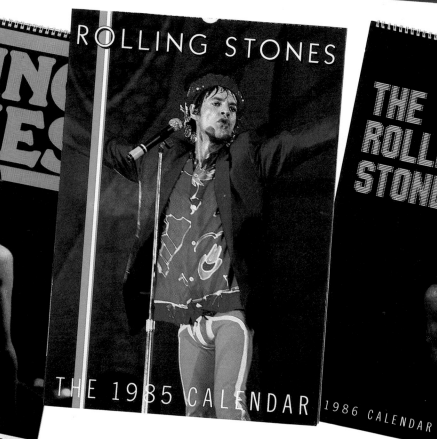

ROLLING STONES

THE 1985 CALENDAR

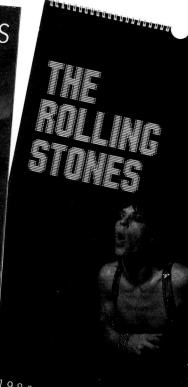

THE ROLLING STONES

1986 CALENDAR

The True Adventures of **THE ROLLING STONES**

by **STANLEY BOOTH**

"If you've never bought a book about rock and roll, no matter - this is the one you've been waiting for" **PLAYBOY**

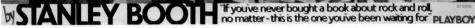

The Rolling Stones
MINIATURE ALBUM COLLECTION
BUBBLE GUM RECORD INSIDE

The 1980s produced a bumper crop of top-flight Stones memorabilia. There was the lurid tongue-shaped telephone, jigsaw puzzle, watch, key ring, and even a Stones-approved car deodorant. The Japanese came up with some very collectible match boxes.

OPPOSITE BELOW There was also a Rolling Stones miniature album collection featuring bubble gum records inside the meticulously reproduced sleeves.

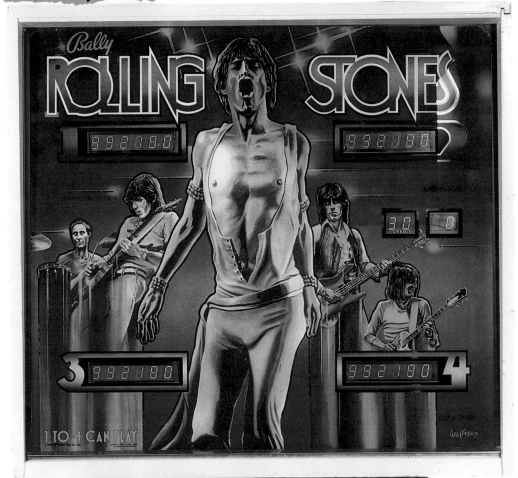

The largest and rarest piece of Rolling Stones memorabila is this pinball machine made by Bally, circa 1982. Hit a gold score and it plays your favourite Stones track.

ABOVE The magazine *Beggars Banquet* has become the only official Rolling Stones fanzine. The Stones have allowed unique access to its editor, Bill German, who faithfully reported inside information on tour dates, record releases, and other exclusive tidbits.

BELOW Part of the Fan Club package was a selection of autographed photographs of the boys. Although offered to fans worldwide, the club was aimed chiefly at the American market. Strangely, it lasted only twelve months.

RIGHT In 1983 the official Rolling Stones Fan Club was formed, the first since the early 60s. The fan club package included a membership card, several postcards, and a special 7" record with a 'personal' message from the Stones.

BELOW Three video releases capturing the Stones live on film. *Let's Spend The Night Together* was a dazzling documentary of the Stones' record-breaking 1981 US tour. Using twenty cameras and the latest 24-track audio, the film features twenty-five hot songs, several never before performed. *Rewind* is a visual 'greatest' hits compilation and contains the controversial TV-banned video of 'Undercover Of The Night.'

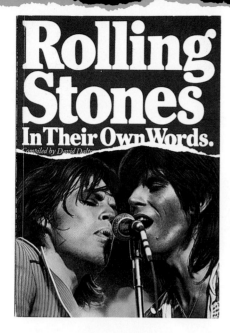

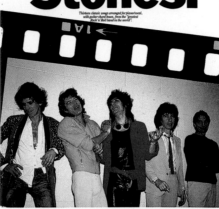

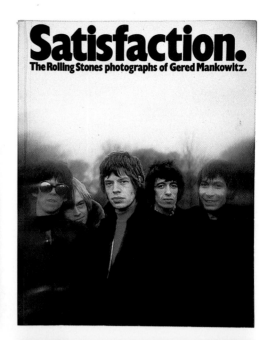

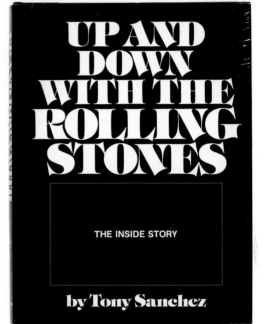

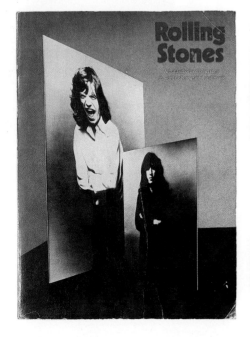

A variety of books about the Stones have been published over the years. Pictorially, the Stones always give book-buyers a good run for their money (see overleaf for more examples).

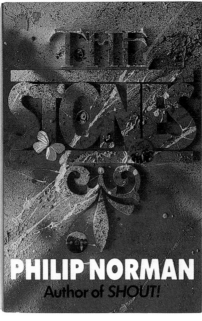

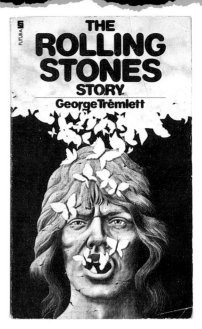

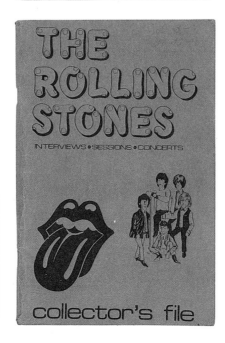

ON MORE THAN 200 RECORDS

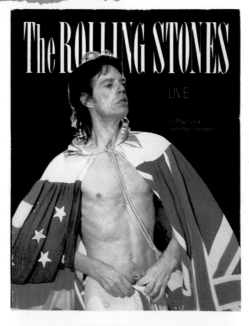

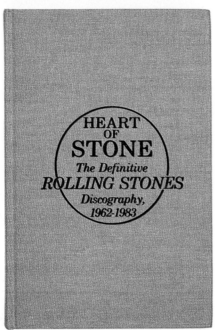

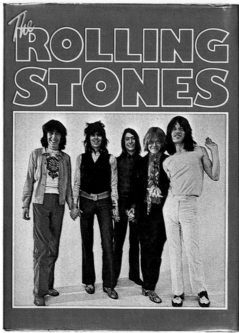

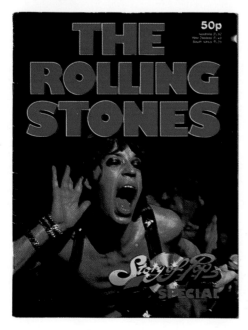

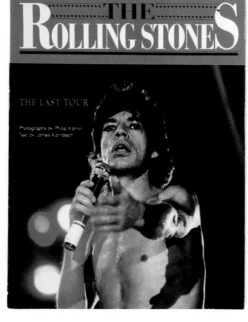

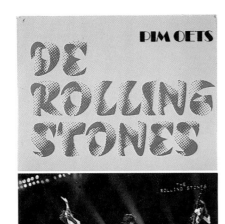

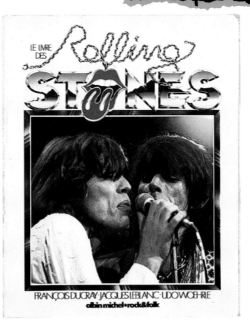

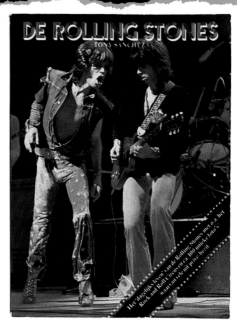

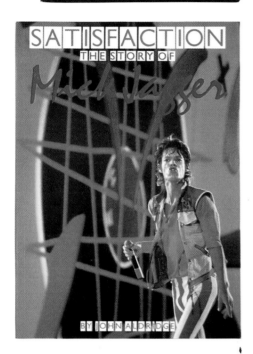

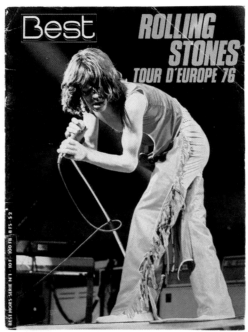

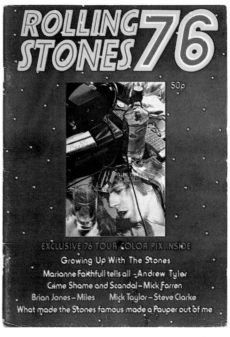

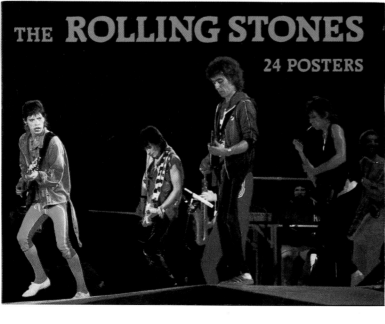

In the seventies, limited edition picture discs became very profitable. Although the Stones only issued
one bona fide picture disc, *Still Life*, the naughty bootleggers had a field day (above and opposite).

Commencing in 1980, the Rolling Stones issued their first limited edition box set in the United Kingdom comprising their first eight studio albums (bottom, right). Thereafter, box sets of old Decca LPs were issued in Germany (*The Rolling Stones Story*), France (top left), and Italy (middle left). In one of the German editions (*The Rest Of The Best*), the naughty 'Cocksucker Blues' was included but quickly withdrawn. Japan, too, came up with an excellent box set and a splendid book included within (middle right). Finally there was the Reader's Digest compilation which would mark an end to the Decca editions (top right).

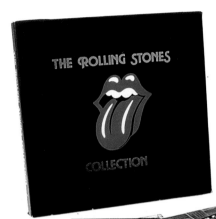

ABOVE AND RIGHT The early London albums were issued in a magnificent black wooden box titled *The Rolling Stones*. The records were all made from the original half-speed masters. The eleven-LP set also included a book of the album covers, as well as a special mat to put on your turntable.

The band repackaged several of their early albums and also released box sets in Australia (above), Spain (right), and in Greece (far right). The Greek box set came in a specially designed blue plastic box with a novel way of spelling 'Goat's Head Soup.'

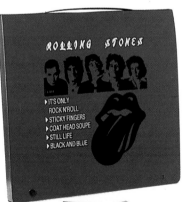

impossible to get a reconciliation when your husband is living with someone else.' On 14 May 1979 Judge Harry Shafer ordered Mick to maintain his wife in a 'sumptuous style' after hearing that he wanted to trim Bianca's monthly allowance.

Throughout the seventies Anita Pallenberg's life had steadily gone downhill. By now saddled with a terrifying drug habit, the formerly precocious beauty was now sadly reduced to an upper-crust junkie. Struggling through her lonely life with Keith Richards' two young children (Keith had long since split with Anita following the trial in Toronto), she was living in an elaborate mansion in Westchester county in upstate New York.

Not suprisingly, the naughty bootleggers also started releasing box sets. The so-called *Black Album* (opposite, above) is an exact replica of the Stones' planned three-album set which was never released. The bootleggers also gave the fans the chance to own a record of an entire live performance (above) just to keep those precious memories alive.

Eclipsing even the Beatles, the Stones are without doubt the most bootlegged group of all time. Although some of the early 'live' albums left quite a lot to be desired, as the technology improved so did the illicit releases. Graphically, the bootleggers have invariably come up with highly creative cover designs, usually on shoestring budgets.

But the event which actually marked the end of the couple's fourteen-year relationship was the suicide of 17-year-old Scot Cantrell in Pallenberg's bedroom while the two were watching television. Without warning the young man placed a .38 calibre revolver to his head and pulled the trigger.

Police investigations subsequently revealed that the gun used in the shooting was stolen, and charged Anita with possession of stolen property and criminal possession of a second unregistered automatic weapon also found in the house. On 31 December 1979 Pallenberg pleaded guilty to possession of the .38 after her attorney convinced the prosecutor to drop the second charge.

She was sentenced to a $1,000 fine on the weapons charge and a one-year conditional discharge.

By the summer of 1980 Mick Jagger had finally divorced Bianca, Keith had finished with Anita, Bill Wyman was forever estranged from his wife Astrid, and Ron Wood had replaced first love Krissy with Jo. Only Charlie, it seemed, was still happily ensconced with his lady Shirley and their two daughters.

Despite the band's domestic turmoil, they were definitely on the upswing musically. On 20 June 1980 a new single, 'Emotional Rescue,' was issued from the album of the same name (released just three days later) to rave reviews and brisk ⮕

new MUSICAL EXPRESS

April 24, 1976   U.S. 95c/Canada 55c   15p

Would you buy a Stones ticket from this man?

CHARLIE WATTS & HIS FABULOUS ROLLING STONES: NEW ALBUM P.5; THE 'OTHER' STONE P.8/9

LONDON, WEDNESDAY MAY 19 1976

Rolling Stone quizzed aft
KEITH RIC
ARRE
DRUGS

EVENING NEWS REPORTER

NG STONE Keith Richard
arrested today on the eve of
'oup's sell-out concert at Earls
's.
his Bentley was involved in a crash
he M1 and police said later that they
taken away a
'stance' found
he car.
was only a slight
ent and 33-year-
Richard was unhurt.
Thames Valley police
man said that a
ay patrol car
at the scene and
icers spoke with

'Ambassadors' to China . . . Charlie Watts, Mick Jagger, Keith Richard, Ronnie Wood, and Bill Wyman

Stones bandwagon rolls to China

By HOWARD FOSTER

THE Rolling Stones are to tour China next spring.
The invitation was extended to the band's leader, Mick Jagger, as he chatted over a cup of tea with the Chinese Ambassador in Washington.
It is an astonishing breakthrough for the wild men of pop.
The Stones have always been seen 'rtain countries as symbols

playing to people who haven't to an large degree been exposed to music.'
Stones publicist Keith Altham s the Chinese had named five cities t would like the band to visit.
'Unfortunately, they wanted Stones to go there this autumn but t were still recording their new album now planning to fly to Pe weeks with a tea

---

sales. That autumn another forty-five, 'She's So Cold' (backed by 'Send It To Me'), was hustled out to a similar response.

Without doubt the most traumatic happening of 1980 was the senseless murder of John Lennon on the evening of 8 December. All over the world people were devastated, but the Stones especially so. 'I don't want to make a casual remark right now, at such an awful moment for his family,' Mick Jagger commented to reporters in Paris.

Bill Wyman, meanwhile, recalled his first meeting with the often caustic singer. '[It was] in March 1963, when the Beatles came down to see the Stones in this dingy club called the Station Hotel in Richmond. They stood in line in their little

leather coats, and later came up to the flat; we stayed up all night talking about music, and we became good friends. John knew where he was going, and was very strong; he really got it together. He was a very determined guy. He will be sadly missed by the world.'

On 4 March 1981 yet another Stones anthology was released, with the rather uneven album *Sucking In The Seventies*. Not surprisingly, numerous record stores throughout North America banned the album simply for its rather suggestive title.

By the summer, however, there was a bit of new music on the burner with the raunchy *Tattoo You* and its initial single, the provocative 'Start Me Up' backed by 'No Use In Crying.' Once

BBC BAN FOR THE STONES?

THE ROLLING STONES are this week waiting to find out whether or not the BBC intends to ban the video of their new single, "She Was Hot", from peak viewing hours.

The video has already been banned by America's influential MTV cable music channel. But the BBC will not consider its suitability for "Top Of The Pops" screaming

But its content may have to be reconsidered for suitability for shows like Top Of The Pops which attract younger audiences.

A spokesman for the BBC said: "We wouldn't be making any decision about it until the record is in the Top 40."

MTV have a long track record of bans. Some time ago, the station

MICK CASTS A SPELL

From BOB HART in Vienna

MICK JAGGER'S angular body seemed to be trying to escape from the glittering silk jump-suit he wore as he hurled himself into the wild climax of his stage act.

At 30, he is almost twice the age of the youngsters who packed into a Viennese hall at the weekend to see if he could still do his stuff.

Lights

play four Wembley concerts next weekend.

He told me: "It worked out fine. Felt great. I have not been nervous about this tour at all."

He has no intention of ever being a very old rock and roll singer.

"But I am not quitting yet," he said.

"I love performing and I love being on the road.

Time

Kurinoff, sent from the Russian Ministry of Culture, must have been impressed.

There are six songs from the Stones' brilliant new Goat's Head Soup album in the act. But there is old

● BLUBBER - LIPS rock star Mick Jagger is number one at kissing, his sexy screen lover revealed last night.

● Sexy Anita Morris, star of the steamy Rolling Stones video She Was Hot, said: "Those lips just make you melt when he presses them against yours."

JAGGER'S TOP OF THE KISSERS

Truckin' along on the Stones roadshow

Full report pages 33–39

NEW STONES

again, like so many times before, the Rolling Stones dutifully headed out on the road, this time opening the tour at JFK Stadium in Philadelphia before a capacity crowd of 90,000. Needless to say, the fifty-city tour did big business at the box office, grossing the band a record-breaking $50 million for their twelve-week efforts.

By the time 1982 rolled around, the Stones were unquestionably the hottest thing going on the concert stage, if not in record stores. On 11 January the torrid 'Hang Fire' backed by 'Neighbours' became the second single culled from *Tattoo You*, and raced up the charts in America. From this point on the Rolling Stones simply continued cashing in their chips,

touring fourteen countries in Europe with determined ferocity.

On 25 August 1983 the Stones made rock 'n' roll history once again by signing the biggest, most potentially lucrative deal ever with the multi-national CBS Records, raking in a cool $25 million advance against royalties.

On Hallowe'en eve the Stones officially presented the world yet another new single with 'Undercover Of The Night' (and 'All The Way Down'). Their new album, *Undercover*, was then released in both the US and the UK. Recorded in Paris at EMI Marconi, the ominous title referred to the dark world of military dictatorships, a theme explored in their video for the title track. Said a BBC spokesman: 'It is exceedingly violent all the ▷156

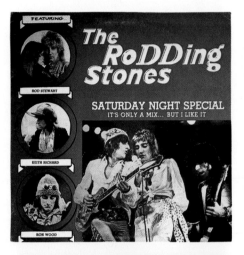

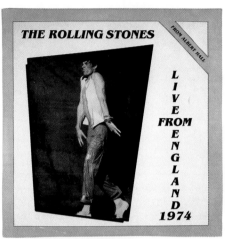

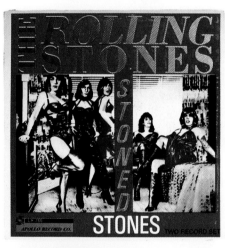

After a time bootlegs became an important staple to the collector, giving enthusiasts the opportunity to experience the Stones as nature never intended. As ever, bootlegs are a double-edged sword, cheating the artists out of millions in royalties, but affording obsessed fans entry into the most private recesses of the musicians' minds (see also pages 152–153).

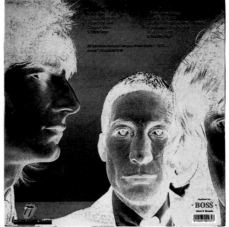

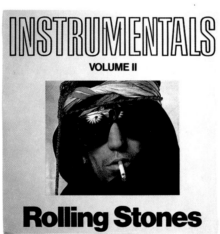

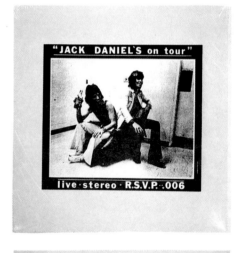

Often, bootlegged studio outtake albums were more interesting than many official releases, the songs 'Hey Claudine' and 'Gangster Maul' being prime examples. In addition, 'Lonely At The Top,' 'Sweet Home Chicago,' and 'Drift Away' (all from the bootleg *Lonely At The Top*) would have comprised a terrific Stones LP. *Accidents Will Happen*, too, is a milestone in bootleg history.

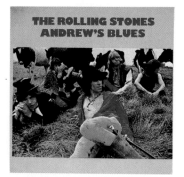

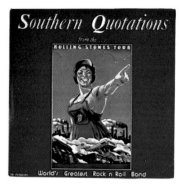

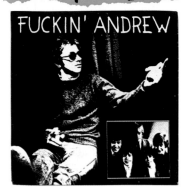

Slowly Rockin' On

LIVE IN OAKLAND '69

WHEN THE WHIP
GOES DOWN

Not only did bootleggers produce illicit albums, they also released an array of unauthorized 7" singles – from picture discs/flexis to multicoloured vinyl box sets. As the examples on this and the opposite page show, the ever-inventive bootleggers have invariably made a strong graphic statement on their picture sleeves, sometimes with more than a hint of good humour.

ROLLING
STONES
NEW SINGLE
ANGIE/SILVER TRAIN

ROLLIN
OUR OF

th May	APOLLO, GLASGO
th May	APOLLO, GLASGO
2th May	APOLLO, GLASGO
4th May	GRANBY HALLS,
15th May	GRANBY HALLS,
17th May	NEW BINGLEY HA
18th May	NEW BINGLEY HA

way through, and we couldn't consider it for 'Top Of The Pops' which goes out in the early evening.' As usual, Mick Jagger himself had the last word: 'A lot of "Undercover Of The Night" was inspired by things I read about all the people who've disappeared in Argentina.'

Later broadcast on Britain's Channel 4, with the offending scene of Mick's make-believe assassination by masked terrorists removed ('for the public good'), Jagger went on to defend the piece. 'It follows the song. The song is about repression, it's

about violence. We're not trying to dress it up and sell the record with advertising clichés. There's no gratuitous violence in it at all. We're not trying to glamorize violence either. We only want to make something interesting that has a valid point.'

Despite the naysayers, the LP *Undercover* went to number one in Britain on 18 November, peaking respectably in the fourth position in the US. Although the band released yet another single at the top of 1984 ('She Was Hot' backed by 'Think I'm Going Mad'), the really big news was the birth of

The Rolling Stones

Goat's Head Soup

STONES ROPE 1976

TICKETS

GLASGOW £3.50, £3.00, £2.50 inc. VAT
AVAILABLE ONLY BY POSTAL APPLICATION
(and limited to 2 per person)
from : BOX OFFICE,
APOLLO CENTRE,
GLASGOW

STAFFORD, LEICESTER all tickets £3.00 inc. VAT
LONDON £4.00, £3.00, £2.00 inc. VAT
AVAILABLE ONLY BY POSTAL APPLICATION
(and limited to 6 per person)
from: G. P. PRODUCTIONS,
P.O. BOX NO. 4TL

Mick and Jerry's first child together, Elizabeth Scarlett, at the Lenox Hill Hospital, New York, on 2 March 1984.

Also on the home front, Ron Wood formally said 'I do' to the lovely Jo Howard on 3 January 1985, while Keith's lady, Patti Hansen, gave birth to a little girl, to be named Theodora Dupree, on 18 March.

Putting a profound damper on all these heart-warming familial goings-on was the news that came from Britain that Charlie Watts had shattered his leg in three places while rummaging around in his cavernous basement in rural Devon on 19 August 1985. Probably just a minor outbreak of bad karma, though, as a joyful Jerry Hall gave birth on 28 August to a little boy upon whom Mick would bestow the grand name James Leroy Augustine Jagger.

All such auspicious tidings, however, were almost completely obliterated when, on 12 December 1985, Ian Stewart suddenly dropped dead of a heart attack in his doctor's waiting room in west London. He was waiting for a check-up as he had been suffering from a severe respiratory disease. He was just forty-seven years old.

1971 UK TOUR

MARCH

4	City Hall, Newcastle-Upon Tyne (2 shows)
5	Free Trade Hall, Manchester (2 shows)
5	Free Trade Hall, Manchester
6	Coventry Theatre, Coventry, West Midlands (2 shows)
8	Green's Playhouse, Glasgow, Scotland
9	Colston Hall, Bristol (2 shows)
10	Big Apple, Brighton, Sussex
12	Empire, Liverpool, Merseyside (2 shows)
13	University, Leeds, North Yorkshire
14	Chalk Farm Roundhouse, London (2 shows)
26	Marquee Club, London

1972 US TOUR

JUNE

3	Canadian Pacific Coliseum, Vancouver, British Columbia
4	Coliseum, Seattle, Washington (2 shows)
6	Winterland, San Francisco, California (2 shows)
8	Winterland, San Francisco, California
9	Hollywood Palladium, Los Angeles, Hollywood, California
10	Pacific Terrace Centre, Long Beach, California
11	Inglewood Forum, Los Angeles, California
13	International Sports Arena, San Diego, California
14	Civic Arena, Tucson, Arizona
15	University of New Mexico, Albuquerque, New Mexico
16	Coliseum, Denver, Colorado
18	Metropolitan Sports Center, Bloomington, Indiana
19	International Amphitheatre, Chicago, Illinois
20	International Amphitheatre, Chicago, Illinois
22	Municipal Auditorium, Kansas City, Kansas
24	Tarrant County, Fort Worth, Texas
25	Hoffheinz Pavilion, Houston, Texas
27	Municipal Auditorium, Mobile, Alabama
28	University of Alabama, Tuscaloosa, Alabama
29	Municipal Auditorium, Nashville, Tennessee

JULY

4	Robert F. Kennedy Memorial Stadium, Washington D.C.
5	The Scope, Norfolk, Virginia
6	Coliseum, Charlotte, North Carolina
7	Civic Arena, Knoxville, Tennessee
9	Kiel Auditorium, St. Louis, Missouri
11	Rubber Bowl, Akron, Ohio
13	Cobo Hall, Detroit, Michigan
14	Cobo Hall, Detroit, Michigan
15	Maple Leaf Gardens, Toronto, Ontario, Canada (2 shows)
17	Forum, Montreal, Quebec, Canada
18	Boston Gardens, Boston, Massachusetts
19	Boston Gardens, Boston, Massachusetts
20	Spectrum Sports Arena, Philadelphia, Pennsylvania
21	Spectrum Sports Arena, Philadelphia, Pennsylvania
22	Civic Arena, Pittsburgh, Pennsylvania
24	Madison Square Garden, New York City
25	Madison Square Garden, New York City
26	Madison Square Garden, New York City

1973 WINTER TOUR

JANUARY	18	Inglewood Forum, Los Angeles, California
	21	International Center, Honolulu, Hawaii (2 shows)
	22	International Center, Honolulu, Hawaii
FEBRUARY	5	Football Club Stadium, Hongkong (2 shows)
	11	Western Springs Stadium, Auckland, New Zealand
	13	Milton Park Tennis Courts, Brisbane, Australia
	14	Milton Park Tennis Courts, Brisbane, Australia
	17	Kooyong Tennis Courts, Melbourne, Australia
	18	Kooyong Tennis Courts, Melbourne, Australia (2 shows)
	20	Memorial Drive Park, Adelaide, Australia
	21	Memorial Drive Park, Adelaide, Australia
	24	Western Australia Cricket Ground, Perth, Australia
	26	Royal Randwick Racecourse, Sydney, Australia
	27	Royal Randwick Racecourse, Sydney, Australia

1973 EUROPEAN TOUR

SEPTEMBER	1	Stadthalle, Vienna, Austria
	3	Eisstadion, Mannheim, West Germany
	4	Sporthalle, Cologne, West Germany (2 shows)
	7	Empire Pool, Wembley, London
	8	Empire Pool, Wembley, London (2 shows)
	9	Empire Pool, Wembley, London
	11	King's Hall-Belle Vue, Manchester, UK
	12	King's Hall-Belle Vue, Manchester, UK
	13	City Hall, Newcastle, UK (2 shows)
	16	Apollo Theatre, Glasgow, UK
	17	Apollo Theatre, Glasgow, UK
	19	Odeon, Birmingham, UK (2 shows)
	24	Eishalle, Innsbruck, Austria
	25	Festhalle, Bern, Switzerland
	26	Festhalle, Bern, Switzerland (2 shows)
	28	Olympiahalle, Munich, West Germany (2 shows)
	30	Festhalle, Frankfurt, West Germany (2 shows)
OCTOBER	2	Ernst Merck Halle, Hamburg, West Germany (2 shows)
	4	Bejlby Riiskonhallen, Aarhus, Denmark
	6	Skandinavium, Gothenburg, Sweden
	7	Brandby Hallen, Copenhagen, Denmark (2 shows)
	9	Grugahalle, Essen, West Germany
	10	Grugahalle, Essen, West Germany
	11	Grugahalle, Essen, West Germany
	13	Ahoy Hall, Rotterdam, Netherlands
	14	Ahoy Hall, Rotterdam, Netherlands (2 shows)
	15	Sport Palais, Antwerpen, Belgium (2 shows)
	17	Foret Nationale, Bruxelles, Belgium (2 shows)
	19	Deutschlandhalle, Berlin, West Germany

1975 TOUR OF THE AMERICAS

JUNE	1	Dunkirk Hall, Baton Rouge, Louisiana (2 shows)
	3	Convention Center, San Antonio, Texas
	4	Convention Center, San Antonio, Texas
	6	Arrowhead Stadium, Kansas City, Missouri
	8	County Stadium, Milwaukee, Wisconsin
	9	Civic General Auditorium, St. Paul, Minnesota
	11	Boston Gardens, Boston, Massachusetts
	12	Boston Gardens, Boston, Massachusetts
	14	Municipal Stadium, Cleveland, Ohio
	15	Municipal Auditorium, Buffalo, New York
	17	Maple Leaf Gardens, Toronto, Canada
	18	Maple Leaf Gardens, Toronto, Canada
	22	Madison Square Garden, New York City
	23	Madison Square Garden, New York City
	24	Madison Square Garden, New York City
	25	Madison Square Garden, New York City
	26	Madison Square Garden, New York City
	27	Madison Square Garden, New York City
	29	Spectrum Sports Arena, Philadelphia, Pennsylvania
	30	Spectrum Sports Arena, Philadelphia, Pennsylvania
JULY	1	Capital Center Arena, Largo, Maryland
	2	Capital Center Arena, Largo, Maryland
	4	Memorial Stadium, Memphis, Tennessee
	6	Cotton Bowl, Dallas, Texas
	9	Inglewood Forum, Los Angeles, California
	10	Inglewood Forum, Los Angeles, California
	11	Inglewood Forum, Los Angeles, California
	12	Inglewood Forum, Los Angeles, California
	13	Inglewood Forum, Los Angeles, California
	15	Cow Palace, San Francisco, California
	16	Cow Palace, San Francisco, California
	18	Center Coliseum, Seattle, Washington
	19	Hughes Stadium, Fort Collins, Colorado
	23	Stadium, Chicago, Illinois
	24	Stadium, Chicago, Illinois
	26	University Assembly Center, Bloomington, Indiana
	27	Cobo Hall, Detroit, Michigan
	28	Cobo Hall, Detroit, Michigan
	30	The Omni Coliseum, Atlanta, Georgia
	31	Coliseum, Greensboro, North Carolina
AUGUST	2	Gaton Bowl, Jacksonville, Florida
	4	Freedom Hall Coliseum, Louisville, Kentucky
	5	Williamsburg, Virginia
	6	Hampton Coliseum, Hampton Roads, Virginia
	8	Rich Stadium, Buffalo, New York

1976 EUROPEAN TOUR

APRIL	28	Festhalle, Frankfurt, West Germany
	29	Festhalle, Frankfurt, West Germany
	30	Muensterlandhalle, Muenster, West Germany (2 shows)
MAY	2	Ostseehalle, Kiel, West Germany
	3	Deutschlandhalle, Berlin, West Germany
	4	Stadhalle, Bremen, West Germany
	6	Foret National, Brussels, Belgium
	7	Foret National, Brussels, Belgium
	10	Apollo Theatre, Glasgow, UK
	11	Apollo Theatre, Glasgow, UK
	12	Apollo Theatre, Glasgow, UK
	14	Granby Halls, Leicester, UK
	15	Granby Halls, Leicester, UK
	17	New Bingley Hall, Stafford, UK
	18	New Bingley Hall, Stafford, UK
	21	Earls Court Arena, London
	22	Earls Court Arena, London

	23	Earls Court Arena, London
	25	Earls Court Arena, London
	26	Earls Court Arena, London
	27	Earls Court Arena, London
	29	Footballstadium, Den Haag, Netherlands
	30	Footballstadium, Den Haag, Netherlands
JUNE	1	Westfalenhalle, Dortmund, West Germany
	2	Sporthalle, Cologne, West Germany (2 shows)
	4	Pavilion de Paris, Paris
	5	Pavilion de Paris, Paris
	6	Pavilion de Paris, Paris
	7	Pavilion de Paris, Paris
	9	Palais des Sports, Lyon, France
	11	Plaza de Totros Monumental, Barcelona, Spain
	13	Parc des Sports, Nice, France
	15	Hallenstadion, Zurich, Switzerland
	16	Olympiahalle, Munich, West Germany
	17	Olympiahalle, Munich, West Germany
	19	Neckarstadion, Stuttgart, West Germany
	21	Zagreb, Yugoslavia
	22	Zagreb, Yugoslavia
	23	Stadthalle, Vienna, Austria
AUGUST	21	Open Air Festival, Knebworth, UK

1978 US TOUR

JUNE	10	Civic Center, Lakeland, Florida
	12	Fox Theatre, Atlanta, Georgia
	14	Capitol Theatre, Passaic, New Jersey
	15	Warner Theatre, Washington D.C.
	17	J.F.K. Stadium, Philadelphia, Pennsylvania
	19	Palladium, New York City
	21	Hampton Coliseum, Hampton Road, Virginia
	22	Convention Center, Myrtle Beach, South Carolina
	26	Coliseum, Greensboro, North Carolina
	28	Mid South Coliseum, Memphis, Tennessee
	29	Rupp Arena, Lexington, Kentucky
JULY	1	Municipal Stadium, Cleveland, Ohio
	4	Rich Stadium, Buffalo, New York
	5	Orchard Park, New York State
	6	Masonic Hall, Detroit, Michigan
	8	Soldiers Field, Chicago, Illinois
	10	Civic Center, St. Paul, Minnesota
	11	Checkerdome, St. Louis, Missouri
	13	Superdome, New Orleans, Louisiana
	16	Folsom Field, Boulder, Colorado
	18	Tarrant County, Fort Worth, Texas
	19	Hoffeinz Pavilion, Houston, Texas
	21	Community Center, Tucson, Arizona
	23	Anaheim Stadium, Anaheim-Los Angeles, California
	24	Anaheim Stadium, Anaheim-Los Angeles, California
	26	Oakland Coliseum, Oakland, California

1981 US TOUR

SEPTEMBER	25	J.F.K. Stadium, Philadelphia, Pennsylvania
	26	J.F.K. Stadium, Philadelphia, Pennsylvania
	27	Rich Stadium, Buffalo, New York
OCTOBER	1	Metro Center, Rockford, Illinois
	3	Folsom Field, Boulder, Colorado
	4	Folsom Field, Boulder, Colorado
	7	Jack Murphy Stadium, San Diego, California
	9	Memorial Coliseum, Los Angeles, California
	11	Memorial Coliseum, Los Angeles, California
	14	The Kingdome, Seattle, Washington
	15	The Kingdome, Seattle, Washington
	17	Candlestick Park, San Francisco, California

18	Candlestick Park, San Francisco, California
24	Tangerine Bowl, Orlando, Florida
25	Tangerine Bowl, Orlando, Florida
26	Fox Theatre, Atlanta, Georgia
28	Astrodome, Houston, Texas
29	Astrodome, Houston, Texas
31	Cotton Bowl, Dallas, Texas

NOVEMBER

1	Cotton Bowl, Dallas, Texas
3	Freedom Hall, Louisville, Kentucky
5	Brendon Byrne Arena, Rutherford, New Jersey
6	Brendon Byrne Arena, Rutherford, New Jersey
7	Brendon Byrne Arena, Rutherford, New Jersey
9	Hartford Civic Center, Hartford, Connecticut
10	Hartford Civic Center, Hartford, Connecticut
12	Madison Square Garden, New York
13	Madison Square Garden, New York
16	Richfield Coliseum, Cleveland, Ohio
17	Richfield Coliseum, Cleveland, Ohio
19	Checkerdome, St. Louis, Missouri
20	Unidome, Cedar Falls, Iowa
21	Civic Center, St. Paul, Minnesota
23	Rosemont Horizon, Chicago-Des Plaines, Illinois
24	Rosemont Horizon, Chicago-Des Plaines, Illinois
25	Rosemont Horizon, Chicago-Des Plaines, Illinois
27	Carrier Dome, Syracuse, New York
28	Carrier Dome, Syracuse, New York
30	Silverdome, Pontiac, Michigan

DECEMBER

1	Silverdome, Pontiac, Michigan
3	River Boar (President), New Orleans, Louisiana
5	Superdome, New Orleans, Louisiana
7	Capital Center Arena, Largo, Washington D.C
8	Capital Centre Arena, Largo, Washington D.C
9	Capital Centre Arena, Largo, Washington D.C
11	Rupp Arena, Lexington, Kentucky
13	Sun Devil Stadium, Phoenix-Scottsdale, Arizona
14	Kemper Arena, Kansas City, Kansas
15	Kemper Arena, Kansas City, Kansas
18	Hampton Coliseum, Hampton Roads, Virginia
19	Hampton Coliseum, Hampton Roads, Virginia

1982 EUROPEAN TOUR

MAY

26	Capitol Theatre, Aberdeen, UK
27	Apollo Theatre, Glasgow, UK
28	Green's Playhouse, Edinburgh, UK
30	100 Club, London

JUNE

2	Feijenoord Stadion, Rotterdam, Netherlands
4	Feijenoord Stadion, Rotterdam, Netherlands
5	Feijenoord Stadion, Rotterdam, Netherlands
6	Niedersachsenstadion, Hanover, West Germany
7	Niedersachsenstadion, Hanover, West Germany
8	Waldbuehne, Berlin, West Germany
10	Olympiastadion, Munich, West Germany
11	Olympiastadion, Munich, West Germany
13	Hippodrome d'Auteuil, Paris
14	Hippodrome d'Auteuil, Paris
16	Stade Gerland, Lyon, France
19	Ullevi Stadium, Gothenburg, Sweden
20	Ullevi Stadium, Gothenburg, Sweden
23	St. James Park, United Football Club, Newcastle, UK
25	Wembley Stadium, London
26	Wembley Stadium, London
27	Ashton Gate Park, Bristol UK
29	Festhalle, Frankfurt, West Germany
30	Festhalle, Frankfurt, West Germany

JULY	1	Festhalle, Frankfurt, West Germany
	3	Prater Stadion
	4	Muengersdorter Stadion, Cologne, West Germany
	5	Muengersdorter Stadion, Cologne, West Germany
	7	Estadio Vincent Calderon, Madrid, Spain
	9	Estadio Vincent Calderon, Madrid, Spain
	11	Stadio Communale, Turin, Italy
	12	Stadio Communale, Turin, Italy
	15	St. Jakob Stadion, Basel, Switzerland
	17	Stadio San Paolo, Naples, Italy
	20	Parc Des Sports, Nice, France
	24	Slane Castle, Slane, Dublin, Ireland
	25	Roundhay Park, Leeds, UK.

1986

FEBRUARY	23	Tribute for Ian Stewart. 250 invited guests, 100 Club, London

Harvey Goldsmith Entertainments Limited

2nd Floor, Avon House,
360-362 Oxford Street
London W1R 1FB
Telephone: 01-409 1984

Telex: 22721
Answerback: HGENTS

26th May 1982

Mr Lusher
Tyneside Piano Co
34 Wellhead Terrace
Ashington
Northumberland

Dear Mr Lusher,

ROLLING STONES CONERT - NEWCASTLE UNITED FOOTBALL CLUB, ST JAMES PARK -
WEDNESDAY 23RD JUNE 1982

I am writing to confirm the order placed by Mr Bob Taylor, Stage Manager
at Newcastle City Hall, for the 5'6" Challon piano to be used at the above
concert.

We would like the piano to be delivered to the backstage area at the Leazes
End of the football ground on the morning of Tuesday 22nd June and collected
on the morning of Thursday 24th June.

Mr Taylor has advised that your quote for the hire of the piano, including
delivery and collection, is £70 and we would be pleased if you would send
your invoice direct to this office at the above address at your earliest
convenience.

Thanks for your help in this matter".

Yours sincerely,

163

For the Rolling Stones, the dawning of 1986 signalled a time of great trial. At a private memorial to their beloved road manager Ian Stewart at the 100 Club in London on 23 February, the Stones spontaneously launched into a blistering, emotionally charged set, reminiscent of their early days in Richmond. Jeff Baker of the *Daily Star* reported: 'They played with the guts and energy of a teenage garage band. There was none of the super-slick, high-tech sound of their recent albums. This was the Stones going back to their roots, playing muddy and dirty, ripping through the old classics.'

After the show, Mick and Keith were spotted leaving the club, buoyant and joking, prompting one spokesman to headily predict: 'The chances of the Stones getting together are 100 per cent better; the band is keen to lay bets that they'll be gigging within eighteen months. A week ago I would have said there was no possibility at all.'

Two days later Eric Clapton presented the band with a Lifetime Achievement Award at the Grammys in Los Angeles. The boys accepted the honour at London's Rooftop Garden Club while the premiere of their new video, 'Harlem Shuffle,' was beamed to a world-wide audience. Featuring a host of sexy cartoon felines slithering across a smokey Harlem ballroom, the clever promo featured both live action and animation sequences. 'Harlem Shuffle' was the initial release off *Dirty Work*, and the first work distributed by Columbia/CBS. It reached number three and four on the British and American charts, spawning hopes of the band's first tour in five years.

Such hopes, however, were quickly dashed when Mick coldly informed Keith via telegram that he would not be touring in favour of producing his second solo album. Reaction from the volatile Richards came swift and heated: 'If Mick tours without the band I'll slit his throat!' Jagger fired back: 'I don't need this bunch of old farts,' setting off a high profile feud that would continue over the better part of the next three years. 'I was surprised Keith was so upset when I wanted to do something outside the band,' Jagger would comment in a cooler moment. 'He'd already done this thing with the New Barbarians. The difficult thing about growing up,' he continued, 'is you start off with this gang of people and it's very childish to think you can remain with them forever.'

Charlie Watts, though, seemed to feel Jagger had no idea how this crippling blow affected the highly sensitive Richards. 'That one decision virtually folded up twenty years of a band,' he proclaimed. 'More than any of us, Keith's whole life was the Stones. He took it very badly.'

In the midst of the maelstrom the group stoically assembled at Elstree Studios to shoot the video for their next single, 'One Hit (To The Body).' The on-screen scuffle between Mick and Keith was designed to parody the non-stop media hullabulloo over their rocky relationship. In truth, though, it resembled a ⇨

OPPOSITE ABOVE One of the first official promotional posters produced after the Stones signed to CBS.

OPPOSITE The Stones bid farewell to Toronto after the momentous 4 December 1989 concert.

steamy fifteen-rounder that would have made fight promoter Don King proud. Explained Richards: 'The relationship was pretty shabby at that point. We got to the end of our tether with each other. So we were gonna make this video and the director [Russell Mulcahy] suggested we use some of the energy that was obviously already there. It was a fairly good portrayal of the situation at the time.'

Although *Dirty Work* peaked in the top five on both the American and British charts, by Rolling Stones standards it did not do well. The unexpected death of Ian Stewart ('the glue of the whole set-up,' according to Keith), the heated in-fighting, plus lack of any sustained collective promotion would adversely affect the group for the next five years.

From there the seriously fractured group spun out in divergent directions. Ron Wood soon found his dance card filled with a host of short-term projects. In New Orleans he participated in a television special with Fats Domino, followed by rehearsals with David Letterman's affable sidekick Paul Shaffer and drummer Steve Jordan for a stint on NBC's 'Friday Night Videos.' He also jammed, as did Bill Wyman, with close mate Rod Stewart on stage at Wembley Stadium for an off-the-

cuff Faces reunion that delighted 60,000 wildly loyal fans. Just ten days later Woody guested with Bob Dylan for three consecutive nights at New York's Madison Square Garden. In between he teamed up with Keith to produce Aretha Franklin's spirited cover of the band's classic, 'Jumpin' Jack Flash.'

Charlie Watts, as ever quietly avoiding any and all controversy, seized the opportunity to book an eight-date east coast tour for his thirty-three member orchestra. Jo Jo Laine was on hand at New York's swank Ritz with former Stones producer Jimmy Miller for one of Watts' Big Apple performances: 'I really think he has no idea what a terrifically talented drummer he is.'

Bill Wyman, too, was busy stirring up his own headlines at the time. In a kiss and tell *News of the World* spread, sixteen year-old Mandy Smith revealed an affair with the Stones' bassist that began at the age of thirteen. The Kensington schoolgirl told of meeting the middle-aged rocker at a Mayfair disco and how she and her sister schemed to fix him up with their thirty-eight year-old mother. Except it wasn't mummy who caught Bill's fancy. At a subsequent dinner at the Smith's swanky Muswell Hill home, the forty-six year-old musician only had eyes for the coltish Mandy, who Wyman later spirited off to an exclusive

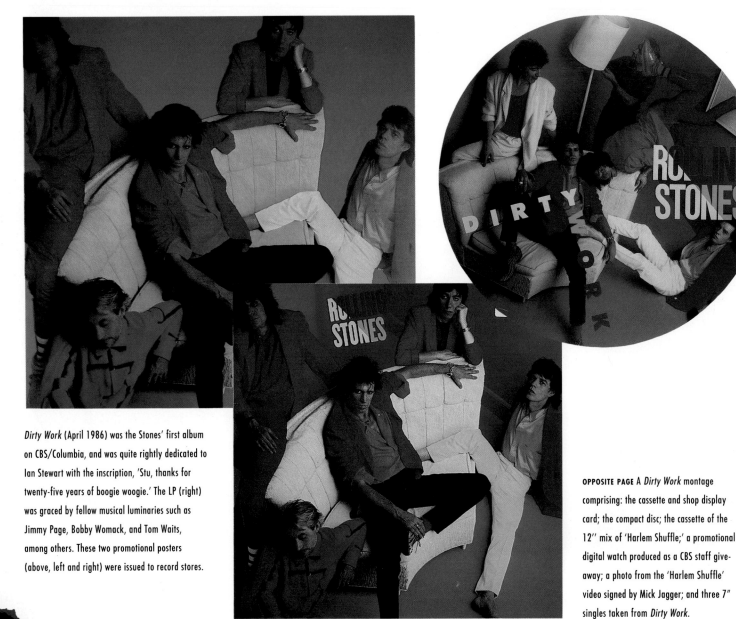

Dirty Work (April 1986) was the Stones' first album on CBS/Columbia, and was quite rightly dedicated to Ian Stewart with the inscription, 'Stu, thanks for twenty-five years of boogie woogie.' The LP (right) was graced by fellow musical luminaries such as Jimmy Page, Bobby Womack, and Tom Waits, among others. These two promotional posters (above, left and right) were issued to record stores.

OPPOSITE PAGE A *Dirty Work* montage comprising: the cassette and shop display card; the compact disc; the cassette of the 12" mix of 'Harlem Shuffle;' a promotional digital watch produced as a CBS staff give-away; a photo from the 'Harlem Shuffle' video signed by Mick Jagger; and three 7" singles taken from *Dirty Work*.

nightclub for a double date with Keith and Patti Richards.

The affair began with Mandy discreetly moving in with her Rolling Stone heart-throb, while he footed the bill for her upscale private Kensington school. 'My mother approved of the relationship with Bill,' Mandy revealed. 'He knew the risk he was taking but it didn't occur to me.' By August of 1986, however, the London teenager had dumped Wyman for a 'penniless beach boy,' claiming that paranoia over his public image kept her home all alone. 'In the end I felt so lonely and it didn't seem right,' she reasoned.

After the story hit the stands, Scotland Yard moved in, questioning Mandy, Patsy Smith, and an understandably uptight Wyman. Fearing an adverse public response, Wyman laid low behind the iron gates of his home in the South of France until the incident had blown over. As it turned out, Mrs Smith had no intention of implicating Bill in any wrongdoing, admitting she had given the liaison her blessing.

Turmoil continued to haunt the Stones as 1987 rolled along. In Barbados to work solo on the album he'd begun at Wisseloord Studios in Holland, Jagger was hit with the news in February that Jerry Hall had been arrested at the island's

Grantley Adams Airport on possession of some twenty pounds of marijuana. Hall had been notified by airline officials that an unlabelled package had arrived for her from Mustique. When the puzzled model requested the parcel be opened, the high-powered hemp was discovered. Barbados police and customs officials instantly slapped the Texas beauty into a cell overnight before Jagger could post a $5,000 bail the next morning.

Following a thirty-one-day enforced stay on the island and three court appearances in mid-February, the case against Hall collapsed when customs supervisor Casper Walcott admitted he had lied under oath. He testified that detectives had asked him to be on the look-out for the package containing the pot and that Ms Hall was a victim of a 'police ambush.' Highly distraught over the incident, Jerry complained she'd lost well over $200,000 in modelling assignments during the trial.

Around the same time Keith was having his own problems back in New York. While laying down some tracks at Studio 900 on 19th Street with keyboardist Ian Neville and drummers Steve Jordan and Charley Drayton (music which would eventually comprise his first solo album), a fierce fire broke out, forcing the musicians to flee the building. As billows of ▷ 169

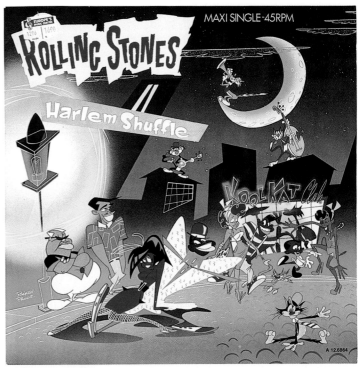

The Stones' first single from *Dirty Work* (above left) was an upbeat version of the Bob and Earl 1969 classic 'Harlem Shuffle,' issued in March 1986. The sexy, blues-inspired romp was released as a 12" (picture sleeve) single (above), a cassette single, and a limited edition 7" single with a wrap-around poster sleeve.

The combatative song 'One Hit (To The Body)' was the next single pulled from *Dirty Work* and released world-wide in May 1986 (bottom left). 'Winning Ugly' was a single released in Canada only in January 1987 (below). As usual, store display posters were produced for the album and singles (opposite).

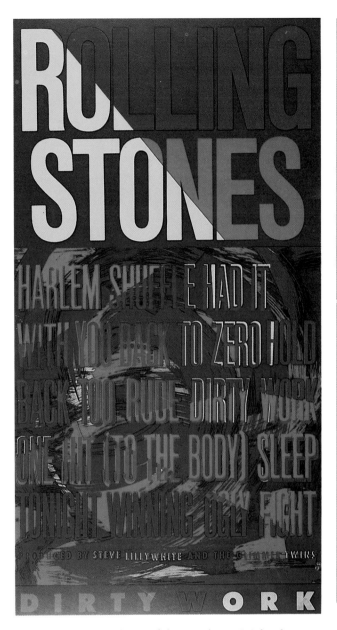

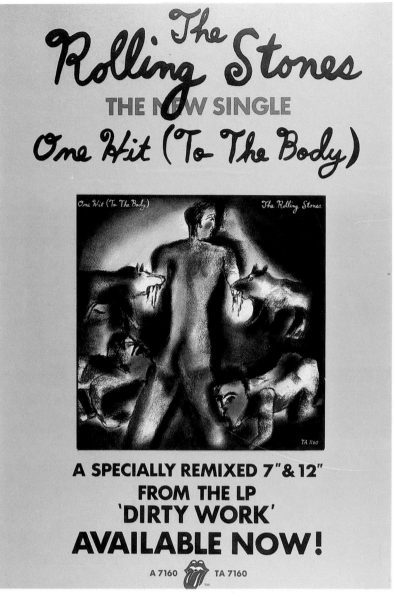

thick smoke poured out of the windows, Richards was seen exiting the burning studio laden with as much equipment as he could carry. Typically unfazed, the laid-back guitarist and his mates launched into an impromptu jam in the street until firemen arrived, much to the delight of the neighbourhood kids.

Woody, it seemed, was also under the gun after the London *Sun* alleged he had spent the night with a young model he had allegedly picked up at a well-known London hot spot. For the usually mellow guitarist the timing was particularly distressing as he was on solid marital ground with his wife Jo, and in the process of forging his own solo career with an album several months in the making. On top of that, he'd recently been hired as a journalist for Italian television, conducting a series of interviews with music's elite, including Prince, David Bowie, and Peter Gabriel. The tawdry publicity was, of course, the very last thing he needed, so he promptly issued a writ for libel against the newspaper. 'Usually I just laugh about things that are written about me,' he said, 'but this has gone too far. I have never even met this girl, let alone gone to bed with her. Anyway, my writ number is 13/13, which I think will prove to be doubly unlucky for them.' The action paid off a year later as the High Court in London awarded Wood a public apology in

The Sun plus an undisclosed sum for libel damages.

Thereafter, a period of relative tranquillity settled over the band throughout the spring and summer of 1987. Mick Jagger was busy shooting promotional videos for his forthcoming singles 'Let's Work' and 'Say You Will,' as well as composing with the Eurythmics' Dave Stewart. Charlie Watts, meanwhile, was enjoying the success of his *Live at Fulham Town Hall* album recorded at the Fulham Town Hall in London. Still out and about with his newly formed big band, the self-effacing drummer played an array of venues from the Hollywood Bowl to the Pistoia Blues Festival in Italy.

Keith, meanwhile, had landed his own deal with Virgin and was acting as musical director on *Hail! Hail! Rock 'n' Roll*, a film documentary about his idol Chuck Berry. Teaming up with venerable director Taylor Hackford of *Officer and a Gentleman* fame, Richards sought to 'pay Berry back [for] every lick ever stolen from him.' Despite his obvious elation at working with his boyhood hero, Keith admitted Berry wasn't always the easiest person to get along with: 'I've been doing it my way for sixty years!' Chuck would spit at Richards' rather tentative attempts to direct him. Berry's well-recorded obsession with money also surfaced as he referred to his collection of vintage guitars as ⇨

On 31 August 1989 the Stones rolled into Grand Central Station, New York, to promote the release of their new album, *Steel Wheels* (above), as well as their first world tour in seven years. Limited editions were now very much the order of the day, with *Steel Wheels* issued in America in a special limited edition CD steel case (above right). In the UK, a 10" picture disc of the press conference in New York was later issued (right, front and back shown). The ubiquitous tongue logo (below) was again used for promotional purposes, and here to display the CD.

merely 'tax deductions.' Many of the moments captured on screen, however, were pure magic, like the old master making Keith play the same passage over and over again until he duplicated the exact effect first heard on record thirty years previously. Nothing, however, could beat the film's free-wheeling jams, with Richards playing lead to Berry's rough-and-ready rhythm, and piano player Johnnie Johnson's sassy boogie woogie keys.

Interestingly, throughout 1987 it was Bill Wyman who managed to hold the Stones together. In April he held a press conference to present details of his new project AIMS, standing for Ambition, Ideas, Motivation, and Success. The novel idea sought to take the Stones' mobile studio around Britain and allow unknown local bands the opportunity to record their music. In addition, Wyman would produce the groups and help them land gigs. The Stones to a man all rallied around the cause, appearing at various AIMS fundraisers, lending a hand in the studio, and giving young hopefuls a few handy pointers.

The uneasy cease-fire, though, would hold just so long. On 14 September came the release of Mick Jagger's second solo album *Primitive Cool*. Two tracks in particular, 'Kow Tow' and

CBS/Columbia embarked on a massive international no-expense-spared promotional campaign on the release of *Steel Wheels*, issuing a wide variety of mouthwatering display material.

'Shoot Off Your Mouth,' were obvious barbs hurled at Keith Richards. Relations between the duelling Stones had so disintegrated that they now spoke only through third parties. 'Mick is very bitter about the row with Keith,' said a friend. 'He's had a real go at him and hopes he listens to the album and realizes the significance.'

Fuelling the acrimonious situation was Jagger's threat to tour on his own, taking along journeyman musician Jeff Beck. 'Great,' snarled Keith upon learning of his former partner's plans. 'Go to Australia in their mid-winter. Go on. I've got other things to do. Go there with your jerk-off band.'

Richards, no doubt, was secretly snickering when Mick's tour (slated for an early October start) had to be postponed. At the last minute, apparently, Beck had a blow up with Jagger that sent the legendary guitarist off in a stormy huff. Venting his side of the story in *The Sun*, Beck complained: 'I quit the tour because Mick offered me peanuts to play with him. It was laughable, an insult. I wanted to teach him a lesson because if you want the best you have to pay for it. The kind of money he offered is what you pay an ordinary session musician. Mick's problem is that he's a meanie. He's no better than a glorified accountant. He counts every penny. For someone with his money I ⇨

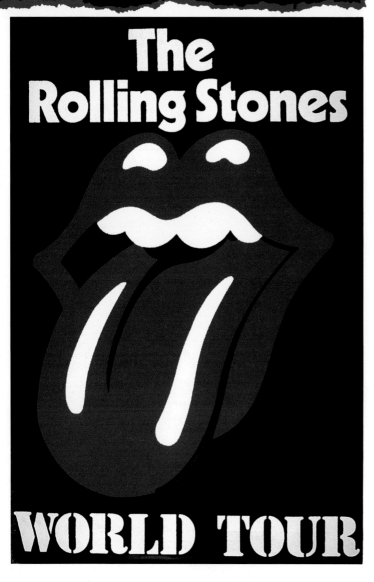

The Rolling Stones

WORLD TOUR

can't believe how tight he is. I'd still love to go on tour with the old geezer. He's just got to make me a proper offer.'

Unfortunately, contending with Beck wasn't all Jagger had to worry about. Fan reception to *Primitive Cool* seemed to indicate that Jagger's efforts fell far short of the chemistry he enjoyed with his former band mates. Though the project received some critical acclaim, *Cool* managed to reach only number eighteen on the British charts and an anaemic forty-one on its American counterpart. On the singles charts the eclectic album failed to generate even one modest hit.

On 14 November 1987 CBS re-released the entire Rolling Stones back catalogue at a time when one had to wonder if the band's glory days seemed to be permanently behind them. With the new tensions at breaking point the inevitable question lingered: Would the world's greatest rock 'n' roll band ever play together again?

In spite of his mounting musical woes, Jagger maintained a high profile as 1988 opened with the induction of the Beatles into the Rock 'n' Roll Hall of Fame. Taking the podium at the Waldorf Astoria, Jagger introduced the Fabs as 'the four-headed monster' and went on to lead a rousing version of 'I Saw Her Standing There' with George Harrison, Ringo Starr, and Bruce Springsteen, among others. The evening's musical highlight, though, focused on a sizzling rendition of 'Satisfaction' backed by the incomparable Jeff Beck.

Mick Jagger's first ever solo tour began in Japan on 15 March at Osaka's Castle Hall before 11,000 squealing fans. The seven-date tour netted a gate of 250,000, adding up to a cool £1,000,000 per night.

On 30 May 1990 a pre-recorded live show was broadcast on American TV. A segment of this concert had been shot in sensational 3-D. Thus the need for the special Rolling Stones 3-D glasses, and tasty Rolling Stones popcorn (below).

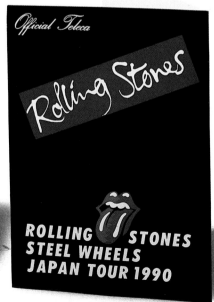

While in Osaka, Mick found time to catch Tina Turner's show, even taking the stage for a hot, raunchy rendition of 'Honky Tonk Women.' The evening, though, took a bizarre turn when Jagger learned that Australian entrepreneur Gunter Roth had offered $20 million for the rock star's ashes upon his death. It seemed the eccentric Gunter intended to market a rather gruesome 'limited edition' gold plated egg timer to the late Stone's fans. Strange world.

Between tour dates Jagger flew back to New York to answer charges of plagiarism in a pesky suit that had been pending for the past sixteen months. Jamaican reggae musician Patrick Alley accused Mick of copyright infringement on his song 'Just Another Night.' Alley claimed Jagger pilfered the tune, which had appeared on the totally forgettable 1982 LP *Just a Touch of Patrick Alley.* Alley was after $7 million in profits from the 1985 *She's the Boss* album. Jagger, of course, hotly denied the charges.

In the much publicized four-day proceedings at White Plains Federal Court, Jagger introduced demo tapes of the song to trace its musical evolution. As part of his defence, Mick also sang several numbers before the judge. In addition, Sly Dunbar, who drummed on *She's the Boss* (and ⇨ 176

TOP *The Atlanta Journal* advertised a Stones feature.
ABOVE In 1989 a set of silver commemorative coins was issued.
RIGHT Labatts sponsored the Canadian leg of the tour.
BELOW The Japanese produced a phone card, and a special 3″ CD tin.

ROLLING STONES MIXED EMOTIONS

THE ROLLING STONES ARE BACK 'MIXED EMOTIONS' THE BRAND NEW SINGLE

7 · 12 · CD

RELEASE DATE: AUGUST 21ST

With the release of the single 'Mixed Emotions' in August 1989, collectors everywhere were set running madly to obtain not only the 12" and 7" versions, but also the cassette single, CD single (in both 3" and 5" formats), other special editions in tins, promotional CDs, and even a promotional maxi disc (12").

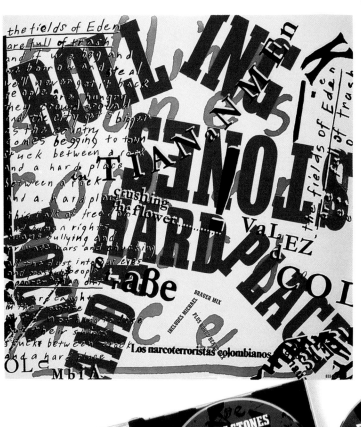

'Rock And A Hard Place' (November 1990), like 'Mixed Emotions,' was specially packaged for the collector. Instead of a tin package, however, the no-holds-barred single came in a boxed set with a free poster and a dye-cut sleeve of the famous tongue logo. Three promotional CDs were issued to radio stations only (above and left).

whom Alley testified played on his record as well), brought his kit to court to demonstrate the different beats used on each version. On 26 April Jagger was formally cleared of the charge. He commented: 'If you're well known, people take shots at you. But the trial was a bit of a waste of time for everyone.'

However, the Stones lost their battle to bar the sale of an extremely rare three-track 1962 group single of Muddy Waters's 'Soon Forgotten,' Jimmy Reed's 'Close Together,' and Bo Diddley's 'You Can't Judge A Book.' The tracks were on an old EMI disc acetate recorded in London at Curly Clayton's studio, with Tony Chapman on drums. Bill Wyman spearheaded the full-tilt legal action, but his efforts fell short as the disc sold for a whopping £6,000 at auction in London later that year.

'Almost Hear You Sigh' (February 1990) became the third single taken from *Steel Wheels*. Interestingly, the video was made with no two Stones appearing in the same shot together. With this release, the collectible tin was reintroduced and in the UK a gold 5" CD was issued.

'Terrifying,' the Stones' next single, was released in May 1990 on CD with bonus tracks 'Start Me Up' and 'Shattered.' One to look out for before the price skyrockets is the Dutch 12" promo (right column, front and back shown).

Legal hassles behind them, things were stirring behind closed doors. In May, all five Stones gathered at the Savoy Hotel to discuss future plans for the band. Though he would never publicly admit it, Jagger was now operating from a position of profound weakness. Not only had his two solo albums bombed, but an American tour, already booked, was cancelled in anticipation of poor ticket sales. On top of that a planned autobiography (for which Jagger had reportedly received a $100,000 advance) was deemed unfit for publication and scrapped. 'His majesty,' as Keith liked to dub his big-lipped buddy, had suddenly tumbled from his throne and there was nowhere else to go. Clearly Jagger needed the Rolling Stones.

Three months later, a victorious Mick was telling the press that the Stones would soon be going into the studio to record a new album with a world tour to follow. But as Jagger flew off to start his seventeen-date Australian tour, beginning on 22 September in Brisbane, Keith Richards' long-awaited solo album, *Talk Is Cheap*, was released. Unfortunately, old wounds were opened. This time Keith seized the opportunity to answer Mick in song, as with the track 'You Don't Move Me.'

What makes you so greedy
Makes you so seedy
Now you want to throw the dice
You already crapped out twice.   ⇨

I played it to him in New York,' recalled Richards. 'He talked all the way through it. Then I went to the john, and as I was coming out I saw him dancing in the front room. So I went back to the john and slammed the door loud. . . He can be a real asshole. He has to play little games. Mick's not about to give you anything. He'll be flip. Which is exactly the reason why we didn't go on the road behind *Dirty Work*. He wanted to compete on a different level.'

Richards apparently felt he had good reason to be upset. He explains: 'Mick suddenly called up saying "Let's put the Stones back together." So I'm thinking, just as I'm in the middle of an album. Boy what are you trying to do, screw me up? *Now* you want to talk about putting it back together?'

In truth, Keith was very much enjoying his new-found freedom. 'I never wanted to do a solo record until I started doing it,' he admitted, 'and by working with all these cats I found the nucleus of another great band.' *Talk is Cheap* proved it had surprising staying power, remaining on the American charts for a solid nineteen weeks, reaching a respectable twenty-four, bettering the disappointing solo efforts of his superstar comrade. 'Keith made the kind of solo record that has thus far eluded the Rolling Stones – full of great songs, energy, and innovation,' hailed Charlie, obviously proud as hell.

Buoyed by the early critical acclaim, Keith hit the road with his new band, dubbed appropriately the X-Pensive Winos, with Steve Jordan on drums, Charley Drayton on bass, talented Ian

Neville at the keyboards, and super-sideman Waddy Watchel playing guitar. The Winos played a sold-out fourteen-date run across the United States, gathering steam as they rolled into the Hollywood Paladium and finally New Jersey's Brendan Byrne Arena before 22,000 appreciative fans on 17 December.

As for the other band members, they too were getting used to life without the 'ball and chain,' as Jagger constantly referred to the Stones. Charlie was enjoying continued success with his orchestra, and made it clear it wasn't always a pleasure being part of the world's greatest rock 'n' roll band. 'With the Stones we do nothing but hang around,' he expressed sardonically. 'Work five years then hang around for twenty.'

By this time Ron Wood had linked up with his boyhood idol, the trail-blazing Bo Diddley, for some heavy-duty, Delta-style rock 'n' roll. Calling themselves the Gunslingers, the duo hit the road from November of 1987 through to July of 1988. The three-leg tour began with fifteen US dates in small, intimate halls like Chicago's Riviera and New York's Ritz, before moving on to two weeks in Japan and a month of European cities.

Of all the Stones, it was Bill Wyman who wandered farthest afield during this period. Ironically, he did very little playing, seeking to focus instead on various charitable projects. Although his AIMS project had to be shelved in June of 1988, he forged ahead with other charitable ventures. In February, Wyman

CBS released a limited edition box set to coincide with the European leg of the tour, now entitled The Urban Jungle Tour. Issued only as a promotional item, the striking box contained a CD and a cassette of *Steel Wheels*, a 12" single of 'Terrifying,' tour dates for Europe and, yes Stones fans, the by now statutory stickers.

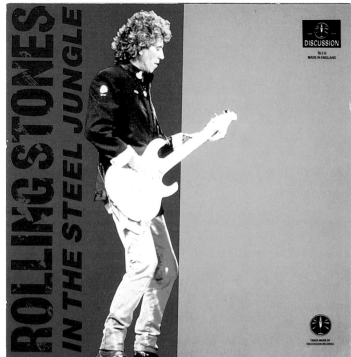

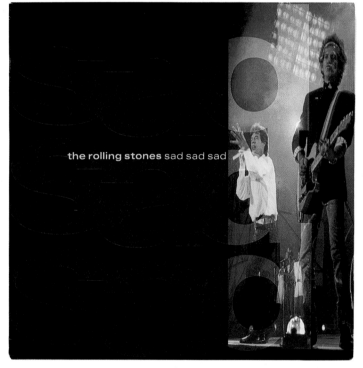

TOP On 22 March 1990 the Urban Jungle Tour was announced. A limited edition interview album was subsequently released in Britain only (front cover left, back cover right).

ABOVE The fifth and final single taken from *Steel Wheels* was 'Sad Sad Sad,' and was released as 7" and 12" singles, and as a CD in the Netherlands only.

rounded up big names Phil Collins, Kenny Jones, and Elvis Costello to pitch in for a show for the Great Ormond Street Hospital that benefited the Sick Children's Wishing Well Appeal – by all reports it was a resounding success.

However, as the year wound down, there were disturbing rumbles from the normally introspective bassist. During the very public feuding between Mick and Keith, Wyman stepped into the arena quick to condemn the Glimmer Twins: 'Mick is the guilty one,' he pointed out. 'He has decided to do his own thing and be famous in his own right. I don't know if we will ever go back on the road. That depends on Mick and Keith becoming friendly again. They're the problem.' Later, in the magazine *People*, Wyman more than hinted at his dissatisfaction with the music business overall: 'The last thing you need worry about is how well you play,' he remarked sarcastically. 'All you have to do

is act at being a pop star. The record companies have actually gone backwards in the last ten years. They used to promote original groups who became world famous. Now they churn out stuff which is indistinguishable from the dross you hear in American supermarkets.'

Rumours were swirling as the Stones gathered in Barbados in January 1989 to discuss a possible reunion album and tour. Richards, still basking in the recent success of his solo venture, had to be talked into the meeting by his manager Jane Rose. 'I told my wife I'd be back in either two weeks or twenty-four hours,' said Keith. 'Because I'll know in twenty-four hours whether this thing is going to work or if we were just going to start cattin' and doggin'.' Ron Wood, apparently, had his own doubts, admitting: 'I never lost any sleep over it because I know how these guys work. They operate on a whim, a feel.' ⇨

No one, in fact, seemed able to predict just what the Stones would actually do. The past instability of the group provided open season for speculation on several possible replacements and additions to the band. A string of Who's Who of rock's reigning stars were said to have an inside track on joining the Stones, from U2's Adam Clayton, Mark King of Level 42, to the ridiculous notion that funky rhythm & blues performer Terence Trent D'Arby would replace Jagger merely on the basis that he'd sung 'Honky Tonk Women' at Bill Wyman's hospital benefit nearly a year before.

The speculation took on a far more serious tone when Mick Taylor showed up with the band at the Waldorf, on 18 January, for the Stones induction into the Rock 'n' Roll Hall of Fame. Bill Wyman was conspicuously absent. The increasingly difficult bassman had five days earlier announced his decision to snub the ceremony, stating that the award was 'too little, too late.' Hall of Fame officials then tried to prevent the band from performing unless another bassist could be substituted, so Ron Wood quickly tapped his old mate Mick Taylor. The scuttlebutt in the music community foolishly had it that Taylor would permanently rejoin the band, with Woody sliding over to bass.

Rumours aside, one major uncertainty was put to rest when Mick Jagger took the podium to confirm that the Stones were indeed reuniting. 'We're not ready to hang up the number yet,' he grinned. That set the stage for an evening few in the audience would soon forget. As befits the stature of the band it could only be rock's elder statesman, Pete Townshend, who eloquently gave the group's induction speech: 'To me the Stones will always be the greatest. The Stones epitomize rock fame. Even though they're all now my friends, I'm still a fan. Guys, whatever you do,' he ended, 'don't grow old gracefully, it wouldn't suit you.'

Accepting the award on behalf of the group, Jagger paid a moving tribute to both Brian Jones and Ian Stewart before expressing his own feelings about the honour: 'It's slightly ironic that tonight you see us on our best behaviour, but we've been awarded [this] for twenty-five years of bad behaviour. Jean Cocteau once said, "Americans are funny people. First you shock them, then they put you in a museum." '

The encore that followed could only be described as electrifying. The jubilant musicians fairly rocked out of their tuxedos in a five-song jam that featured Tina Turner, Stevie Wonder, and Little Richard. To everyone present one thing was abundantly clear: the Rolling Stones were back in a big way.

BELOW The elaborate Steel Wheels press kit illustrates the professional way the Stones presented their pre-tour publicity.

In anticipation of their first tour in seven years, the Stones signed the most lucrative rock 'n' roll contract in history. Following weeks of intense, war-like bidding between Canadian promoter Michael Cohl of Concert Productions International (CPI) and established pop mogul Bill Graham, the Toronto-based whiz kid landed the deal, presenting a package that guaranteed the Stones a whopping $65 million. The forty-one year-old Cohl (who orchestrated recent mega-comeback tours by the Who and Pink Floyd) secured merchandising rights through his $400 million Brokum Group. With Cohl accompanying the band to each gig and personally overseeing every detail (including the sale of a $39.95 limited edition silver coin with embossed portraits of the emperor-like Stones) he himself was about to haul in profits of over $40 million.

These big business Stones, however, quickly drew sharp criticism. Upon learning that Labatts, Budweiser, and MTV had signed on as corporate sponsors, seasoned rock critic Dave Marsh spoke his mind: 'It cheapens and degrades the whole process by turning the artistic experience into a pimping experience. If Mick Jagger can't make a profit from a concert without Michael Cohl selling his ass to a beer company, he's incompetent.' Even Keith Richards winced when he contemplated what he termed 'the rag trade,' referring to $28 Stones tank tops and $450 leather jackets on the racks of J. C. Penney and Macy's. 'Of course we want to make some bread,' he acknowledged, 'but we don't want to come off as some kind of company.'

Putting the dollars and cents behind them, the band was anxious to get on with the business of making music. Hunkering down at the exclusive Eddy Grant Studio complex in Barbados, Mick and Keith composed an astounding forty songs in just five weeks, highlighted by a whirlwind two-week marathon that produced fifteen top-notch 'keepers' for the album. 'The songs just tumbled out,' said Keith. 'First we screamed and yelled at each other. We needed to clear the air. Then we sat down with our guitars and something entirely different took over. You can't define it; it's something that always happens. I just start banging out a little riff. He'll go, "That's nice," and he'll come up with a top line. I'll get to the bridge and suddenly everything seems to pop. Fifteen songs in two weeks. That's not bad for a couple of old geezers.'

The duo's new-found dedication to the project took Mick, Keith, and Ron to Tangier, Morocco, to record a track called 'Continental Drift' backed by the Master Musicians of Joujouka. More than anything, this was the band's long overdue tribute to Brian Jones, who some twenty years before had first recorded the pipe-playing prophets of the bawdy god Pan.

Thus it was with renewed energy that the Rolling Stones gathered at George Martin's Air Studios in Montserrat for the whole month of April 1989 to record their as yet untitled album. The sessions were filmed by television director Lorne Michael of 'Saturday Night Live' fame for a documentary ▷184

RIGHT T-shirt and sweatshirts issued by sponsors and Columbia Records.

ROLLING STONES STEEL WHEELS

THE NORTH AMERICAN TOUR 1989

ROLLING STONES STEEL WHEELS

THE NORTH AMERICAN TOUR 1989

A further selection of T-shirts, sweatshirts and jackets from the momentous Steel Wheels Tour.

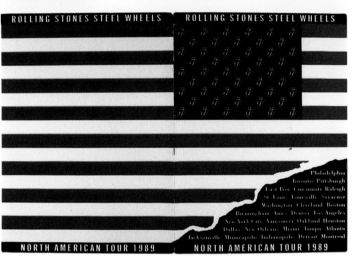

entitled *The Return of the Rolling Stones*, to be broadcast during the band's upcoming tour.

Even the often aloof Bill Wyman was exhibiting a noticeably improved frame of mind. The on-again off-again soap opera romance with Mandy Smith was now definitely a go. Taking a day off from recording to fly to Antigua, Wyman held a press conference to confirm he'd proposed to the nineteen year-old on Easter Sunday in a phone call from Barbados. 'I accepted immediately,' cooed the willowy blonded ingenue. 'It was really romantic. I'm delighted and so is he.'

While in Amsterdam for a group meeting, a drunken brawl erupted between the usually unruffled Charlie Watts and Mick Jagger. According to sources, Keith and Mick had gone out to a local pub and didn't get in until 5am. A thoroughly souped Jagger stomped into Charlie's room shouting, 'Is that my little drummer boy there? Why don't you get your arse down here!' Keith picks up the story: 'Mick was dead drunk – and Mick drunk is a sight to behold! Charlie was fast asleep and Mick shouted at him. Charlie shaved, put on a suit and tie and came down and grabbed him and went BOOM! Charlie dished him a walloping right hook. He landed in a plateful of smoked salmon and slid along the table towards the window. I caught his leg just in time to save him from flying out into the canal below.'

By mid-May, the band was hard at work mixing the new album at Olympic Studios in Barnes. Richards took a short break to receive the Living Legend statuette at the first ⇨ **187**

1989 STEEL WHEELS US TOUR

AUGUST	12	Toad's Place, New Haven, Connecticut
	31	Veteran's Stadium, Philadelphia, Pennsylvania
SEPTEMBER	1	Veteran's Stadium, Philadelphia, Pennsylvania
	3	Exhibition, Toronto, Canada
	4	Exhibition, Toronto, Canada
	6	Three Rivers Stadium, Pittsburgh, Pennsylvania
	8	Alpine Valley, East Troy, Wisconsin
	9	Alpine Valley, East Troy, Wisconsin
	11	Alpine Valley, East Troy, Wisconsin
	14	Riverfront Stadium, Cincinnati, Ohio
	16	Carter Finley Stadium, Raleigh, North Carolina
	17	Busch Stadium, St. Louis, Missouri
	19	Cardinal Stadium, Louisville, Kentucky
	21	Carrier Dome, Syracuse, New York
	22	Carrier Dome, Syracuse, New York
	24	RFK Stadium, Washington D.C
	25	RFK Stadium, Washington D.C
	27	Municipal Stadium, Cleveland, Ohio
	29	Sullivan, Boston, Massachusetts

OCTOBER	1	Sullivan, Boston, Massachusetts
	3	Sullivan, Boston, Massachusetts
	5	Legion Field, Birmingham, Alabama
	7	Cyclone Field, Ames, Iowa
	8	Arrowhead, Kansas City, Kansas
	10	Shea Stadium, New York City
	11	Shea Stadium, New York City
	18	Coliseum, Los Angeles, California
	21	Coliseum, Los Angeles, California
	22	Coliseum, Los Angeles, California
	25	Shea Stadium, New York City
	26	Shea Stadium, New York City
	28	Shea Stadium, New York City
	29	Shea Stadium, New York City

OPPOSITE TOP Tour programmes for Canada and the US.
LEFT AND BELOW A collection of Japanese stickers and publicity material; **RIGHT** A Japanese souvenir programme and a guest pass for the Tokyo Dome (below right).
BOTTOM Japanese tour programme with printed signatures.

NOVEMBER			DECEMBER		
	1	B.C. Place, Vancouver, Canada		3	Sky Dome, Toronto, Canada
	2	B.C. Place, Vancouver, Canada		4	Sky Dome, Toronto, Canada
	4	Alameda, Oakland, California		6	Hoosier Dome, Indianapolis, Indiana
	5	Alameda, Oakland, California		7	Hoosier Dome, Indianapolis, Indiana
	8	Astrodome, Houston, Texas		9	Silverdome, Detroit, Michigan
	10	Texas Stadium, Dallas, Texas		10	Silverdome, Detroit, Michigan
	11	Texas Stadium, Dallas, Texas		14	Olympic, Montreal, Canada
	13	Superdome, New Orleans, Louisiana		17	Convention Center, Atlantic City, New Jersey
	15	Orange Bowl, Miami, Florida		19	Convention Center, Atlantic City, New Jersey
	16	Orange Bowl, Miami, Florida		20	Convention Center, Atlantic City, New Jersey
	18	Tampa Stadium, Tampa, Florida			
	21	Grant Field, Atlanta, Georgia			
	25	Gator Bowl, Jacksonville, Florida			
	26	Death Valley Stadium, Clemson, Utah			
	29	Metro Dome, Minneapolis, Minnesota			
	30	Metro Dome, Minneapolis, Minnesota			

1990 STEEL WHEELS JAPAN TOUR

FEBRUARY		
	14	Korakuen Dome, Tokyo
	16	Korakuen Dome, Tokyo
	17	Korakuen Dome, Tokyo
	19	Korakuen Dome, Tokyo
	20	Korakuen Dome, Tokyo
	21	Korakuen Dome, Tokyo
	23	Korakuen Dome, Tokyo
	24	Korakuen Dome, Tokyo
	26	Korakuen Dome, Tokyo
	27	Korakuen Dome, Tokyo

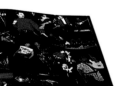

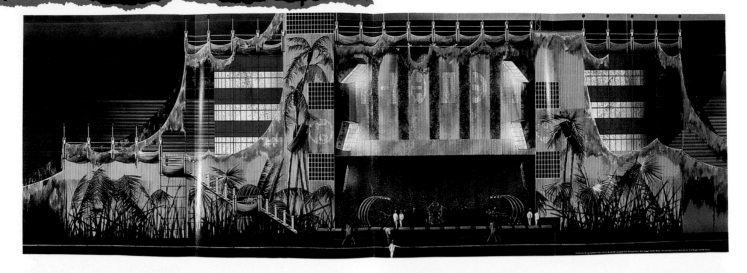

ROLLING STONES

URBAN JUNGLE

Tour Dates

JULY 4 · LONDON WEMBLEY STADIUM
JULY 6 · LONDON WEMBLEY STADIUM
JULY 7 · LONDON WEMBLEY STADIUM
JULY 9 · GLASGOW, HAMPDEN PARK
JULY 11 · CARDIFF ARMS PARK
JULY 13 · LONDON, WEMBLEY STADIUM
JULY 14 · LONDON WEMBLEY STADIUM
JULY 18 · NEWCASTLE

JULY 20 · MANCHESTER, MAINE RD.
JULY 21 · MANCHESTER, MAINE RD.
JULY 22 · EXCLUSIVE BROADCAST
ON SKY TELEVISION 8PM
JULY 28 · EXCLUSIVE BROADCAST
ON SKY TELEVISION 5PM

ROLLING STONES

URBAN JUNGLE

EUROPE 1990 + GUEST

DI. 31. JULI 1990 WIEN PRATERSTADION
EINLASS: 16.00 UHR / BEGINN: 18.30 UHR

DER VORVERKAUF HAT BEGONNEN!
SONDERZÜGE MIT DISCO- UND BUFFETWAGEN AUS GANZ ÖSTERREICH!
Eintrittskarten und Sonderzugtickets in jeder CA in ganz Österreich, telefonische Bestellung
TICKET EXPRESS 0222/505 23 24, Bestellkupons in der KRONEN ZEITUNG.

Sponsored by
TDK Produced by ROCK PRODUCTION with THE BCL GROUP
CLUB Ö3

annual International Rock Awards held at New York's Armory. Before a world-wide audience, Richards and his X-Pensive Winos performed 'You Keep A-Knockin' and 'Whip It Up,' including in the mélée an all-star line up of Eric Clapton, Dave Edmunds, Clarence Clemons, and Jeff Healey.

Having announced the date for their wedding as 5 June, Bill and Mandy snookered everyone by secretly marrying three days earlier in a civil ceremony at Bury St Edmonds, Suffolk. Curiously, the only guests in attendance were the couple's witnesses – Bill's son Stephen and Mandy's sister Nicole. Wyman didn't even tell his mother Kathleen until after the brief fifteen-minute ceremony. 'I'm very disappointed they didn't invite me,' confessed the seventy-six year-old Mrs Perks, adding, 'I suppose it's typical of Bill, though. He's always been a bit of a rebel.'

The newlyweds, however, weren't to be denied their golden day. On 5 June their marriage was blessed at the Anglican Church of St John the Evangelist in Hyde Park Crescent, London, before 170 relatives and close friends. Afterwards, Bill and Mandy held an all-star reception at the Grosvenor House Hotel, inviting 400 guests that included such luminaries as Elton John, Eric Clapton, Paul Young, Mike Rutherford, plus, of course, all the Stones, their wives, and kids. Jagger surprised everyone by bestowing a reported £200,000 genuine Picasso as a wedding gift for the happy couple.

On 11 July, before 500 reporters and scores of exhilarated fans, the Rolling Stones arrived by train at New York's Grand Central Station in an open flatcar to announce the Steel Wheels Tour, named after their forthcoming album. Naturally, the deadline-hungry journalists shouted out a barrage of gripping questions:

'Is this your final tour?'

'I've been asked this since 1966,' answered Jagger. 'I don't see this as a farewell concert. It's the Rolling Stones in 1989. It won't be our last tour.'

'Where are the girls?' shot a reporter.

'You've got the wrong group. We're all married,' cracked Bill in response to a question about his energy level. He retorted, 'Ask my wife.'

'Are you reuniting for the money?' barked another.

'No, that's the Who,' Ron Wood was quick to answer.

Following their grand entrance, the band scurried away separately to gather their families and drive two hours to the tonied hills of Washington, Connecticut, where they would spend the next eight weeks rehearsing for the tour. According to the locals, they landed like an army, booking an entire hotel for the staff alone, three houses for their families, and taking over a former girls' academy, the Wykem Rise School, for rehearsals. Security guards installed fitted steel gates at the secluded facility plus closed-circuit TV to keep curious intruders and fans at bay. ⇨ 190

OPPOSITE The extravagant design for the Urban Jungle stage (top). Tour poster and concert promo poster for the 31 July 1990 concert at Vienna (middle). The elaborate Urban Jungle press kit included a CD and 7" single of 'Rock And A Hard Place' (below).

ABOVE Promo poster for the European leg of the Budweiser-sponsored Urban Jungle Tour, and the official tour poster on sale at all European dates above.

Urban Jungle T-shirts and the tasteful (and extremely rare) inscribed baseball jacket produced to accompany the tour.

The glitzy entourage did not sit well with residents in the remote upper-crust town. They soon banded together to form a 'Roll the Stones Out of Town' action group to protest the invasion of their privacy and to complain that the band had indiscriminately bought up property to house their entourage. One resident said: 'It's like the marines have moved in and taken over. You're afraid to take a walk because Stones security goons will stop and question who you are and what you're doing.'

In preparation for the rugged workout he'd encounter performing back to back two-and-a-half hour shows, Jagger hired a personal trainer to whip him into shape. 'Of course, if you just stand there like Bill, you can't get tired,' he joked. Matt Clifford, the Stones' young pianist, recalled Jagger putting all the band through taxing vocal exercises as well as strictly looking after their diet. The Stones' taskmaster had Charlie Watts so wound up over the group's new health kick that when a visitor walked up to shake his hand he was momentarily startled. 'Sorry,' he mumbled nervously, 'I thought you were going to take my pulse.'

Following two solid months of rehearsals, plus the shooting of the videos 'Mixed Emotions' and 'Rock And A Hard Place,' the band played an impromptu concert at a small club in nearby New Haven, before leaving for New York. Things were really happening fast now. On 15 August, ABKCO Records released a four-album compilation, *The Rolling Stones Singles Collection: The London Years*, to cash in on the group's burgeoning popularity. The handsome set contained all the band's singles from 1963 to 1971, digitally re-mastered, complete with a glossy seventy-two page illustrated booklet.

Just two days later the first single off *Steel Wheels*, 'Mixed Emotions,' was released on Rolling Stones Records in Britain and the US simultaneously. In the best tradition of the band, the record catapulted immediately to number five on the American charts, a healthy indication that the Stones had not yet lost their touch.

It was obvious though that the band didn't need a hit record in order to bring back their fans. Tickets to the Steel Wheels Tour (going at $28.50 a crack) were selling at a phenomenal

1990 URBAN JUNGLE TOUR

MAY	18	Feyenoord Stadium, Rotterdam, Netherlands
	19	Feyenoord Stadium, Rotterdam, Netherlands
	21	Feyenoord Stadium, Rotterdam, Netherlands
	23	Niedersachsen, Hannover, West Germany
	24	Niedersachsen, Hannover, West Germany
	26	Wald Stadium, Frankfurt, West Germany
	27	Wald Stadium, Frankfurt, West Germany
	30	Mungersdorfer, Cologne, West Germany
	31	Mungersdorfer, Cologne, West Germany
JUNE	2	Olympic Stadium, Munich, West Germany
	3	Olympic Stadium, Munich, West Germany
	6	Olympic Stadium, Berlin, West Germany
	10	Alvalade, Lisbon, Portugal
	13	Olympic Stadium, Barcelona, Spain
	14	Olympic Stadium, Barcelona, Spain
	16	Calderon, Madrid, Spain
	17	Calderon, Madrid, Spain
	20	Velodrom, Marseille, France
	22	Parc des Princes, Paris, France
	23	Parc des Princes, Paris, France
	25	Parc des Princes, Paris, France
	27	St Jacob, Basel, Switzerland

JULY	4	Wembley Stadium, London
	6	Wembley Stadium, London
	7	Wembley Stadium, London
	9	Hampden Park, Glasgow, UK
	16	Arms Park, Cardiff, UK
	18	St. James Park, Newcastle, UK
	20	Maine Road, Manchester, UK
	21	Maine Road, Manchester, UK
	25	Flamenio, Rome, Italy
	26	Flamenio, Rome, Italy
	28	Delle Alpi, Turin, Italy
	31	Prater, Vienna, Austria
AUGUST	3	Eriksberg, Gothenberg, West Germany
	4	Eriksberg, Gothenburg, West Germany
	6	Valle Hovin, Oslo, Norway
	7	Valle Hovin, Oslo, Norway
	9	Idretspark, Copenhagen, Denmark
	13	Weisensee, Berlin, West Germany
	14	Weisensee, Berlin, West Germany
	16	Parstadion, Galsenkirchen, West Germany
	18	Straiiov Stadium, Prague, Czechoslovakia
	24	Wembley Stadium, London
	25	Wembley Stadium, London

rate. Four dates at New York's Shea Stadium (300,000 tickets in all) sold out in a record six hours. The same scenario was reported in several other cities across the country.

Excitement was mounting as the band arrived in Philadelphia in late August for the kick-off concert at Veteran Stadium on the 31st. Almost right up until showtime, Jagger was busy overseeing the lighting team, re-working the choreography, and even charting the song order. 'It got to the point,' he explained, 'where I plotted all the tempos on a graph. I'm afraid the quiet sequence ('Ruby Tuesday,' 'Play With Fire,' and 'Dead Flowers') is going to bore this east coast crowd.'

Despite last-minute fretting over sound systems, set designs and the nearly impossible task of keeping rehearsal venues top secret, the boys were in surprisingly good form for the shows. Mick and Keith each sat down together for extended interviews, indicating that the past was now soundly behind them. 'It was really easy working with the guy again,' Jagger told reporters. 'Though Keith is more sensitive than me, we didn't have any major rows.' Of his three-year sabbatical from the group Mick admitted: 'I was feeling very stilted with the Stones. I felt I had to go and work with other people to get revitalized and I think it actually worked. It created a tremendous ruckus in the Stones, totally unnecessary really. Everyone made far too much fuss about it. I think they all should have been a bit more indulgent.'

Richards spoke along the same lines: 'Hell, we needed a break. Mick needed to find his feet out there and see what it's like, if he thought he could live without us, and I had to find out and do it too. I learned a lot of things by being the don, the top man. I learned more self discipline and a sense of responsibility. We both grew up.'

Just two days before their first concert came the eagerly-awaited release of *Steel Wheels*, the band's thirty-fourth album. Produced by Mick and Keith under the now familiar ⇨

A selection of tickets from the Urban Jungle Tour.

OPPOSITE ABOVE The official Urban Jungle Tour programme (1990) and inserts for Budweiser and TDK.

OPPOSITE BELOW A large printed canvas bill-board produced for stadium display.

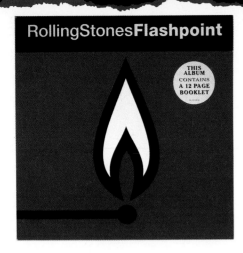

In April 1991 the Stones' fifth live album, *Flashpoint*, was released (left, front and back cover shown). Possibly their best ever, it also contained studio tracks 'Highwire' and 'Sexdrive.' 'Highwire' (opposite page, top left, 12" shown) was the first single taken off the album and immediately raised some eyebrows. It was thought the song was anti-Gulf War and so was subsequently banned by the BBC. Indeed, when it was shown on British television's 'Top of the Pops' the first verse was cut entirely. Mick and Keith later stated that it was not all about war, but rather about how war gets going. **BELOW** The large *Flashpoint* display boxes distributed to record stores.

pseudonym of the Glimmer Twins (along with Chris Kimsey) many feel that this album conveys the original drive, soul and sense of fun that energized the band in its glory days in the sixties. From Keith's buttermilk guitar work on 'Almost Hear You Sigh' to Mick's infectious harmonica chugging over Ron Wood's steel guitar in the country-blues 'Break The Spell,' even hard-core Stones fans had to admit that, just maybe, the band's self-imposed sabbatical may have been a blessing in disguise.

Before a capacity crowd of 55,000, almost evenly split between old and new fans, the Rolling Stones opened their current tour in the dark, as a cacophonous blend of percussive sounds revved up into a roar worthy of a 747. A wall of flames ignited across the foot of the stage. Suddenly, with a boom, the lights flashed on and the Stones cranked into gear as Keith Richards rumbled boldly into 'Start Me Up.'

Mick Jagger, resplendent in a white bow tie and green leather tails, strutted about the almost three-hundred-foot stage whose design, mammoth steaming airducts, steel girders and bright orange catwalks, looked like something out of the movie *Alien*. For two-and-a-half hours the band rolled through a crowd-pleasing mix of their greatest hits, interwoven with cuts from the new album. The undisputed highlight came when two fifty-five-foot inflatable dolls in provocative attire hovered over the stage as Jagger pranced and howled out 'Honky Tonk Women.'

While the scene inside the stadium was festive, outside an ugly incident arose when drunken fans, angry over the ticket shortage, (an estimated two million vied for some 110,000 seats), clashed with police, resulting in twenty-eight arrests and fifty-two injuries. It was a grand night, though, for the ever-present scalpers, who picked desperate fans clean to the tune of $2,000 per precious ticket. But the most bizarre and potentially frightening occurrence unfurled when the Hell's Angels issued a death threat against Mick Jagger, a twenty-year vendetta stemming from the ugly events of the ill-fated Altamont Festival. Police kept a twenty-four hour watch on the marked superstar; fortunately nothing unpleasant came to pass.

On a more positive note, the reviews for opening night were almost universally spectacular. Rock critic Tom Moon of the *Philadelphia Inquirer* wrote: 'Five middle-aged English dudes led 64,000 Yanks through a fantastic two-and-a-half hour party sing-song. The fireworks were superfluous. This concert was hotter than any Roman candle.'

USA Today's Edna Gundersen added: 'In a year swarming with sixties legends from the Who to Boy Dylan to Paul McCartney, the Stones threaten to storm the nineties unchallenged as the world's greatest rock 'n' roll band, a mantle bestowed on them in 1969 and disputed by almost no one.'

As the Stones barnstormed throughout North America,

conquering every major stadium in Canada and the States and raking in millions, it appeared they could do no wrong. The unending media blitz made sure it had every last angle covered, from the bi-plane towing a Rolling Stones/Steel Wheels banner circling over every city on the tour, to the deluxe press kit featuring a twenty-eight page chronology of virtually every important date in Stones history. For those who couldn't get seats, Lorne Michael's documentary *It's Only Rock 'n' Roll* was being networked all across the country. On radio, a three-hour special, 'The Rolling Stones Story,' was broadcast on the same date that *Steel Wheels* sped to number one on the charts.

Despite all the glitz, however, something far more profound was happening up on stage. On the surface they looked and sounded very like the same old Stones, grinding through steamy classics like 'Paint It Black,' 'Brown Sugar,' 'Sympathy For The Devil' – Mick even broke a long time vow never to perform 'Satisfaction' again. There was the patented Jagger sneer, the erotic androgynous prancing, he and Keith playing off each other, ever the perfect foils. But these were clearly not the Rolling Stones of the sixties or seventies. Keith, whose only turn at lead vocal in the past had been on 'Happy,' was singing several songs on this tour in a voice still ragged as a cheese grater, but with a renewed confidence gleaned from his successful solo experience. Mick, traditionally only a vocalist on

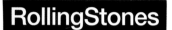

'Sexdrive' (not released in Britain) was the second single culled from *Flashpoint*. The naughty video for the suggestive single, (directed by Julian Temple), was almost immediately banned by MTV and had to be re-shot. Instead of 'Sexdrive,' the Stones released 'Ruby Tuesday' in the UK. The last single the Stones were to release on CBS was to be 'Jumpin' Jack Flash,' which was issued only in The Netherlands.

stage, played a wide assortment of instruments, including guitar. This new give and take was never more evident than on 'Blinded By Love,' where the two wandered through harmonies purposefully and effectively off-key, resulting in a weirdly contorted beauty.

For the band as a whole there seemed a stunning new awareness, maturity, and overall togetherness exemplified to moving heights in their final number 'Slipping Away,' a soulful ballad about dying far more potent than 'As Tears Go By' or even 'Moonlight.' This was the band's profound 'everyman' sound, a shadowy celebration of life's journey, its tough ⇨

A mouthwatering selection of *Flashpoint* promotional and official releases, the most sought-after being a 5" five-track promo CD titled *Too Great To Make You Wait*. 5" and 3" CDs and cassette singles were now becoming commonplace, and *Flashpoint* was no exception.

choices, bitter struggles, and unholy compromises. The song was also meant as a tribute to Brian Jones and, more pointedly, Ian Stewart. 'It has taken us all this long to reconcile being able to put the Stones together without him,' said Keith. 'Nobody knows much about Stu out there, but to the boys in the band the Stones were his group. In a way we're all still working for Stu.' 'None of us really believe he's gone,' echoed Ronnie. 'I'm sure even during this Steel Wheels Tour every night we all think of him and in a way dedicate the show to him. We think he's up there criticizing us.'

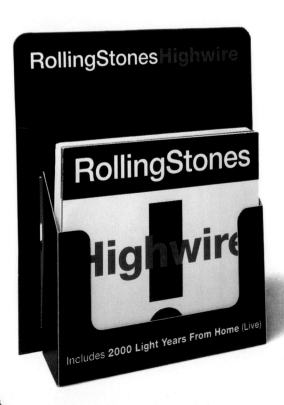

This was a far different tour in another way as well. Replacing the standard backstage fare of smoke, drink, and all manner of illicit pharmaceuticals of past tours was a simple post-concert spread of mineral water and salad, with beverages no more potent than coffee. Pianist Matt Clifford revealed that after-show activities among these older, wiser Stones was in fact downright boring. Apart from Keith and Ron, who'd generally gather the band's horn players and host night-long drinking sessions, the Stones were a tame bunch these days. 'Mick would go to his room and then sometimes he and I would go out to dinner or watch a movie,' related Clifford. 'Bill used to work on his autobiography 'till three or four in the morning. And Charlie would disappear into his room and sketch his bed or something. He has this book where he's made a drawing of virtually every bed in every hotel room.'

This wasn't to say that the Stones weren't up to a little night-life, however. During their stay in Los Angeles, the guys partied it up with old mates Eric Clapton and Bruce Springsteen, who stopped by for a friendly game of snooker. The guest list for the after-concert bash, held at trendy Mortons, boasted Hollywood celebs Barbra Streisand, Meryl Streep, and Michael Douglas. In a rather humorous case of mistaken identity Guns 'N' Roses (the Stones opening act) was barred from the restaurant as ruffians trying to crash the exclusive eatery.

The Rolling Stones, however, saved their best for last. Their 19 December show (the second of three at Atlantic City's Convention Center) was a cable TV pay-per-view special. After the first nine songs Jagger took the mike and announced: 'They've come all the way east to get their tattoos touched up!' Out pranced Axl Rose and Izzy Stradlin' of Guns 'N' Roses to join in on 'Salt Of The Earth' from the Stones' classic, *Beggars Banquet*. It marked the first time the band had ever performed the song live. Invited guests also included Eric Clapton and blues master John Lee Hooker for the gritty 'Boogie Chillun.' The sizzling performances resulted in the most successful pay-per-view show to date.

The next night it was all over, leaving the Stones to count their haul – a tidy $140 million for playing sixty-one shows before 3.2 million fans in thirty-three cities. Not half bad for five gritty geezers from London's sprawling suburbs.

Following a much-needed two-month holiday, the Rolling Stones were back on the road for their 10 February show at the 50,000-seat Tokyo Korakuen Dome. Earlier that month, in the same venue, Buster Douglas had unseated Mike Tyson for the heavyweight crown, and now the Stones were out to show off a little musical muscle of their own.

Banned from Japan for years due to prior drug arrests, the Stones were greeted with a rampaging mania not seen since the Beatles first conquered America. Japanese concert-goers gleefully paid $70 a ticket and stood cheering wildly throughout the concert before quietly filing out of their seats at the show's end, section by section.

Unfortunately, the group's stay was marred by tragedy as Keith's mother-in-law suffered a heart attack and was forced to remain in a Tokyo hospital even after the tour's conclusion. Later, Bill Wyman had to tend to his gravely ill father back in London, who finally passed away just days after the tour ended.

Their fourteen-day stint at the Korakuen Dome earned the band a cool $30 million. They could have easily sold another two week's worth of tickets, but were forced to move on as their old mate Mr McCartney was coming to town with his own travelling roadshow.

The band took two months to re-group before launching their European tour. Opening in late May in Rotterdam and finishing up in Prague that August, the most memorable ⇨

The Rolling Stones as they were in this 1990 promotional photograph (above). To promote *Flashpoint* a wonderful selection of goodies was created, including *Flashpoint* matches, *Flashpoint* sparklers, a *Flashpoint* Zippo lighter, and a great *Flashpoint* metal badge.

The CD itself was issued in two editions, one American and the other English. The US release came in a leather wallet with a second CD of rarities entitled *Collectibles*. The British CD contained music and interviews recorded during the Urban Jungle Tour.

performance was their 6 July homecoming at Wembley Stadium before a capacity crowd of 72,000. For this special occasion the show underwent a complete facelift. The Stones dubbed the British leg the Urban Jungle Tour, complete with a stage of scaffolding decorated with graffiti and four fierce-looking inflatable hound dogs surplanting the sexy dollybirds.

This rumble in the jungle, however, was interrupted when Richards severed a finger in his right hand with a broken guitar string. The cut soon became badly infected, thus forcing the Stones to reschedule their final two dates.

It was an exhausted but thoroughly satisfied (and decidedly richer) bunch that finally came off the road in the autumn of 1990. While gearing down from their gruelling gypsy ⇨198

A timely three-CD box set, *The Rolling Stones Singles Collection: The London Years* was released by London and included a seventy-four-page booklet containing the lyrics to the evergreen tunes (left). Also shown is the impressive gold disc issued by ABCKO to commemorate sales of more than 500,000 of the album, cassette, and CD of *The Rolling Stones Singles Collection: The London Years.*

To coincide with the European tour, London Records reissued two compilation albums: *Hot Rocks* and *More Hot Rocks*. The ever-favourite 'Paint It Black' was also released as the single.

In The Netherlands, London put out 'She's A Rainbow' backed by '2000 Light Years From Home.'

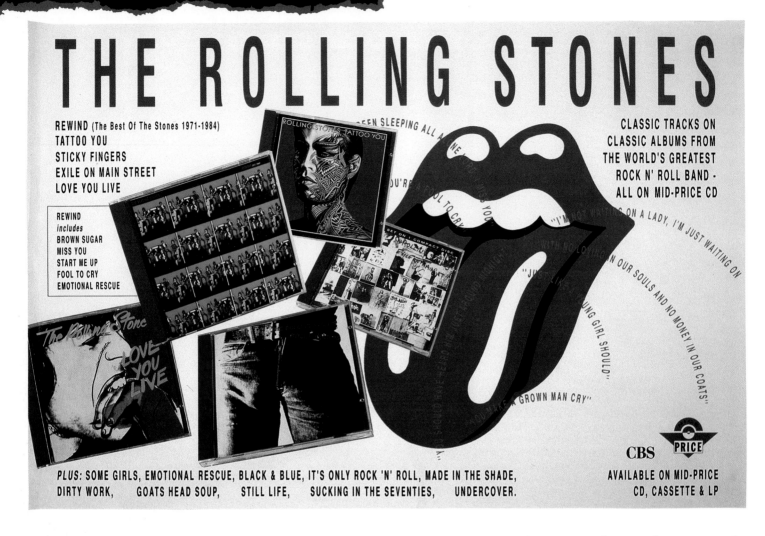

lifestyle, Jagger shocked the entertainment world by marrying Jerry Hall, his live-in love for the past thirteen years. With their fiery courtship played out in public, it seemed Jerry would never drag her man to the altar. 'It's that darn "M" word,' Hall had often sighed in frustration to reporters. And asked just when the long-time couple would finally marry she'd often tease: 'Golly, I'm workin' on it fellas. Would y'all quit rubbin' it in?'

The breakthrough apparently occurred in January, when she and Mick agreed they would finally tie the knot before the year was out. Immediately following the tour the couple jetted off to the Far East and opted for a wedding on the exotic island of Bali. On 21 November 1990, in a ceremony attended by only the couple's children and Stones tour director Alan Dunn, Mick and Jerry exchanged vows before a Balinese Hindu priest. According to the ancient religious rite, Mick even reportedly whacked his bride over the head with a banana.

While one marriage was off and away, another in the Stones family came to an unhappy end. The day after Mick and Jerry's wedding, Bill Wyman announced that his seventeen-month union to Mandy Smith was over. Things had gotten off on the wrong foot when Mandy's mother, Patsy, accompanied the newlyweds on their honeymoon to Venice. Another complication occurred when Mrs Smith began dating Wyman's twenty-three year-old son Stephen. But when Mandy came

The CDs were now flying fast and furious. Not to be outdone, CBS issued all their Stones' albums on CD in a limited edition box set in 1990. This comprised fourteen compact discs covering the Stones' musical history from 1971 through to 1989. Additionally, a bonus CD of rare and previously unavailable tracks was included for good measure.

down with a baffling life-threatening yeast allergy causing chronic fatigue and frightening weight loss, making her unable to join her husband on the road, Wyman finally lost all patience. After spending only five days together in a year-and-a-half, they decided to part. 'A tragic inevitability,' one insider commented.

In the new year, it was back to work for the band as they entered the studio to lay down two new tracks for their upcoming live album from the Steel Wheels Tour. On the eve of the Gulf War, the guys cut their first studio recording in two years, 'Highwire,' a biting commentary on the struggle for political power and oil that, commentators claim, had led to the current conflict:

We sell 'em missiles, we sell 'em tanks
We give 'em credit and you can call up the bank.
It's just a business, you can pay us in crude
You'll love these toys, just go and play out your feuds.

Mick wrote the lyrics at the end of December 1990 over a melody that dated back several years. 'There is a lot of division of opinion between people who think war solves everything and people on the other side who say it never solves anything. In the middle is almost everyone else,' said Jagger. 'I don't want to sound like some cheap history lesson. We built up the armaments up to a point where, thirty years ago, it might have been a very low-key affair. These days it's not low-key and the scenario of a mad dictator in the Middle East has been talked about for as long as I can remember. Someday, one of these guys is going to let loose out there with all this weaponry.'

The single was released 22 February, and instantly became a hot potato when a Conservative member of Parliament rebuked the song as being 'appalling in time of war,' and pressured the BBC to discourage DJs from playing the record. Unfortunately, *Flashpoint*, the fifteen-song live album (plus two new studio tracks) from the Steel Wheels Tour, fell far short of expectations, and did not sell well. Alan Nash of *Stereo Review* dismissed it as: 'so sloppy, uninspired and mediocre that it sounds like the work of a group that passed on while no one was looking.'

Bill Wyman's long suffering autobiography, prophetically titled *Stone Alone*, was published in the autumn. Written with the help of august rock biographer Ray Coleman, the meticulously detailed account drawn from Wyman's trunkfuls of clippings, notes, and mementoes focused on the band's frenzied warp-speed early years. Among other revelations, Wyman divulged he had bedded some 278 women in two years, one of whom in 1966 delivered a baby daughter in Australia, a child he's never known.

It was ironic that, on the heels of the book's release, Wyman counted himself out of the band's $45 million three-album deal with Virgin Records, making the Rolling Stones the highest paid band ever in rock history. 'It's a terrible thing,' Jagger commented on Wyman's desertion. 'I think Bill's kind of had enough of it all, really. He's got enough money and I suppose he feels he's done it all.' Keith Richards, on the other hand, was

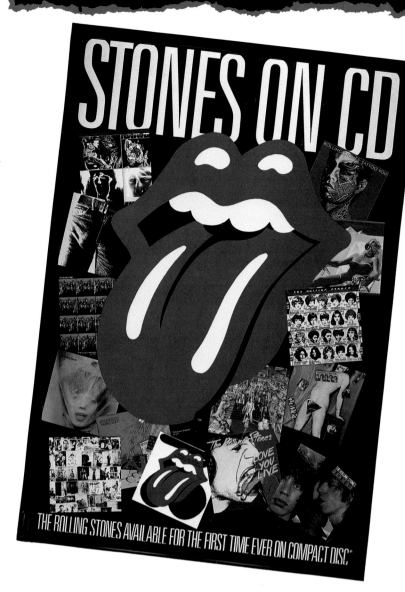

Promotional poster for ABKCO Stones CDs, released in 1986.

hoping the bassist might still have a change of heart. 'I'm assuming he will rejoin the band. I have no desire to change anything within the Stones, but if push comes to shove we'll carry on and make other arrangements.'

What began as an early sixties band of ruffians had turned into a multi-national conglomerate brilliantly managed by Lichtenstein Prince turned adviser, Rupert Lowenstein. In recent economic times when most musical acts have found it difficult even breaking even, the Rolling Stones grossed $90 million in 1989 alone. Even in an off year, the band's valuable catalogue still sells one million copies annually. At a royalty of $1.75 per copy, the Stones stand to haul in $2,000,000 without even playing a single note. Every time a Stones song is played, it's another five cents per airplay, not to mention the substantial income from the band's vast publishing empire.

'I told Mick even if we both said, "I never want to see you again," we'd still have to deal with each other for the rest of our lives,' joked Keith. 'There are too many businesses that demand our attention, too many people who depend on the salaries we pay them. It's like a marriage with no divorce.'

No longer the élite club of young men united under the renegade banner of musical mayhem, the Stones have ⊃ 201

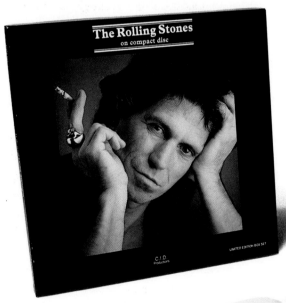

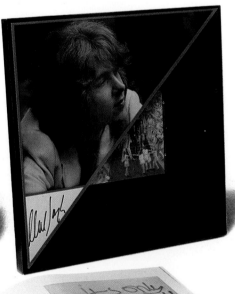

TOP CBS issued two box sets, each containing three CDs of old Stones' albums. France released a 'greatest hits' picture disc CD (above), while Japan was at last beginning to issue some very interesting compilation CDs. Also shown is a special German issue of *Sticky Fingers,* plus a picture disc interview CD of the Stones from the early sixties (CD with orange cover).

LEFT By now everyone knows there is big money to be made in limited editions. *It's Only Rock 'n Roll* (left) was repackaged in a box which included a booklet written and autographed by Carr. The talented Mick Taylor signed both. As with all inscribed memorabilia, these signatures have naturally added to their value. Also shown (far left) is a CD box set of a Keith Richards interview .

finally grown up. When the band gets out of the studio and off the road, it is five very different people who now scatter to families and lives distinctly apart from one another.

These days Ron Wood is settled down with his wife Jo and their children Leah, Tyrone, and Jesse James. Wood was one of two Stones to move back to England in 1986, following Margaret Thatcher's more relaxed tax format. Ronnie, once the carousing madman trashing hotels with Rod Stewart, scoots about Wimbledon in a Volvo these days, and works on solo material in his home studio.

Wood is also an accomplished artist, specializing in portraits of legendary musicians, including his own celebrated mates. Over the years he's had several showings in such hallmark spaces as London's Hamilton Gallery and Christie's Contemporary Art Gallery. He also published a book of his paintings called *The Works* in 1988, for which he received critical acclaim. For two years he owned a successful entertainment complex in Miami, Florida, called Woody's On The Beach, that incorporated a restaurant, art gallery and nightclub. Unfortunately, it closed down in 1989 due to neighbours' unending complaints about the noise.

The unflappable Charlie Watts has also returned from tax exile to the lush countryside of Devon. Watts has never been particularly comfortable with his rock star status – 'There's nothing forced about Charlie, least of all his modesty,' said Keith. 'He's the most ▷ 203

TOP LEFT *Sticky Fingers* was issued in a special limited edition jean bag which contained an insert signed by Mick Taylor; **TOP RIGHT** A super rare collector's item is the CD issued to commemorate the Stones' induction into the Rock 'n' Roll Hall of Fame in 1988; **LEFT** Photographs by Gered Mankowitz were used for the box set of *Between The Buttons*. A certificate signed by Mankowitz was issued with each set.

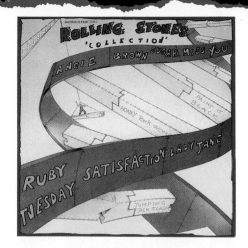

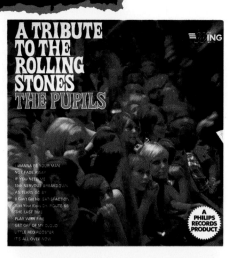

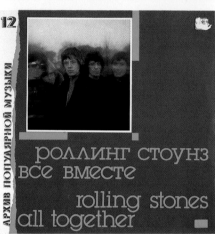

TOP Three long-forgotten albums of Stones-penned material as performed by other artists.
ABOVE By the late 1980s the Soviet Union and other Communist countries were allowing western music to be made readily available to those who sought it. Three examples are shown here, plus the Stones' first CD Soviet-issued CD released in 1992 (opposite left).
BELOW Two colourful bootleg 7"single box sets containing all the fans' favourites.

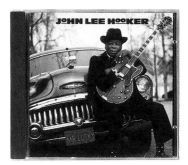

ABOVE Eight CDs containing one or more of the Stones as guest artists. *Stoned Alchemy* and *Rolling Stone Classics* contain numbers later covered by the Stones but here performed by the original artists. The essential *Jagger/ Richard Songbook* features compositions as performed by other artists.

RIGHT AND BELOW Various Stones and Stones-related rarities, including a transparent French flexi-single containing a Mick Jagger interview from the mid-eighties.

BOTTOM The late eighties also saw the release of two German 7″ single box sets covering the Stones' early material.

honest person I know and [he] cannot understand what people see in his drumming.'

Shirley, to whom Charlie's been happily married for twenty-five years, confesses that off the road, with time on his hands, Charlie can turn into something of an eccentric. On one such occasion she recalls Watts coming downstairs in his manor home dressed in white flannels saying he was 'going to watch the cricket.' 'But that's tomorrow,' Shirley reminded him. 'I know,' he replied, 'I'm just practising.'

Among the Rolling Stones, Bill Wyman has been perhaps the hardest to categorize, historically the quietest, yet oddly the one with a sustained reputation as a ladies' man (self-confessed 2,000 conquests in his lifetime), and the Stone who has certainly caused the most consistent controversy over the past five years. Seemingly unobsessed with his music, Wyman has remained commited to charity work. He became deeply involved in the 1988 Kampuchea Appeal and has worked tirelessly for the Starlight Foundation, founded by actress Emma Samms, which grants wishes to terminally ill children. His all-star Bill ⇨ 208

ABOVE The twenty-CD set entitled *The Complete History of the Rolling Stones* was made by Media America Inc for radio Covering the period 1964 to 1989, Jagger has stated that this series is without doubt the most detailed account of the band produced to date.

Keith's legal problems in Canada are cleared up when a judge places him on probation for one year and orders him to do a benefit concert on behalf of the Canadian National Institute for the Blind. Around this time Peter Tosh's <u>Bush Doctor</u> album is released. Mick is the executive producer and shares vocals on the single <u>Don't Look Back.</u>

arly '79 while Mick is vacationing in Martinique, Keith and ood along with Bobby Keys, Ian McLaglen, Stanley Clarke ggy Modeliste form "The New Barbarians" and prepare for a The New Barbarians and the Stones do the benefit concert to fulfill Keith's legal obligations. In June on i released. This the featured album

ABOVE Other radio shows worth tracking down are the *King Biscuit Flower Hour* (top row), the box set titled *The Rolling Stones Up Close* (third row), a four-CD package with music and interviews on the album *Flashpoint*, as well as ABC Radio Networks' four-CD *25th Anniversary Radio Special*. This box set was issued to radio stations across America. As they were never commercially marketed, all such shows are today highly prized by collectors. Bootleggers, as always, are close at the heels of such bona fide recordings (selection shown, bottom three rows).

A selection of bootleg albums from the Steel Wheels/Urban Jungle Tour period. Bootleg box sets are today possibly more sophisticated than even the official releases. *Atlantic City '89*, for instance, featured a great sound, great packaging, and of course great memories.

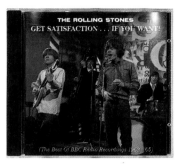

A Last Bow or *The Final Bow* (left) may perhaps be the most elaborate bootleg ever. Issued in a wooden box containing two CDs, the package also included a miniature bottle of Jack Daniels and a booklet of photographs, all of which were mounted on a genuine leather base. **BELOW** Four bootleg picture disc CDs, and at the top of the page are a selection of bootleg compact discs.

ABOVE A terrific live boot is *Hampton '81*.
BELOW Videos, like CDs, have become an important part of the rock 'n' roll industry. '25 x 5', the definitive history of the Rolling Stones on video, should not be passed by.

'The Rolling Stones Story' is less satisfying, containing primarily early, familiar footage. 'Best' is a promotional video comprising fourteen clips of Stones classics shot in atmospheric black-and-white.

Wyman XI Charity Cricket Matches attract such lauded participants as Eric Clapton, David Essex, and Mike Rutherford, and have earned upwards of £25,000 per event for the foundation. Wyman has also dabbled in various business enterprises, such as the Atlanta nightclub, La Brasserie (along with Ringo Starr), and his very own upmarket hamburger joint in London, appropriately called Sticky Fingers.

Perhaps the greatest puzzle in Stonedom, though, is the flamboyant Mick Jagger. Doing the 'old married man' routine, something he once vehemently condemned ('Marriage is a terrible drag'), has now evolved into the great pleasure of his life. Insiders say that what Jerry Hall gives Mick is something the restless high-flying Bianca lacked – nesting instincts. 'I went to see her once when she was modelling and working very hard,' remembers a friend, 'and she and Mick were about to go spend a weekend in France. On the bed she had perfectly folded all his shirts, pants, underwear, and even socks. Jerry was a wild girl, but she's also a natural homemaker.'

The often crusty Jagger has also taken a direct hand in raising his children. Daily he drops off his daughter at school in Roehampton before tutoring his son on the finer points of ping-pong. Mick has found himself having to keep a tight rein on twenty year-old Jade, however, a dark petite replica of her mother Bianca. At sixteen there was the much publicized dismissal from the posh public school, St Mary's, for running off to meet her boyfriend, John Aster, the illegitimate son of

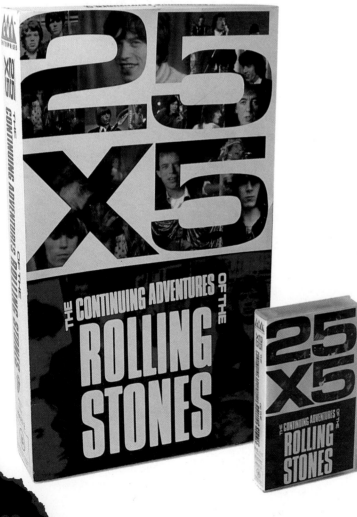

disgraced Gannex peer Lord Kagan. Jade was also called on to testify in court as a witness in a cocaine case for which young Aster served three months for drug possession. Later, Daddy had to stop her from accepting the film role of a young prostitute. 'He always has time for all his children,' says a member of the venerated Guinness family. 'He's fair, warm, and giving, though he's not spoiling and quite good at reading the riot act.'

Outside the studio and away from the bad-boy stage image, Jagger now moves in the highest levels of the British aristocracy, hobnobbing regularly with Prince Charles and Lord Jacob Rothschild, chairman of the National Gallery. He's used his influence to organize a National Music Day and to better children's education.

'He's very conservative now,' reveals West End art dealer Christopher Gibbs. 'He talks about architecture, literature, and his children's schools all the time,' quite a far cry from the motley teenage hellraiser who was once photographed in the sixties urinating against a gasoline pump shouting with a defiant snarl, 'We piss anywhere, man!' Jagger's near obsession with real estate has found him collecting a £500,000 home in Mustique, a Georgian manor in the London suburb of Richmond, a $2,000,000 Manhattan brownstone, plus a seventh-century château in the Loire valley complete with formal gardens.

These days, Jagger is seriously pursuing an acting career, having recently played a futuristic bounty hunter in the January 1992 release *Freejack* with Emilio Estevez. His first film in more than twenty years, Mick is now looking to do one movie a year, as well as write and produce films. Freejack director Geoff Murphy believes Jagger has what it takes: 'The camera loves him,' he says. 'If you had him in the back row, seventh spear-carrier from your left, your eyes would still go to him the moment he appeared. He's that strong.'

If Jagger stands out as the most chameleon-like member of the band, then it's Keith Richards who, twenty-five years

To accompany the tour film *At the Max* (which contains fifteen Stones classics) the band issued a press kit, the usual array of clothing, and a badge, among other items.

At the Max was shot utilizing the special IMAX process, viewable in only a handful of theatres. It requires a 100-foot curved screen which fills the viewer's peripheral vision.

THE ROLLING STONES—STEEL WHEELS TOUR.
PHOTO CREDIT: Paul Natkin

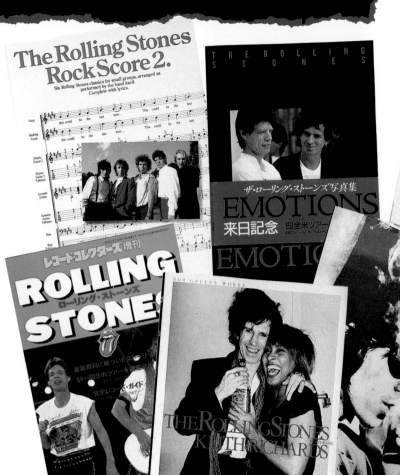

A plethora of books and magazines have appeared since 1986 describing in fine detail the turbulent life and times of the Rolling Stones. Although the Stones did not play Japan until 1990, they nevertheless garnered a huge following there. The magazine *Stone People* kept the fans informed of the band's every move since the early seventies.

later, still embodies the streetwise, scrapping maverick that is the hallmark of the Rolling Stones. This is perhaps most evident in his band, the X-Pensive Winos. For Richards, who virtually lives on live performance, this is his element: roughcut, on the edge, always just the slightest element of danger. 'I play rock 'n' roll, that's what I do,' he has said often. 'Just point me in the direction of the nearest rock band. The Winos allow me to do things the Stones can no longer do. They keep me in touch with the basics of playing to people without too much fuss and bother and just enjoying yourself.'

Richards has recently laid down roots in Westport, Connecticut, with his wife, Patti Hansen, and their two daughters, Theodora, six, and four year-old Alexandra. Twenty-one year-old Marlon and nineteen year-old Angela from his relationship with Anita Pallenberg currently reside in England with their mother. 'With Patti, this is the big one,' he sighs. 'We have a good thing going. It just seems to work.' For a man who wears a skull ring and whose look, reputation, and life experience are more befitting of a sea-roving pirate than loving family man, Keith insists it's a misguided to buy into this image: 'I have two little girls who beat me up. I mean, sometimes I

wake up in the middle of the night and there's both my kids in the bed. Family is a special thing. This is a very rootless life if you're on your own. The only thing you've got to hold on to is family. Believe it or not, this is the way I've always dreamed married life should be. Because I'm away a lot, I never mind coming back to an active nest.'

For this well-heeled band of five primordial rockers, the Rolling Stones represent something quite different now – they are a piece of the whole, certainly not the entire pie. Bound by their new deal to deliver their first album in 1993, the Stones will soon skyrocket headlong into their fourth decade, still making rock history.

Already that promise is being fulfilled with the Stones' participation with IMAX, the deluxe giant screen film format. *The Rolling Stones at the Max*, their concert movie of the Steel Wheels Tour, is the first full-length feature utilizing this revolutionary new system. As ever, audiences are flocking to see these sky-high Stones rocking out of a sixty-storey screen. After more than a quarter of a century, the world's greatest rock 'n' roll band, it seems, is still a phenomenal attraction.

And poor Charlie Watts just can't figure it out. 'People just love to come out and see the Stones,' he says, baffled. 'I really don't know why, and I'm sure I never will.'

Throughout the sixties, the individual Stones made no secret of their desire to work outside the often rigid structure of the group. Mick and Keith, of course, already had an outlet for their excess energies, composing a string of songs for artists such as Gene Pitney, who scored a sizeable hit with Jagger/Richards' 'That Girl Belongs to Yesterday.'

The pair were also equally active as producer/arrangers, lending their talents to a variety of Andrew Oldham's off-the-wall projects. Anybody buying the single 'To Know Him Is To Love Him' by Cleo and the Andrew Loog Oldham Orchestra in 1964 might well have been surprised to hear Jagger singing lead vocals. Similarly, the album *Today's Pop Symphony*, by the obscure Aranbee Orchestra, boasted the 'Musical Direction' of Keith Richards.

As time passed, the Glimmer Twins' creative workload increased. Andrew Oldham's Immediate Records, in fact, made constant use of Mick and Keith, with the two writing and producing records by Chris Farlowe, Twice As Much, Charles Dickens, and several others.

They also continued working closely with Marianne Faithfull. Three years before the Stones issued their own version of the nightmarish 'Sister Morphine' on *Sticky Fingers*, Keith contributed a chilling guitar solo to Marianne's own heartfelt version. Faithfull's first-ever single, 'As Tears Go By,' was likewise penned by the ambitious duo. As with 'That Girl Belongs To Yesterday,' the tune was recorded and released some time before the Stones themselves dared even try for the charts with their own version.

Back in May 1964, the *New Musical Express* reported that Brian Jones was composing with Andrew Oldham, and that one of their works was about to be recorded by guitarist Jet Harris. Three weeks later, the same paper claimed that Brian himself was going to be making a record on his own.

Neither project panned out, but towards the end of his tragically brief life, Jones did finally stir himself into activity. In 1967, German film director Volker Schlondorff asked Brian to write a score for the movie *Mort und Totschlad* (released in America as *A Degree of Murder*). The movie's star was Anita Pallenberg, who very likely persuaded Schlondorff to give Brian the chance, and then made sure he followed the project through.

With ace guitarist Jimmy Page and pianist Nicky Hopkins helping out, Jones wrote and arranged the full-length score, embracing everything from country and western to Eastern raga. He played harmonica, autoharp, sitar, dulcimer, and organ, with the only vocals on the soundtrack provided by Peter Gosling. He was the lead singer with Moon Train, a band that had recently been discovered by Bill Wyman.

Jones, however, was immensely insecure about his work, and indeed his position within the group. He often claimed to be writing songs, but never actually played them to the rest of the group. 'I just can't,' he would say, 'because they'll never, never record them, so I won't play any for them.'

Even the movie soundtrack, though it was Germany's ⇨214

Evening News

London
Thursday,
July 3, 1969.
No. 27,204   5d.

Anna, girl in a black bikini, gives him the
kiss-of-life after drama of rescue dive

BRIAN JONES DIES
N POOL AFTER
MIDNIGHT PARTY

By HARRY JONES

RIAN JONES, 27-year-old ex-guitarist
the Rolling Stones, died today after
midnight bathe in the swimming pool
his 15th century Sussex farmhouse
Hartfield, tucked away in a fold of
e rolling Ashdown Forest.

Jones, who suffered from asthma, almost
tain   h of an attack of
e com
ck
ala
Wit
out 2
s mo
er c

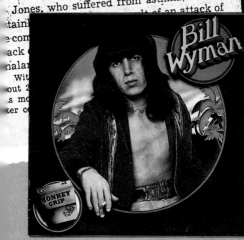

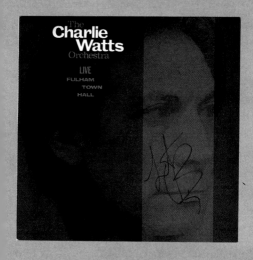

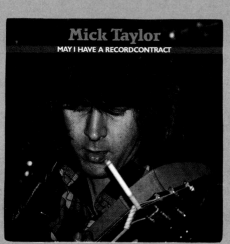

Charlie Watts: 'the one-off, merchant...'

Brian Jones

BRIAN JONES WEDDING
Dylan named best man!
by Rod

Brian Jones quits Stones
By DOUGLAS MARLBOR...

'Jumpin' Jack sound si...
But we're just

THE CHILD: Born before pop was heard of
by DON SHORT

THE P... PO... COR...

entry at the Cannes Film Festival, worried him – especially after it was rejected by the most unlikely audience imaginable. Visiting Gibraltar with Jagger, Faithfull, Richards, and Pallenberg, Brian got it into his head to play some of his music to the Rock's celebrated apes. 'He turned on the tape recorder,' says Marianne, 'and the monkeys, with a collective shriek, ran pell-mell away, tearing off into the distance. Brian took it as a terrible rejection. He screamed at the monkeys, trying to get them to come back, and when they wouldn't he began to revile them in terrible language. "The monkeys don't like my music! Fuck the monkeys! Fuck the monkeys!" I tried to comfort him but there was no stopping his outburst.'

Jones made just one other non-Stones recording, on 8 June 1967, when Paul McCartney invited him to play on 'You Know My Name (Look Up My Number),' a strange knockabout song which the Beatles had been trying to record for some time. McCartney expected Brian to bring along his guitar but instead, he turned up with his sax, looking very, very nervous. His contribution to the song, as it eventually was released in 1970

Let It Be appeared shortly before the end of this very curious Monty Pythonesque track.

Jones' only other solo work of note, indeed, the best-known of all his outside projects, is ironically one on which he personally had no active musical involvement. In 1965, Brian took a holiday in Morocco with his girlfriend Linda Lawrence. While there, and again on subsequent visits, Jones heard some of the traditional tribal music of the area. In the spring of 1968 he returned with engineer Glyn Johns intending to record the G'naoua tribe in Marrakesh.

The tapes, which Jones intended to mix together with an American soul rhythm section, were never released, but Brian was still keen to commit the country's unusual minstrels to vinyl. Later that same year he encountered the Master Musicians of Joujouka, members of a nomadic Berber tribe high in the Moroccan mountains.

'It was Brian's intention to learn to play Joujoukan music like the natives and then adapt it to the Stones' recordings,' says Anita Pallenberg. Armed with his tape recorder, girlfriend Suki

Jones drowned while drunk and drugged

Mick IS a modern 'Kelly' in his battle with society

ANITA ON BRIAN

'He was a tortured personality. Insecure and totally paranoiac'

●● I was surprised at some of the support we got. It helped to balance things up ●●

Poitier and mates Brion Gysin and George Chkiantz, Jones recorded great chunks of the week-long fertility ritual, later dubbed the Rites of Pan.

Back in England, Jones decided to present the music in two forms. Side one of the LP would feature the Master Musicians with the original tapes fed through a phaser; side two would represent the 'Pipes of Pan' as they were originally performed.

Jones was justifiably proud of the record, writing the accompanying liner notes and preparing the artwork for its eventual release. He even had a handful of acetates produced to be aired by British and American radio, and for a short time it looked as though Track Records was going to issue the album. Unfortunately, contractual difficulties arose, and *Brian Jones Presents the Pipes of Pan at Joujouka* was not released until 1971, two years after Jones had passed away.

Around the same time that Brian was working on his Moroccan tapes, Bill Wyman was busying himself producing a group called the End – and in one of those curious twists of fate which seem to dog the Stones, two of that band's songs have

become almost inextricably associated not with Bill but with Brian. 'Shades of Orange' and 'Loving Sacred Loving' have both appeared on Rolling Stones bootlegs, where they are clearly described as Brian Jones solo performances!

Like Jones, Wyman often found the Stones a very restrictive band to work in. A reasonably prolific songwriter himself, he was seldom given the opportunity to publicly display his talents. The group recorded several of his songs, but it was 1967 before one was released. It was 'In Another Land,' from *Their Satanic Majesties Request*.

By 1973, Wyman was rapidly approaching the end of his artistic tether. 'I was getting so depressed I was thinking about leaving the band because it was no fun,' he later remembered. Common sense, though, prevailed and instead he resolved to record a solo album, entitled *Monkey Grip*, to be released on the Stones' own label. 'I felt like I was on my own out in the wilds somewhere,' Wyman said, 'and I couldn't get back to being one of the lads. I needed to get away from being a Rolling Stone.'

That he certainly did. Neither *Monkey Grip*, nor *Stone* ⇨

Stone me! Stars are dazzled by silver Di

MAURICE CHITT

DAILY EXPRESS Thursday April 4 1991

Watts is plugging into jazz

DRUMMER Charlie Watts, 49, got some real Satisfaction yesterday when he launched a jazz album.

The Rolling Stone, who plays with a jazz group in his spare time, revealed his latest record is based on hits by soprano sax player Charlie "Bird" Parker.

He played tracks from the record at Ronnie Scott's club in London's West End.

And he sho... daughter Serap... that whatever he... his career is definit... not All Over Now.

Picture: RICHARD YOUNG

The Life and Times of a Rolling Stone

By ANNE NIGHTINGALE

Alone which he recorded two years later, could be called unqualified successes, either musically or commercially. Today, both records are better remembered for the handful of unique promotional films which Wyman made to accompany them – strumming his guitar while around him a bevy of archetypical seventies dollybirds sway, pout, and gyrate.

Peter Rudge, the band's eternal road manager, remembers: 'Keith freaked when Bill released *Monkey Grip*. I'd never seen him so upset. He was enraged because the Stones are a group, and they don't have misses, they don't have flops, they don't produce anything *average*. And Keith didn't want that to be a reflection on the band.'

Neither, though, did Wyman. He *needed* to make those records for his own reasons, to assert his hard-fought-for musical independence. He didn't even ask any of his fellow Stones to pitch in on either project. Instead he recruited an army of other superstar friends including Van Morrison, Sly Stone, Stephen Stills, and Joe Walsh to help him out. And when it was all over, he settled back into the band, happy to have made a musical statement of his own – for the moment anyway.

For several years thereafter, Wyman continued to murmur about leaving the band. He'd been in the pop business too long, he would say, and it held nothing left to interest him. Another step in a different direction came when he agreed to write the soundtrack for a movie called *Green Ice*, released in 1981. But while he was recording this he came up with a song which he felt might perhaps have other applications: '(Si Si) Je Suis Un Rock Star' was a blatantly commercial, hilariously self-deprecating song, charting the life and loves of a pop star, sung in a combination of cockney English and atrocious French.

Signing a contract not with Rolling Stones Records but with A & M, Wyman then astonished himself and the rest of the world by landing a Top Twenty hit in Britain, and a number one around Europe. When the Stones toured Britain later that same year Jagger even introduced him as 'Mr (Si Si) Je Suis Un Rock Star himself,' while the tape of songs played during intervals included Wyman's latest solo hit, 'A New Fashion.'

It was the early years of the video boom, and Wyman embraced the new technology more completely than even the Stones. All three singles which were eventually pulled from the

Foodies: Ronnie Wood and Keith Richards with their wives Jo and Patti outside Mosimann's last night

Night out for Stones could bring £30m satisfaction

by Caroline Davies

VETERAN rockers the Rolling Stones had much to smile about as they dined at London's most exclusive restaurant club.

The final bill could come to £30 million. And Virgin boss Richard Branson seems intent on picking up the tab.

As the battle to sign the rock world's hottest band reaches fever pitch, Branson's men were hoping to tempt the ageing superstars with a meal and a contract that will keep them going till the grand old age of 65.

No doubt German record giants Polygram would love to have caught a careless crumb of conversation dropped indiscreetly at Mosimann's — the club run by top TV chef Anton Mosimann, where it costs £400-a-year just to look at the menu.

Polygram are Virgin's main rivals in the race to sign up the Stones, whose deal with Sony, the world's biggest record label, has expired leaving them up for grabs.

... the beams from Mick Jagger, 48, ...hards, 47, Ronnie Wood, 44, and ...nothing

ANITA ON KEITH

ANITA AND KEITH: They tried to rid the... ...ar heroin addiction, but failed

'Free and easy, but tough, he loved sex, drugs and drinking'

because she was fascinated by his talent. 'But he was a tortured personality,' she now says. 'Insecure as hell. He was totally paranoiac.'

Ronni Money, an ex-dancer and one of Jones's close friends, recalls the evening Brian introduced her to Anita.

Anita's first words were: 'So who's this one? Another one of your one-nighters? I thought I'd met all of them by now.' Brian whirled round and smashed her in the face. 'You can't talk to Anita like that, you bitch!' he yelled at her. Her nose was pouring blood and the waiters were using napkins to try to keep the blood off her dress. That's how we met.'

...on, Brian... ...and I had a big fight...

would physically attack me. Keith wanted to drive the 2,000 miles to Marrakesh in his Bentley and we thought it might be a lark. When we got to the South of France, however, Brian became ill, developed a high fever, and — by the time we reached Toulon — came down with pneumonia and had to be hospitalised. It was Brian who suggested that we drive on without him to Tangier, where we should wait for him by the Hotel Minzah.

'That meant that Keith and I would be alone. By the time we reached Valencia, we could no longer resist each other, and Keith spent the night in my room. In the morning, I realised as did Keith — that we were creating an ...unenviable situati...

EXCLUSIVE
By LOUISE GANNON and DAVID WIGG

ROLLING Stone Bill Wyman last night looked set to quit the legendary rock group after almost 30 years.

As the band signed a £20 million deal with Richard Branson's Virgin Records it was revealed that Wyman had refused to add his signature.

'Bill has come to no decision as to his future with the group,' said Stones' publicist Bernard Doherty.

But other sources said Wyman, 55, was fed up with 'the hassle' and 'being messed around by the band' and wanted to settle down.

Yesterday aides were ...rching for the bass ... snoop for his ...

Wyman set to quit as Stones sign up for £20m

Bill Wyman album were accompanied by brilliant videos: 'Rock Star' played on the song's lyric, with Wyman attempting to pick up several young girls in a variety of exotic locals; 'A New Fashion' utilized a series of disconnected images to illustrate the lyrics; but most alluring was 'Come Back Suzanne,' which cast Wyman as a failed house-husband, desperately trying to keep the house in order after his lady has walked out. Compared to the Stones' own videos, which at this stage still relied on the old 'band in front of a curtain' routine, they might well have come from another planet!

If Wyman's solo success was built around humour and self-deprecation, his next project was deadly serious. Midway through 1982 he started AIMS, intent upon giving new bands a break. Wyman even started his own record label, Ripple, as an outlet for the fresh young talent he hoped to discover.

It was an admirable affair, but when AIMS's sponsor, the drink company Pernod, withdrew from the project the whole thing collapsed, with Ripple's only release of note being yet another Bill Wyman single, 'Visions.'

Wyman returned briefly to soundtrack work, this time for a film called *Digital Dreams*. The following year, 1986, he launched another ambitious musical spectacular – Willie and the Poor Boys. This unique project was intended to raise money for ARMS, a charity researching Multiple Sclerosis – the disease which had devastated one of Bill's (and Ron Wood's) closest friends, Ronnie Lane. Wyman had been involved with ARMS since 1983, when he played a series of all-star benefit concerts staged at the Royal Albert Hall with Jimmy Page, Chris Rea, and Andy Fairweather-Lowe. Willie and the Poor Boys subsequently released an album, single, and seven-song in-concert video, and while the venture was not the commercial success it deserved to be, it did at least highlight ARMS's admirable work.

Way back in 1965, Charlie Watts, like Wyman, was wondering whether there was more to life than the constant touring and recording grind which the Stones' regimen demanded. His response was to publish a book of cartoons entitled *Ode To A High-Flying Bird*, and dedicated to the late jazz great, Charlie Parker. The book was a considerable success, and seemed to satisfy for a time Watts' need for ⇨ 222

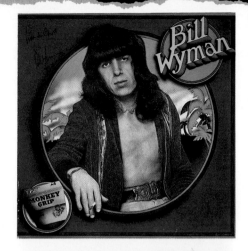

Bill Wyman was the first Stone to strike out on his own. His initial solo release came in May 1974 with an album entitled *Monkey Grip*. Two singles were released from this album, 'Monkey Grip Glue' and 'White Lightnin'.' Two years later Bill gave us his second musical offering, aptly titled *Stone Alone*. Singles lifted from the album were, 'A Quarter to Three' and 'Apache Woman.' Unlike his first album, which charted for only one week, this one didn't even show. Wyman's third LP, simply titled *Bill Wyman* (1982), gave us the delightful '(Si Si) Je Suis Un Rock Star' which climbed the charts to number fourteen. The next single, 'Come Back Suzanne,' failed even to dent the charts while 'A New Fashion' crept to number thirty-seven. His fourth solo single, 'Visions,' was released in June 1982 (a limited edition picture disc was issued in March of that same year). In 1984 Wyman released a six-song video, including '(Si Si) Je Suis Un Rock Star.' A year later Bill's all-star rhythm and blues group Willie and the Poor Boys put out a brilliant album on Bill's Ripple Label, with all proceeds from the LP generously donated to ARMS (Action for the Research into Multiple Sclerosis). A seven-track video of the album was later released (see page 220) — a must-have if only for the fifties suits and sideburns.

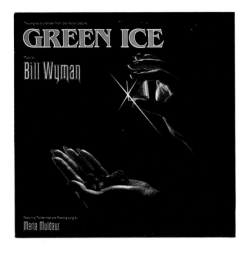

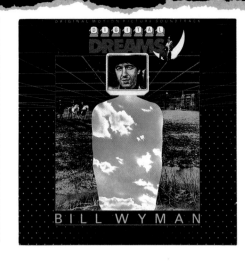

Wyman's film score for *Green Ice* was released in 1981, while in 1983 Wyman actually starred in the 'western' *Digital Dreams*. The soundtrack album, issued as a promo, is very hard to find. A year later the album *Drinkin' TNT 'n' Smoking Dynamite* was released featuring Wyman, Buddy Guy and Junior Wells. In 1983 the ARMS tour hit the road with Ronnie Lane, Jeff Beck, Eric Clapton, Joe Cocker, Andy Fairweather-Low, Kenny Jones, Jimmy Page, Paul Rodgers, Charlie Watts and, Bill Wyman.

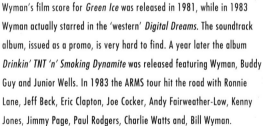

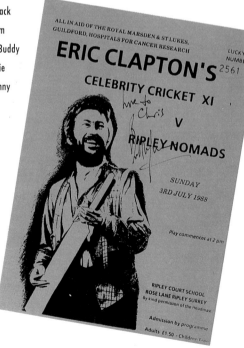

PROGRAMME

THE PERNOD AIMS PROJECT
FINALISTS

THE WORKS
AN AMERICAN IN PARIS
SOMEONE SHOUTED
MOLA MOLA
THIS PERFECT GIFT
LORRY DOGS

CHRIS REA

JIM DAVIDSON

BILL WYMAN'S ALL STAR BAND
FEATURING:
BILL WYMAN RONNIE WOOD KENNY JONES
PHIL COLLINS RAY COOPER IAN DRURY
EDDY GRANT ALAN CLARK

Bill Wyman's XI cricket team always finds time for charity work, while Bill's AIMS project (Ambition, Ideas, Motivation, Success) was set up in 1987 to encourage new bands. The gala night at the Royal Albert Hall raised much-needed cash for the Great Ormond Street Hospital for Children, London.

A natural archivist and collector, Wyman finally showed his hand with the comprehensive autobiography *Stone Alone (The Story Of A Rock 'n' Roll Band)*. Published in 1990, the book (co-authored by pop veteran Ray Coleman) neatly covers the years 1962 to 1969.

TOP In 1989, *Hello* magazine commemorated Bill and Mandy's wedding.

LEFT A montage of Bill Wyman-related videos and CDs.

ABOVE The very first Wyman bootleg CD titled *Rock 'n' Roll Is Made Of This*

ABOVE Back and front details of T-shirt and decorated coffee mug.

LEFT AND RIGHT Rare biker style leather jacket bearing the legend It's Only Rock 'n' Roll.

On 21 May 1989 Bill Wyman opened the high-class hamburger joint Sticky Fingers in the up-market Kensington area of London, adorned with a cornucopia of Stones-related memorabilia.

an extra-curricular life. Between 1965 and 1977, Charlie made only one other excursion outside the group, producing an album for the People's Band in 1970. 'I could live without the Rolling Stones,' Watts once commented. 'But I wouldn't especially want to.'

By 1977, with the Stones' own future looking grim as a result of Keith Richards' latest drug bust, Watts began stepping out with a series of makeshift jazz and big band outfits. One of these, which featured the deadpan drummer behind Bob Hall and George Green, was released as a limited edition LP in 1978. Inspired by the success of the venture, Watts finally formed his own group, Rocket 88, with Ian Stewart, Alexis Korner, and Dick Morrissey on tenor sax.

In May 1979 the band débuted at London's Venue theatre, predictably drawing a predominantly Stones-worshipping audience but winning it over regardless, fusing jazz and blues in a cool musical fog. Unfortunately, Rocket 88 barely survived the year. A series of concerts in Europe followed, but by December, with the Stones now back in action (*Emotional Rescue* was due for release), it was all over. A Rocket 88 live album, recorded in Germany that summer, was subsequently released in 1981.

In 1983 Watts joined Wyman on stage for the first ARMS benefit, and in 1986, with the Stones lying moribund, he again began thinking of a solo career. The recent deaths of Ian Stewart and Alexis Korner, however, discouraged Watts from simply resurrecting the Rocket 88 concept. Instead he formed a twenty-nine-piece band, the Charlie Watts Orchestra, and a year's worth of live work was topped by the release of *Live* ⇨ **226**

Mick Jagger – actor.
Shown above is an invitation
for the premiere of *Ned Kelly* (1970) and
(top) a Belgian film poster. The soundtrack LP
featured Mick singing a stirring rendition of 'Wild Colonial Boy.'
Not missing out, the American magazine *Hit Parader* featured
'notorious Ned' in 1971 – a true collector's item.

TOP From the stunning film *Performance* (1970) came the first solo 'Stone' single, 'Memo From Turner' (November 1970).

LEFT AND ABOVE Jagger's first solo LP, *She's The Boss* (March 1985), gave us three singles: 'Just Another Night,' 'Lucky In Love,' and 'Hard Woman.' **BOTTOM RIGHT** To coincide with the album, Mick employed the skills of director Julian Temple to make a video containing songs from the album. Titled 'Running Out Of Luck,' the steamy thriller was burdened with an adult-only certification. Look out for Mick's sometime-future partner Jerry Hall in a cameo performance as a dancer.

MICK JAGGER

Primitive Cool, Mick Jagger's second solo album, was let loose upon the world in August 1987. Produced by Dave Stewart and Keith Diamond, the LP also features some great guitar from veteran virtuoso Jeff Beck. The initial single 'Let's Work' went to number thirty-one in the English charts and came in the usual formats as well as a special 7" edition with a wrap-around poster sleeve. A specially packed cassette single from Holland was also made available. 'Throwaway' (December 1987) became Jagger's second single and was issued both as a 7" picture disc and a CD single. The final 45 off the album was 'Say You Will' (opposite page), issued only in Europe and the US. The compact disc of *Primitive Cool* was released as a picture CD and included a free 1988 CBS calendar.

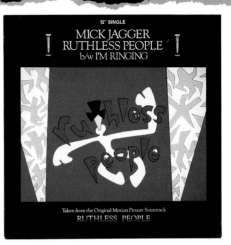

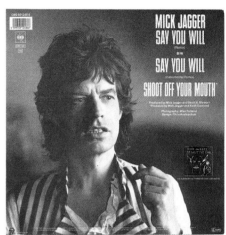

Mick Jagger enjoyed his first solo number one after teaming up with David Bowie for their rousing rendition of 'Dancing In The Streets' (August 1985). This, however, was not Jagger's first notable work with another artist. Way back in 1984 he scored a minor hit with the Jacksons on a song entitled 'State of Shock.' In July 1986 Mick recorded the theme to *Ruthless People*, a high-powered black comedy starring Danny De Vito and Bette Midler. In Australia a compact disc of Jagger's solo 12" mixes was released, as well as a cassette titled *The Very Best of Mick Jagger*.

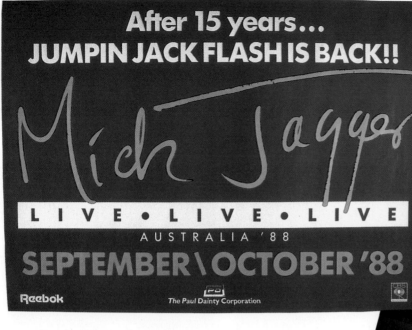

at Fulham Town Hall, a fine documentary of Watts' most personally fulfilling venture yet.

Throughout the sixties, the possibility of Jagger leaving the group in favour of working in movies had kept the band's fans on tenterhooks. Both *Ned Kelly* and *Performance* spawned new Jagger recordings. 'Wild Colonial Boy' from *Kelly* was an adaptation of a much-loved Australian folk song, but raised few commendations when released on the film's soundtrack. 'Memo From Turner' from *Performance*, however, was something else entirely. Written by Jagger and Richards, the song was first tried out by the Stones themselves some time before work on *Performance* began. Aided by members of Traffic, it was recorded but shelved (though eventually appearing on the *Metamorphosis* album in 1975). Jagger later re-recorded it for the movie.

The song was also released as a single in 1970 and narrowly missed the British Top Thirty, establishing it as the worst-performing single yet released under the Stones' banner. 'Memo' has become so inextricably bound up with the band that when London Records compiled their three-disc collection of Stones A and B sides in 1989, they had no hesitation in including the chilling track.

Throughout the seventies, Jagger contented himself merely with appearing on other artists' records, as on the chorus of Carly Simon's 'You're So Vain' (amid rumours that the song was actually about him). He also guested on an album by veteran Heavy Metal guitarist Leslie West and sang lead on 'I Can Feel The Fire,' a song from Ron Wood's first solo album *I've Got My Own Album To Do*. Keith Richards also appears on the record, singing his own 'Act Together.'

But Jagger's most significant contribution was perhaps to reggae star Peter Tosh's 1978 single '(You Gotta Walk) Don't

Determined to find his own star as a solo artist Jagger toured Japan, Australia, and New Zealand. Mixing in his solo songs with several Stones classics, Mick also threw in a few relative oddities including 'Foxy Lady,' and performed 'Wild Colonial Boy' (just for Australia), as well as an instrumental titled 'Deep Down Under' to introduce the Australian TV special. Collectable tour programmes and promoters' posters shown above.

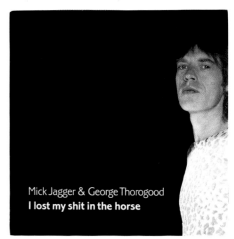

Mick Jagger & George Thorogood
I lost my shit in the horse

Look Back.' Released on Rolling Stones Records, the song was essentially a Jagger/Tosh duet, and gave Tosh – who was later murdered by burglars at his Kingston, Jamaica home – his first and only hit record.

In 1984 Jagger made another guest appearance, this time on the Jacksons' 'State of Shock' single. Emboldened by its unexpected success, he immediately set about recording a full solo album. Like Wyman and Watts, Jagger went outside the Stones for accompanying musicians – Jeff Beck, Sly & Robbie, Herbie Hancock, and Nile Rodgers were all co-opted for Jagger's first album, *She's The Boss,* which was recorded in New York and the Bahamas and unveiled early in the new year with the single 'Just Another Night.'

Fears that Jagger solo would sound much the same as Jagger with the Stones proved unjustified – and perhaps a shade optimistic. Without the benefit of Keith Richards' searing guitar, and shorn of the faithful Wyman/Watts rhythm section, Jagger embraced a clean-cut disco sound, brash, breezy, and not a little embarrassing for hard-core rock fans. It was perhaps fitting that 'Just Another Night' should fare no better in the British charts than 'Memo From Turner,' again coming to rest at number thirty-two; in America, however, ⇨

Limited edition picture discs were very much the order of the day and Jagger was no exception. The majority of these are of medium quality and, nine times out of ten, of interview material. Jagger has also appeared on several bootleg albums and CDs as a solo artist. A selection is shown here.

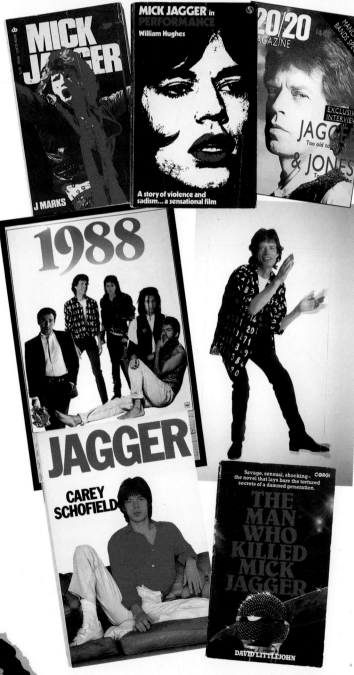

it raced to the edge of the Top Ten, out-performing almost every Stones single of the decade.

Shortly after *She's The Boss* appeared, Mick guested at the Live Aid concert in July 1985 at the Philadelphia venue. It was his first ever solo performance. With Hall and Oates behind him, and Tina Turner making a whirlwind guest appearance towards the end of the set, it proved that in concert Jagger was still a force to be reckoned with – even if the music wasn't particularly extraordinary.

Live Aid also premiered Jagger's next single, a sexy duet with David Bowie performing the old Martha Reeves standard 'Dancing in the Street.' Accompanied by a video which featured the duo looking like a pair of old queens camping it up in their pajamas, 'Dancing in the Street' was an instant, predictable, hit. It gave Jagger his first number one since 'Honky Tonk Women' in 1969, reached number seven in the US, and created so much interest in the wayward Stone that it immediately established *She's The Boss* among the year's most successful albums.

Jagger's next outing, the raucous theme to the Bette Midler movie *Ruthless People* was only a modest hit. Mick received more exposure when he guested in the video for Midler's cover of the Stones' 'Beast of Burden.' It seems surprising, then, that Jagger chose to continue pursuing his solo career even after the Stones made their 1986 comeback LP *Dirty Work*.

Ignoring Keith Richards' demands for a tour, Jagger pressed ahead with *Primitive Cool*, an album which paired him with a new songwriting partner, the talented Dave Stewart of the Eurythmics. He was also planning a full solo tour, ignoring Richards' renewed demands that it was once again time to take the Stones back out on the road. For a time one couldn't open a magazine without reading of the bitter enmity which apparently festered between the pair concerning *Primitive Cool*, released amid very real fears that the Rolling Stones had finally reached the end of the line.

As if to pile insult onto injury, Jagger's live repertoire, once he finally made it out on his own, scarcely extended beyond the Stones' catalogue. Ridiculous though it may sound, the world's most accomplished concert performer seemed out of his depth. He has not mentioned a solo singing career in public since, with film acting once again occupying his spare time.

What Jagger lacked throughout his solo career, however, was a reliable, steadfast foil. The burden of carrying the show totally on his own just seemed too great – even at Live Aid, it was the arrival of Tina Turner on stage that brought the best out of him. What he needed was . . . Keith Richards.

Richards, on the other hand, has spent much of his career proving that he didn't actually need *anybody*. His lead vocal contributions to the Stones' own albums are often the first track many fans go to, and over the years he has not disappointed them – 'Happy,' 'Before They Make Me Run,' 'Indian Girl,' and

TOP Marianne Faithfull finally surfaced in 1979 with the excellent album *Broken English*.
LEFT AND OPPOSITE TOP An assortment of books about Mick Jagger. One of the better books is Carey Schofield's *Jagger*, published in 1983.

'Little T & A' are often rated among the band's finest. The Stones' own label seemed happy to highlight this side of the band – a promotional single of 'Before They Make Me Run' was released in 1978, with a Keith Richards interview on the B-side and the sleeve depicting Keith wearing a 'Who the fuck is Mick Jagger?' T-shirt.

Several other Stones songs are also indelibly stamped with the guitarist's unmistakable imprimatur. In 1970, Richards celebrated his birthday by organizing an all-star jam on 'Brown Sugar,' a song which the Stones wouldn't officially release for close to another year but which snuck out on bootleg under Keith's own name all the same.

A few years later, he and Alexis Korner collaborated on a stunning version of 'Get Off Of My Cloud,' and in 1977, while awaiting the outcome of his celebrated Toronto bust, Richards stockpiled a number of solo recordings, many of which are also familiar under-the-counter releases.

Keith did his best though to downplay his solo ambitions. 'If I made a solo album I'd only hire the band to play on it,' he used to say, 'so why bother?'

Not until 1978 did Richards finally, and officially, take the solo plunge. With Ron Wood, Ian McLagen (another ex-Faces member), Stanley Clarke, and long-time Stones collaborator Bobby Keys, Keith formed the New Barbarians, initially to play the concert for the blind which the Toronto court had ordered. The group so enjoyed the experience, however, that they remained together, and throughout the first half of 1979 successfully toured the US. (They also made one British appearance, supporting Led Zeppelin at the Knebworth Festival in Hertfordshire.)

In the midst of this activity, Rolling Stones Records released Keith's two year-old recording of Chuck Berry's seasonal 'Run Rudolph Run' – in February, which may account for its poor chart placing! It was a slice of vintage rhythm & blues. But it was the B-side, Jimmy Cliff's 'The Harder They Come,' which received the most attention, illustrating as it did Keith's other great love – reggae.

' "Harder They Come" was just a quick snatch of tape between two other songs we did during a break. There's a couple of mistakes in it, but I don't care. Some of the records I like best have mistakes all over them,' Keith later commented. Hopes that the single might preface a full Keith Richards album were premature, however, as were those raised by the guitarist's dalliance with down-home country blues in 1981.

But finally Keith bowed to the pressure, following his much publicized feud with Jagger in 1986. To begin with, Richards let off steam by joining with Aretha Franklin and then with Chuck Berry on two more collaborations – producing and playing on Aretha's spirited remake of the Stones' 'Jumpin' Jack Flash' then taking the role of Musical Director for Chuck Berry's *Hail! Hail! Rock 'n' Roll* film.

The following year he set about recording an album of his own, proving his sincerity by signing a solo recording deal with Virgin that July. In light of Richards' reputation as the ⇨

In 1992 Mick co-starred in the film *Freejack*. Ticket and guest pass for Mick's latest cinematic adventure (above).

Fiercely loyal to the Stones, Keith Richards kept quiet as a solo artist (apart from the 1966 curio *Pop Symphony*). In 1988 he burst upon the scene in a big way when he signed a major deal with Virgin Records. The result was the tremendous eleven-song LP *Talk Is Cheap* (top right). Virgin issued the CD of the album in a limited edition tin of three 3" CDs (bottom). The best promotional issue, however, was a black box set of four singles, with one track on each record, numbered Keith 1–4. The tunes are 'Make No Mistake,' 'Locked Away,' 'Struggle,' and 'Big Enough.' Below is a snappy Rolling Stones business card, the reverse of which contains a good representation of Mick by his buddy Keith.

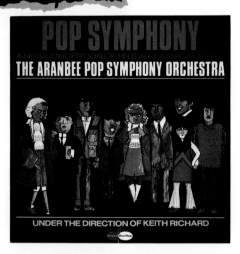

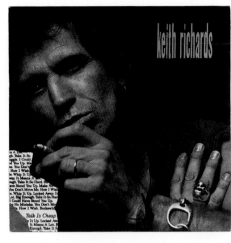

musical power behind the Stones, it was perhaps inevitable that *Talk Is Cheap* (when finally released in 1988) should have got the best reception of the band's solo projects. Certainly it was truer to the group's legacy than anything the others had mustered, a relaxed but nevertheless storming selection of songs, rooted in the general direction of soulful rhythm & blues. True to form, some devastating guitar work was also in evidence. It had taken a long time, but Richards had finally proved that he could make the album his fans had been dreaming about for years.

Much the same was hoped for when Mick Taylor first left the Stones in 1974. Over the course of five years and six albums, Taylor amply demonstrated why he was ranked amongst the finest young guitarists Britain had ever produced. A handful of albums recorded with blues giant John Mayall testify to the talent which brought him to the Stones' attention in the first place (he also issued a solo single in 1965, 'London Town'). Now, as he walked out of the greatest rock 'n' roll band in the world, Taylor mused quietly about his future plans. 'I had a lot more inside me and it needed to get out.' ⟹ 232

The initial single taken from *Talk Is Cheap* was 'Take It So Hard' (October 1988), released in all familiar formats including a 3" CD (shown are the front and back of the 12" single). The next, 'Make No Mistake,' followed some four months later (12" shown, top right). 'You Don't Move Me' (right, back and front shown) was released as 12" promo only in 1988. Other promotional releases issued by Virgin include a picture disc CD of 'Make No Mistake,' plus two additional tunes which never made it as official releases, 'Struggle' and 'You Don't Move Me.' Also shown is the X-Pensive Winos live CD issued March 1992 (below), and various cassette singles and 3" CDs issued around the world.

Unfortunately, it took an awful long time to do so. A projected union with vocalist Carla Bley and Jack Bruce survived for little more time than it took to appear on British television's 'Old Grey Whistle Test,' and it was 1979 before Taylor released his first solo album, *Stranger in this Town*. It was not a great success.

'If only he'd realize what he is, a damn good guitar player,' lamented Keith Richards. 'He's great. I wish he'd stop pissing about trying to be a songwriter, producer, and bandleader.'

Despite press reports of acrimony between Taylor and the Stones, the guitarist remained in touch with them and even made several on-stage appearances at Stones gigs during the 1980s. His rehabilitation was completed when Keith Richards invited him along to play on *Talk Is Cheap*. Taylor repaid the favour by including the Stones' own 'Sway' and 'Silver Train' on promotional versions of his second album, *Live*, recorded with Carla Olson at the Roxy in 1990.

In terms of the Rolling Stones' own history, Ron Wood is still very much the 'new boy' – and that despite the fact that he has now played longer with the group than Brian Jones and Mick Taylor put together.

Woody's solo career got underway while still a member of The Faces. *I've Got My Own Album To Do*, released in 1974,

featured contributions from Jagger, Richards, and Mick Taylor; indeed, the two songs Keith donated were, as Jagger later complained, as good as any he had given the Stones. Keith turned up again on Wood's second album, *Now Look*, one year later in 1975 after Wood had joined the Stones. *Mahoney's Last Stand* reunited Woody with former Face, Ronnie Lane.

Over the next couple of years, the guitarist let his solo career take a back seat as he acclimatized himself to the Stones' ▷ 234

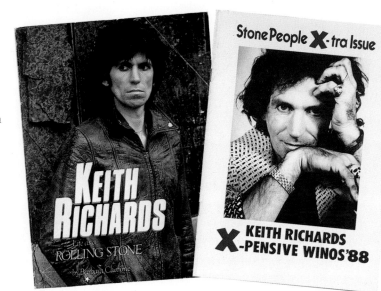

ABOVE A special issue of the Japanese magazine *Stone People* and Barbara Charone's powerful book on Keith.

ABOVE These miniature leather jackets were hand-made for members and close friends of the band. There are reportedly no more than twenty-five in existence.

LEFT Released in America and Japan was a limited box set of Keith's solo tour with the X-Pensive Winos. The US release included a live CD, video, and sixteen-page booklet of photos. Recorded on 15 December 1988 at the Hollywood Palladium, the package also includes a T-shirt shrunk to the size of a bar of soap which, when soaked, expands into glorious full-size.

In February 1979 Keith released his only solo single on Rolling Stones Records, 'Run Rudolph Run.' Two obscure Richards-related singles are by Max Romeo, and the Dirty Strangers. Keith also produced a film about Chuck Berry, titled *Hail! Hail! Rock 'n' Roll*. The rarest interview CD is the 4-CD set *Keith Richards Up Close* (1988). Below is the bootleg CD *Guitar Legends*.

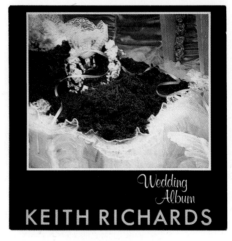
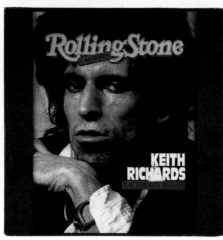

gruelling schedule. In 1978, with memories of the New Barbarians still fresh in his mind, he started work on his fourth album, *Gimme Some Neck*, released in 1979.

Jagger, Richards, and Charlie Watts all dropped by to lend a hand – Watts was eventually recruited to play drums throughout both *Gimme Some Neck* and 1981's *1 2 3 4*. But neither album met with any real success and, since then, Woody has concentrated instead on live work.

During the Live Aid concert, while Mick was cavorting energetically with Tina Turner, Woody and Keith Richards joined Bob Dylan for a short performance which, depending on one's viewpoint, was either the most appalling or courageous effort of the day. Certainly, the sight of the trio struggling through a ramshackle clutch of Dylan oldies was in marked contrast to the bloated self-importance of so many of the concert's other artistes.

Woody also turned up in the brief but almost spectacular Faces reunion which capped one of Rod Stewart's 1986 concerts in London. Then, in late 1987 he joined Bo Diddley – one of the Stones' earliest and most influential idols – for a world tour that spawned the spectacular live album *Live at the Ritz* (released only in Japan.) 'I'd never do any long term solo stuff,' Woody later commented. 'It's purely ideas to get off my back that I can do on my own. The group is definitely much more important to me.'

That feeling has been echoed, at different times, by every member of the group, past and present. It is perhaps worth noting that the bulk of solo Stones material dates from the

Of all the Stones, Keith Richards is the most popular with bootleggers. A selection of their wares are shown. Who is Mick Jagger, anyway?

middle seventies onwards. Before that, the Stones maintained a punishing recording schedule, averaging more than one album a year since 1964. Touring, too, was rigorous and surely debilitating. The last thing any of the group would have wanted to contemplate was adding even more work to their heavy load.

By 1974 the Rolling Stones were slipping imperceptibly into the superstar routine of releasing one album every two or three years, with a mammoth tour to match. Often, what appeared to be a brand new album was, in fact, a record pieced together from tracks recorded many years previous. Out-takes from *Goat's Head Soup*, recorded in 1973 for example, were still appearing on albums as late as 1981 – prompting Mick Taylor to sue for royalties when 'Tops' and 'Waiting On A Friend' both made it on to *Tattoo You*. ⇨ 243

RIGHT Keith Richards acted as producer and musician on Aretha Franklin's version of 'Jumpin' Jack Flash.' A limited edition picture disc was also issued to help boost sales.

TOP AND BELOW A further selection of much sought-after Keith Richards bootlegs.

بارك الله فيك
لا باس
الحمد للـه

Brian Jones presents the Pipes of Pan at
JouJouKa

Brian Jones plays with the Pipes of Pan at
JouJouKa

Brian Jones released only one album on Rolling Stones Records, *Brian Jones Presents the Pipes of Pan at Joujouka* (November 1971). The first pressing was titled *Brian Jones Plays with the Pipes of Pan at Joujouka* (right), but was quickly withdrawn. The first pressings of the album were issued with a four-page booklet (left). Below is the tasteful inside gatefold of this rather strange musical offering.

In 1984 Psychic TV released 'Godstar,' a 12" single taken from an unreleased film about Brian Jones. A double album by various artists, *The Ghost of Brian* (1989), contains cover versions of sixteen classic Stones numbers. Brian's handsome visage adorns this bootleg picture disc containing live Stones material (top right).

Don't Judge Me Too Harshly, a Brian Jones memorial album, was released in 1977 (front and back cover shown above). Many books have been written about Brian, but will we ever know the truth about his death? Westwood One issued a five-album radio show (1983) on Brian Jones titled *Rock & Roll Never Forgets* (below).

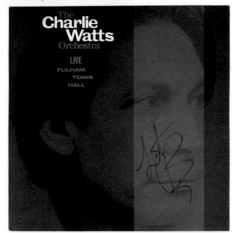

BELOW Two drumming magazines featuring the much-admired Rolling Stones drummer: *Modern Drummer* (August/September 1982) and *Downbeat* (February 1987).

Charlie Watts is one of the most respected rock 'n' roll and jazz drummers in the world; **TOP** In 1970 he produced an album called *The People Band,* released on the Transatlantic label. **BELOW** Early in 1964 Watts wrote and illustrated a book entitled *Ode To A Highflying Bird,* inspired by the music of the late Charlie Parker. In April 1991 the book was re-published with a special CD by the newly formed Charlie Watts Quintet. It was hatched at the very centre of jazz, Ronnie Scott's in Soho, London.

OPPOSITE CENTRE The Charlie Watts Orchestra got together to shoot a fifty-minute jazz video at the Fulham Town Hall, London. The result was the excellent album *Live At Fulham Town Hall,* recorded on 23 March 1986. **OPPOSITE BOTTOM** Charlie next took his quintet to further heights at New York's Blue Note, and then Tokyo's Spiral Hall. In the centre is a signed Japanese tour programme.

Then Charlie was asked by Ronnie Scott if he and the boys would open his new club in Birmingham, England, on 28 October 1991. 'A great honour,' replied Charlie, and there they played for six nights in November.

BELOW A live CD of Charlie's Ronnie Scott show was released in 1992 with very tasteful packaging featuring the members of Charlie's band. **RIGHT** Front and back design of the Quintet T-shirt.

Charlie Watts Quintet 1991

David Green

Gerard Presencer

Brian Lemon

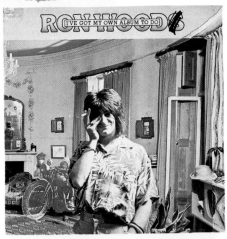

Released in the eighties, *These Birds Are Dangerous* contained six songs by Ron Wood's old band, The Birds. Ron's first solo album, *I've Got My Own Album To Do* (1974) was followed by *Now Look* (1975), and *Gimme Some Neck* (1979). Ron also wrote a soundtrack with Ronnie Lane for the film *Mahoney's Last Stand*. A catalogue of Wood's pictures titled *Ronnie's Art Works* was published in 1991.

ABOVE A signed and unpublished photo of Ronnie performing on stage in Toronto, November 1984.

RIGHT Ron contributed one song to the film soundtrack *The Wild Life* (MCA Records), next to which is a German 12" picture disc single of 'I Can Feel The Fire' (1988).

BELOW Ron's fourth solo album was *1 2 3 4* (September 1981, front and back cover shown, below). On the release of *Gimme Some Neck*, Columbia sent out this notice to radio stations warning that a certain track was not suitable for airplay.

BOTTOM Various Ronnie Wood singles and CDs, including one from Ron's previous group, the Faces. Wood teamed up with Bo Diddley in the summer of 1987 to perform a series of shows in America and Canada dubbed the Gunslingers Tour. Out of this came the lively CD *Live At The Ritz*.

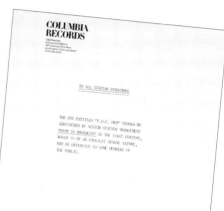

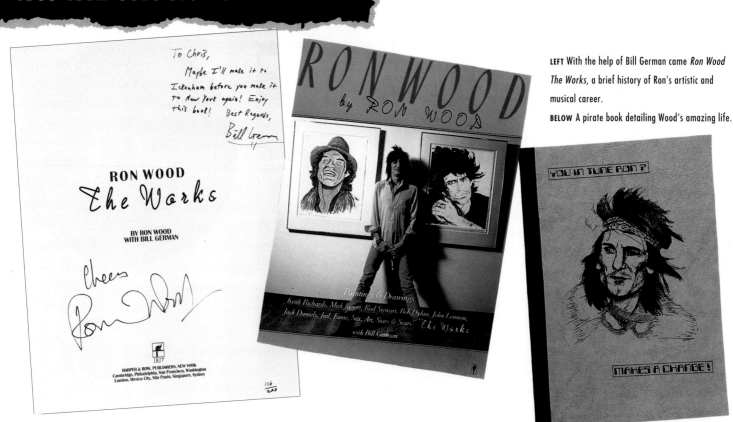

LEFT With the help of Bill German came *Ron Wood The Works*, a brief history of Ron's artistic and musical career.

BELOW A pirate book detailing Wood's amazing life.

BELOW Ads from Japan promoting exhibitions of Woody's imaginative paintings and drawings.

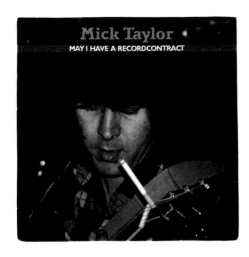

LEFT Mick Taylor's début as a member of the Rolling Stones was on 5 July 1969 at the free concert in Hyde Park, London. Starting out with John Mayall's Bluesbreakers way back in the early sixties, he officially became a Stone on 13 June 1969. He had made only one single (in 1965) called 'London Town.' In 1977 Mick Taylor guested on *Sirkel & Co* (Affinity), and knew he had made it when the bootleg album *May I Have a Record Contract* turned up.

Should the band fall apart tomorrow, there is reportedly enough material still in the vaults to maintain a constant stream of new albums well into the next century without anyone being any the wiser. But life as a Rolling Stone was, and is, punctuated by long breaks from their recording and touring schedules. When Bill Wyman went off to record *Monkey Grip*, he did so in the knowledge that he had some time to himself – not just a few stolen moments between sessions, but weeks stretching into months, maybe even yawning into a lazy year or two.

That Keith Richards was able to create albums which could truly be placed alongside the Rolling Stones at their best in many ways vindicates the individual members' decisions to 'go it alone,' just as it underlined their need to keep the Rolling Stones together.

Even at their worst – and each of the band has in turn admitted that not every song on every album is perfect – the Rolling Stones have maintained a constant and consistently entertaining and challenging barrage of sound. When the sixties demanded revolution, the Stones were there to make the dream at least seem possible. When the seventies screamed for glamour and abandon, the Stones effortlessly stepped into that breach. And if the eighties were the decade when the post-Woodstock idealism and mystique were finally stripped from rock 'n' roll, the Stones aptly commented upon that as well.

Now we are into the nineties, the Stones are bravely stepping into their fourth decade together. Nobody yet knows what demands the final years of the twentieth century will make on us, but whatever they are, the Rolling Stones will probably have a good sense of what is needed, and chances are they'll deliver it right on the money.

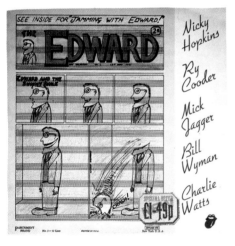

ABOVE Two albums appeared on the Stones label with different members of the band playing with several well-known guest artists. First came *Jamming With Edward!* featuring Nicky Hopkins, Ry Cooder, Bill, Charlie, and Mick. The album came complete with a letter of apology from Mick saying that they 'cut the album while we were waiting for our guitar player to get out of bed.' It was subsequently released in 1972 as a budget-priced LP.

RIGHT The other all-star project was released a year earlier in 1971. *The London Howlin' Wolf Sessions* featured Eric Clapton, Steve Winwood, Bill, Charlie, and, of course, the legendary Howlin' Wolf.

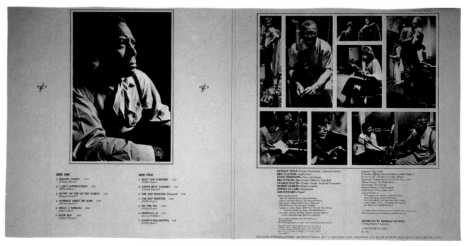

CHARLIE WATTS ORCHESTRA 1986

NOVEMBER	29	Music Hall, West Hartford, Connecticut

DECEMBER	1	Philadelphia, Pennsylvania
	2	Ritz Hotel, New York
	3	Ritz Hotel, New York
	4	Ritz Hotel, New York
	5	Boston, Masssachusetts
	6	Toronto, Canada

CHARLIE WATTS ORCHESTRA 1987

JUNE	13	Jazz Festival, Hollywood Bowl, Los Angeles, California
	23	Avery Fisher Hall, New York

RON WOOD/BO DIDDLEY
GUNSLINGER TOUR 1987

NOVEMBER	4	Newport Music Hall, Columbus, Ohio
	5	Rivera Theater, Chicago, Illinois
	6	Harpo's, Detroit, Michigan
	7	The Agora, Cleveland, Ohio
	8	Holiday House, Pittsburg, Pennsylvania
	10	The Copa, Toronto, Canada
	11	The Grange, Poughkeepsie, New York
	12	The Channel, Boston, Massachusetts
	13	The Living Room, Providence, Rhode Island
	14	Sundance, Long Island, New York
	21	Stone Ballon, Newark, Delaware
	24	The Bayou, Washington D.C.
	25	The Ritz, New York, New York

DECEMBER	19	Woody's On the Beach, Miami, Florida
	20	Woody's On the Beach, Miami, Florida

RON WOOD/BO DIDDLEY
GUNSLINGER TOUR 1988

JUNE	21	Woody's On the Beach, Miami, Florida
	22	Woody's On the Beach, Miami, Florida
	28	Hammersmith Odeon, London

JULY		seven more shows in Italy, Germany, and Spain

MICK JAGGER
TOUR OF JAPAN/AUSTRALIA/NEW ZEALAND 1988

MARCH	15	Castle Hall, Osaka, Japan
	18	Castle Hall, Osaka, Japan
	19	Castle Hall, Osaka, Japan
	22	Karakuen Dome, Tokyo, Japan
	23	Karakuen Dome, Tokyo, Japan
	25	International Exhibition Hall, Nagoya, Japan

SEPTEMBER	17	Kardomah Cafe, Sydney, Australia
	22	Boondall Entertainment Centre, Brisbane, Australia
	23	Boondall Entertainment Centre, Brisbane, Australia
	26	Entertainment Centre, Sydney, Australia
	27	Entertainment Centre, Sydney, Australia

OCTOBER	1	Entertainment Centre, Sydney, Australia
	2	Entertainment Centre, Sydney, Australia
	6	International Tennis Centre, Melbourne, Australia
	7	International Tennis Centre, Melbourne, Australia
	10	Burswood Superdome, Perth, Western Australia
	11	Burswood Superdome, Perth, Western Australia
	14	International Tennis Centre, Melbourne, Australia
	15	International Tennis Centre, Melbourne, Australia
	17	International Tennis Centre, Melbourne, Australia
	21	Entertainment Centre, Sydney, Australia
	30	Stadion Utama Senayan, Djakarta, Indonesia

NOVEMBER	5	Western Spring Stadium, Aukland, New Zealand

KEITH RICHARDS
WITH X-PENSIVE WINOS ON THE ROAD 1988

NOVEMBER	24	Fox Theater, Atlanta, Georgia
	25	Auditorium, North Hall, Memphis, Tennesse
	27	Constitution Hall, Washington D.C.
	29	Beacon Theater, New York

DECEMBER	1	Tower Theater, Philadelphia, Pennsylvania
	2	Tower Theater, Philadelphia, Pennsylvania
	4	Orpheum Theater, Boston, Massachusetts
	5	Orpheum Theater, Boston, Massachusetts
	7	Music Hall, Cleveland, Ohio
	8	Fox Theater, Detroit, Michigan
	10	Aragon Ballroom, Chicago, Illinois
	13	Henry J Kaiser Convention Center, Oakland, California
	14	Universal Amphitheater, Los Angeles, California
	15	Hollywood Paladium, Los Angeles, California
	17	Brendan Byrne Area, Meadowlands, New Jersey

CHARLIE WATTS QUINTET 1991

APRIL	3	Ronnie Scott's, London

JUNE	3	Blue Note, New York

SEPTEMBER	15	Spiral Hall, Tokyo
	16	Spiral Hall, Tokyo
	17	Spiral Hall, Tokyo

OCTOBER	28	Ronnie Scott's Jazz Club,
to NOVEMBER	2	Birmingham, UK

CHARLIE WATTS QUINTET 1992

MAY	4-15	played 11 shows in Brazil, including five shows at the São Paolo Palladium.

JULY	12	Theater of the Living Arts, Philadelphia, Pennsylvania
	14–19	Blue Note, New York
	21	Park West, Chicago, Illinois
	23	Hollywood Palace, California

LONG STORY SHORT

I was resting for a moment after working with my horses recently when Geoffrey rang, ranting about me committing to paper my experiences with the brave young Stones. A more than avid polo enthusiast, my head was a million miles away, absorbed in thoughts of that weekend's upcoming match in Mokulea, when Giuliano Esq. suddenly yanked me back to earth with his off-the-wall request.

'You did know them, didn't you?' he pried.

'Yes Geoffrey.'

'So what were they like? Did you ever play with them?'

'Yes Geoffrey.'

These Americans, I thought to myself, always in such a perpetual hurry (and this one in particular). At any rate, dear reader, what follows is the little that time and memory allow concerning my scant association with Messrs. JaggerRichardsJonesWattsAndWyman. It's only a dribble I'm afraid, but frankly, there's the ponies to see to, the match, and, as always. . . Geoffrey.

The year was 1962 (if memory serves) and the setting, ironically, was the annual polo ball somewhere in snooty Sussex. It was only my second gig with Alexis Korner, and despite the thunderous reaction from the well-pissed crowd, I was still more than a little on edge. That afternoon I had noticed this kid sitting at the back of the band bus and suddenly here he was again, perched on a chair between Jack Bruce and me on stage! 'Who the hell is this guy?' I mouthed to Mr. Bruce as we were wailing away. After a time, Alexis whispered into the mike that a fledgling crooner by the name of Mick Jagger was making his debut that evening. After jumping up and wading through some long-forgotten blues number, young Jagger all but disappeared into the balmy Sussex night.

Perhaps I should mention here that it was another future Stone, Charlie Watts, who was responsible for me drumming for Alexis in the first place. Originally, you see, Mr. Watts had the job but kindly stepped aside when he came to realize my close ties with fellow musos Bruce and the fabulous Dick Heckstall-Smith. Beyond that, I remember meeting up with Charlie somewhere on the Bakerloo Line a few weeks later and him confiding in me that he was having serious doubts about staying in music at all, as it was financially far too 'uncertain.'

My next meeting with Mick was at the Ealing Club, where Korner asked Johnny Parker, Jack, and me if we wouldn't mind passing up our interval to sit in with Jagger while he did a couple of numbers. Now at the time I was still very heavily into smack, and so greatly resented losing my opportunity to nip into the carsey for my regular fix. As a result we intentionally played badly (screwing around with various time changes) so as to confuse poor Master Jagger. Now that particular evening Brian Jones was also in attendance, supporting Mick on the guitar, and it was only thanks to his well-known musicianship that any sense at all was made of the out-of-sync jam. I remember sitting at the back grinning like a cat as Jones shouted out '1-2-3-4!' to Jagger in a frantic effort to keep him even vaguely on time.

Unfortunately, this went on for several more weeks until I had finally had enough and pleaded with Brian to get his bloody finger out and find himself a rhythm section. The very next week thankfully they turned up with a drummer. After their set Brain rushed up to me in the dressing room and blissfully inquired what I thought. 'Yeah, great, Bri,' I muttered, 'but you realize the drummer is absolute shit.' Disappointed, he dragged his ass back out on the floor and directly up to the bar.

Sometime later, Jones invited Jack and me down to see them play at the Cylowrie Club on Windmill Street in London's Soho. Although musically they still had quite a long way to go, in terms of pure charisma and showmanship they were a bloody power-house. Interestingly, in those days it was Brian and not Mick who was generally the centre of attention. Jumping into the crowd, playing guitar while laying on his back, and otherwise creating quite a spectacle. Jones far outshone the still reserved and tentative Jagger who stood quietly at the mike as his musical partner effortlessly and effectively brought down the house.

Several years later, after we were all riding the crest of our newly-found fame, me with Cream and the Stones as the pre-eminent pop idols of the hour, we somehow lost touch. Although I occasionally shared a friendly pint or two with the likes of Wyman and Richards at such celebrity watering holes as the Cromwellian, the Speakeasy, the Bag O' Nails, or the notorious Ad Lib, those were terrifically busy times for all of us and it wasn't really until poor Brian finally passed away that I once again connected with any of the Stones crowd. Now, light years later, I look back on the Rolling Stones with a mixture of profound professional respect, admiration, and, I hope, friendship. But to be honest, I prefer thinking of them as they once were – a tough, ambitious troupe of committed bluesmen laying down the law in a succession of smoky, tatty, little dives tucked away on the grotty side streets of London. Never compromising – always on the make for a tighter riff, a more searing vocal, or a better gig. Back then they were still 'Brian's band,' today they belong to the ages.

God bless you lads. It looks good on ya.

Ginger Baker
Santa Ynez
California 1992

1963

UK Singles

'Come On'/'I Want To Be Loved'	Decca	F11675
'Poison Ivy'/'Fortune Teller' [WITHDRAWN]	Decca	F11742
'I Wanna Be Your Man'/'Stoned'	Decca	F11764

1ST PRESSING LISTED B SIDE AS 'Stones'

Export Singles

'Come On'/'Tell Me (You're Coming Back)' [BLACK LABEL]	Decca	AT 15032

UK Albums

Thank Your Lucky Stars (Vol. 2) [MONO]	Decca	LK 4554

1 TRACK ONLY: 'Come On'

1964

UK Singles

'Not Fade Away'/'Little By Little'	Decca	F11845
'It's All Over Now'/'Good Times, Bad Times'	Decca	F11934
'Little Red Rooster'/'Off The Hook'	Decca	F12014

US Singles

'Not Fade Away'/'I Wanna Be Your Man'	London	9657
'Tell Me'/'I Just Wanna Make Love To You'	London	9682
'It's All Over Now'/'Good Times, Bad Times'	London	9687
'Time Is On My Side'/'Congratulations'	London	9708
'Heart of Stone'/'What A Shame'	London	9725
'I Wanna Be Your Man'/'Stoned' [WITHDRAWN]	London	9641

Export Singles

'Little Red Rooster'/'Off The Hook'	Decca	AT 15040
'Empty Heart'/'Around & Around' [BLACK LABEL]	Decca	AT 15035
'Heart of Stone'/'What A Shame' [PS]	Decca	F22180

UK EPs

'The Rolling Stones'	Decca	DFE 8560
'Five by Five'	Decca	DFE 8590

Export EPs

'The Rolling Stones (Vol. 2)'	Decca	SDE 7501

UK Albums

Ready, Steady, Go! [MONO]	Decca	LK 4577

2 TRACKS ONLY: 'Come On'/'I Wanna Be Your Man'

Saturday Club [MONO]	Decca	LK 458

2 tracks only: 'Poison Ivy'/'Fortune Teller.' 'Poison Ivy' IS THE 1ST TAKE;
2ND TAKE IS ON THEIR FIRST EP 'This Is The Stones' FROM THE 2ND
SINGLE THAT WAS WITHDRAWN]

The Rolling Stones [MONO]	Decca	LK 4605
Fourteen [MONO]	Decca	LK4645

1 TRACK ONLY: 'Surprise Surprise'
PROCEEDS WENT TO THE LORD TAVENER'S PLAYING FIELDS ASSOCIATION

US Albums

England's Newest Hit Makers: The Rolling Stones [MONO]	London	LL 3375
England's Newest Hit Makers: The Rolling Stones [STEREO]	London	PS 375
12 x 5 [MONO]	London	LL 3402
12 x 5 [STEREO]	London	PS 402

1965

UK Singles

'The Last Time'/'Play With Fire'	Decca	F12104
'(I Can't Get No) Satisfaction'/'The Spider And The Fly'	Decca	F12220
'Get Off Of My Cloud'/'The Singer Not The Song'	Decca	F12263

US Singles

'The Last Time'/'Play With Fire'	London	9741
'(I Can't Get No) Satisfaction'/'The Under Assistant West Coast Promotion Man'	London	9766
'Get Off Of My Cloud'/'I'm Free'	London	9792
'As Tears Go By'/'Gotta Get Away'	London	9808

Export Singles

'Satisfaction'/'The Under Assistant West Coast Promotion Man' [PS]	Decca	AT 15043
'Get Off Of My Cloud'/'I'm Free'	Decca	F22265
'Time Is On My Side'/'Congratulations' [BLACK LABEL]	Decca	AT 15039
'The Last Time'/'Play With Fire' [PS]	Decca	F 12104

UK EPs

'Got LIVE If You Want It!'	Decca	DFE 8620

Export EPs

'Got LIVE If You Want It'	Decca	SDE 7502
'Got LIVE If You Want It' [RED LABEL]	Decca	RFE 8620

UK Albums

The Rolling Stones No.2 [MONO]	Decca	LK 4661
Out Of Our Heads [MONO]	Decca	LK 4733
Out Of Our Heads [STEREO]	Decca	SKL 4733
Out Of Our Heads [MONO]	Decca	LK 4725

EXPORT ONLY, FEATURING 'Satisfaction'

US Albums

The Rolling Stones, Now! [MONO]	London	LL 3420
The Rolling Stones, Now! [STEREO]	London	PS 420
England's Greatest Hit Makers [MONO]	London	LL 3430

1 TRACK ONLY: 'Surprise Surprise'

England's Greatest Hitmakers [STEREO]	London	PS 430

PROCEEDS WENT TO THE LORD TAVENER'S PLAYING FIELDS ASSOCIATION

Out Of Our Heads [MONO]	London	LL 3429
Out Of Our Heads [STEREO]	London	PS 429
December's Children (And Everybody's) [MONO]	London	LL 3451
December's Children (And Everybody's) [STEREO]	London	PS 451

1966

UK Singles

'19th Nervous Breakdown'/'As Tears Go By'	Decca	F1233
'Paint It Black'/'Long Long While'	Decca	F12395
'Have You Seen Your Mother, Baby, Standing In The Shadow?'/'Who's Driving Your Plane'	Decca	F12497

LABEL AND COVER CHANGED WITH THIS RELEASE

US Singles

'19th Nervous Breakdown'/'Sad Day'	London	9823
'Paint It Black'/'Stupid Girl'	London	901
'Mother's Little Helper'/'Lady Jane'	London	902
'Have You Seen Your Mother, Baby, Standing In The Shadow?'/'Who's Driving Your Plane'	London	903

Export Singles

'19th Nervous Breakdown'/'As Tears Go By' [PS]	Decca	F12331

Export EPs

'The Rolling Stones' (*Out Of Our Heads* cover)	Decca	SFE 7503
'The Rolling Stones'	Decca	DFE 8650

UK Albums

Aftermath [MONO]	Decca	LK 4786
Aftermath [STEREO]	Decca	SKL 4786
Have You Seen Your Mother LIVE! [STEREO, EXPORT ONLY]	Decca	SKL 4838
Originally entitled: *Hits LIVE* [STEREO, EXPORT ONLY]	Decca	SKL 4495
Big Hits (High Tide And Green Grass) [MONO]	Decca	TXL 101
1ST GATEFOLD SLEEVE		
Big Hits (High Tide And Green Grass) [STEREO]	Decca	TXS 101
1ST GATEFOLD SLEEVE		

US Albums

Aftermath [MONO]	London	LL 3476
Aftermath [STEREO]	London	PS 476
Aftermath, Got LIVE If You Want It [MONO]	London	LL 3493
Aftermath, Got LIVE If You Want It [STEREO]	London	PS 493
Big Hits (High Tide And Green Grass) [MONO]	London	NP 1
1ST GATEFOLD SLEEVE		
Big Hits (High Tide And Green Grass) [STEREO]	London	NPS 1
1ST GATEFOLD SLEEVE		

1967

UK Singles

'Let's Spend The Night Together'/'Ruby Tuesday'	Decca	F12546
'We Love You'/'Dandelion'	Decca	F12654

US Singles

'Let's Spend The Night Together'/'Ruby Tuesday'	London	904
'We Love You'/'Dandelion'	London	905
'She's A Rainbow'/'2000 Light Years From Home'	London	906
'In Another Land'/'The Lantern'	London	907

Export Singles

'2000 Light Years From Home'/'She's A Rainbow'	Decca	F22706
'Let's Spend The Night Together'/'Ruby Tuesday' [PS]	Decca	F12546
'We Love You'/'Dandelion' [PS]	Decca	F12654

UK Albums

Between The Buttons [MONO]	Decca	LK 4852
Between The Buttons [STEREO]	Decca	SKL 4852
Flowers [STEREO, EXPORT ONLY]	Decca	PS 509
Their Satanic Majesties Request [MONO]	Decca	TXL 103
Their Satanic Majesties Request [STEREO]	Decca	TXS 103

US Album

Between The Buttons [MONO]	London	L3499
Between The Buttons [STEREO]	London	PS 499
Flowers [MONO]	London	L3509
Flowers [STEREO]	London	PS 509
Their Satanic Majesties Request [MONO]	London	NP 2
Their Satanic Majesties Request [STEREO]	London	NPS 2

1968

UK Singles

'Jumpin' Jack Flash'/'Child Of The Moon'	Decca	F12782

US Singles

'Jumpin' Jack Flash'/'Child Of The Moon'	London	908
'Street Fighting Man'/'No Expectations' [WITHDRAWN, PS]	London	909

Export Singles

'Street Fighting Man'/'No Expectations' [PS]	Decca	F22825

UK Albums

Beggars Banquet [MONO]	Decca	LK 4955
Beggars Banquet [STEREO]	Decca	SKL 4955

US Albums

Beggars Banquet [MONO]	London	LL 3539
Beggars Banquet [STEREO]	London	PS 539

1969

UK Singles

'Honky Tonk Women'/'You Can't Always Get What You Want'	Decca	F12952
PROMOTIONAL COPIES ISSUED IN A PICTURE SLEEVE		

US Singles

'Honky Tonk Women'/'You Can't Always Get What You Want'	London	910

Export Singles

'Honky Tonk Women'/'You Can't Always Get What You Want' [PS]	Decca	F12952

UK Albums

Through The Past, Darkly (Big Hits Vol. 2) [MONO]	Decca	LK 5019
Through The Past, Darkly (Big Hits Vol. 2 [STEREO]	Decca	SKL 5019
Let It Bleed [MONO]	Decca	LK 5025
1ST ISSUES CAME WITH FREE POSTER		
Let It Bleed [STEREO]	Decca	SKL 5025
1ST ISSUES CAME WITH FREE POSTER		

US Albums

Through The Past, Darkly (Big Hits Vol. 2) [MONO]	London	NP 3
Through The Past, Darkly (Big Hits Vol. 2) [STEREO]	London	NPS 3
The Rolling Stones Promotional Album	RSR	RSD 1
Let It Bleed	London	NPS 4

1970

UK Albums

'Get Yer Ya-Ya's Out!' The Rolling Stones In Concert	Decca	SKL 5065

US Albums

'Get Yer Ya-Ya's Out!' The Rolling Stones In Concert	London	NPS 5

From 1971 all Stones singles and albums were released on their own label, Rolling Stone Records [RSR]; the UK and US covers are identical except for the catalogue numbers. * denotes singles and albums released by Decca and London after the Stones had left.

1971

Singles

'Brown Sugar'/'Bitch'/'Let It Rock' [UK, 1ST PS]	RSR	RS 19100
'Brown Sugar'/'Bitch' [US]	RSR	RS 19100
'Wild Horses'/'Sway' [US ONLY]	RSR	RS 19101

UK Singles

'Street Fighting Man'/'Surprise Surprise'	Decca	F13203*

Export Singles

'Love In Vain'/'Little Queenie' [PS]	Decca	F13126*
'Street Fighting Man'/'Surprise Surprise'/ 'Everybody Needs Somebody To Love' [PS]	Decca	F13195*

Albums

Sticky Fingers [UK]	RSR	HRSS 591-01
Sticky Fingers [USA]	RSR	COC 591-01

UK Albums

Stone Age	Decca	SKL 5084*
Milestones	Decca	SKL 5098*

US Albums

Hot Rocks 1964-1971	London	2PS 606/7*

1972

Singles

'Tumbling Dice'/'Sweet Black Angel' [UK & US]	RSR	RS 19103
'Happy'/'All Down The Line' [US ONLY]	RSR	RS 19104

US EPs

'Rocks Off'/'Sweet Virgin'/'Rip This Joint'/ 'Shake Your Hips'/'Tumbling Dice' [ATLANTIC EP]	RSR	COC-7 22900

Albums

Exile on Main St. [UK]	RSR	COC69 100
Exile on Main St. [USA]	RSR	COC2 2900

UK Albums

Gimme Shelter	Decca	SKL 5101*
Rock 'N' Rolling Stones	Decca	SKL 5149*

US Albums

More Hot Rocks (big hits and fazed cookies)	London	2PS 626/7*

1973

Singles

'Angie'/'Silver Train' [UK & US]	RSR	RS 19105
'Doo Doo Doo Doo Doo (Heart Breaker)'/ 'Dancing with Mr D.' [US ONLY]	RSR	RS 19109

UK Singles

'Sad Day'/'You Can't Always Get What You Want'	Decca	F13404*

US EPs

'Star Star'/'Give Your Love'/ 'Can You Hear The Music'/'100 Years Ago' [ATLANTIC EP]	RSR	COC-7 22900

Albums

Goat's Head Soup [UK AND US]	RSR	COC 59101

UK Albums

No Stone Unturned	Decca	SKL 5173*

1974

Singles

'It's Only Rock 'N Roll'/'Through The Lonely Nights' [UK]	RSR	RS 19114
'It's Only Rock 'N Roll'/'Through The Lonely Nights [US]	RSR	RS 19301
'Ain't Too Proud To Beg'/'Dance Little Sister' [US ONLY]	RSR	RS 19302
'Time Waits For No One' [US, MONO/STEREO, PROMO ONLY]	RSR	PR 228
'It's All Over Now'/'Paint It Black' [WITHDRAWN]	Decca	F 13517

UK EPs

'Brown Sugar'/'Happy'/'Rocks Off'	Atlantic	K19107

US EPs

'Star Star'/'Hide Your Love'/ 'Can Your Hear The Music'/'100 Years Ago' [ATLANTIC EP]	RSR	COC-7 59101

Albums

It's Only Rock 'N Roll [UK]	RSR	COC 59103
It's Only Rock 'N Roll [US]	RSR	COC 79101

1975

UK Singles

'I Don't Know Why'/'Try A Little Harder'	Decca	F13584*

1ST PRESSING CREDITED TO JAGGER, RICHARDS, TAYLOR.

2ND PRESSING CREDITED TO WONDER, WISE, HUNTER, HARDWAY

'Out of Time'/'Jiving Sister Fanny'	Decca	F13597*

US Singles

'I Don't Know Why'/'Try A Little Harder'	ABKCO	ABK 4701*
'Out of Time'/'Jiving Sister Fanny' [US]	ABKCO	SN 4702*

Albums

Made In The Shade [UK]	RSR	COC 59104
Made In The Shade [US]	RSR	COC 79102

UK Albums

Metamorphosis	Decca	SKL 5212*
Rolled Gold	Decca	ROST 1/2*

US Albums

Metamorphosis	ABKCO	ANA 1*

1976

Singles

'Fool To Cry'/'Crazy Mama' [UK]	RSR	RS 19121
'Fool To Cry'/'Hot Stuff' [US]	RSR	RS 19304
'Hot Stuff'/'Crazy Mama' ISSUED AS 12" SINGLE (1ST US)	RSR	RS 4070
PROMOTIONAL ONLY, ON BLACK AND BLUE VINYL		
'Fool To Cry'/'Crazy Mama' [US, WITHDRAWN]	RSR	RS 19303

UK Singles

'Honky Tonk Women'/'Sympathy For The Devil'	Decca	F13635*

Albums

Black And Blue [UK]	RSR	COC 59106
Black And Blue [US]	RSR	COC 79104

1977

EPs

'If You Can't Rock Me'/'Get Off Of My Cloud'/ 'Brown Sugar'/'Jumpin' Jack Flash'/'Hot Stuff'	RSR	EP287
US, PROMO ONLY		

Albums

Love You Live [UK]	RSR	COC89101
Love You Live [US]	RSR	COC 2-9001

UK Albums

Get Stoned: 30 Greatest Hits, 30 Original Tracks	Arcade	ADEP 32

1978

Singles

'Miss You'/'Faraway Eyes' [UK, PS]	RSR	EMI 2802
AS 12" SINGLE ON PINK VINYL	RSR	12EMI 2802
'Miss You'/'Faraway Eyes'[US]	RSR	RS 19307
AS 12" SINGLE	RSR	DK 4609
'Respectable'/'When The Whip Comes Down' [UK, PS]	RSR	EMI 2861
'Beast Of Burden'/'When The Whip Comes Down' [US, WITHDRAWN, PS]	RSR	RS 19309

Albums

Some Girls [UK]	RSR	CUN 39108
ISSUED IN 3 DIFFERENT COLOURED SLEEVES		
Some Girls [US]	RSR	COC 39108
ISSUED IN 3 DIFFERENT COLOURED SLEEVES		
Time Waits For No One: Anthology 1971–1977 [UK]	RSR	COC 59107

1979

Singles

'Shattered'/'Everything Turning To Gold' [US ONLY, PS]	RSR	RS 19310
'Hot Stuff'/'Miss You'	RSR	DK 4616
ISSUED AS 12" SINGLE ONLY		

US Albums

Songs Of The Rolling Stones	London	MPD 1*
PROMOTIONAL ONLY		

1980

Singles

'Emotional Rescue'/'Down In The Hole' [UK, PS]	RSR	RSR 105
'Emotional Rescue'/'Down In The Hole' [US, PS]	RSR	RS 20001
AS 12" SINGLE (PROMOTIONAL ONLY)	RSR	PR 367
'She's So Cold'/'Send It To Me' [UK, PS]	RSR	RSR 106
'She's So Cold'/'Send It To Me' [US]	RSR	RS 21001
AS 12" SINGLE	RSR	12RSR 111

UK Singles

'Singles Collection'	Decca	STONE 1-12*
BOX SET OF 12 7" SINGLES, CAME WITH A POSTER AND BADGE		

Albums

Emotional Rescue [UK]	RSR	CUN 39111
Emotional Rescue [US]	RSR	COC 16015

UK Albums

Solid Rock	Decca	TAB 1*
Album Collection	Decca	ROLL 1*
LIMITED EDITION, BOX SET OF 1ST 8 STUDIO LPs		

1981

Singles

'Start Me Up'/'No Use In Crying' [UK, PS]	RSR	RSR 108
'Start Me Up'/'No Use In Crying' [US]	RSR	RS 21003
'Start Me Up'/'No Use In Crying'	RSR	PR 347
AS 12" SINGLE (PROMOTIONAL ONLY)		
'Waiting On A Friend'/'Little T & A' [UK, PS]	RSR	RSR 109
'Waiting On A Friend'/'Little T & A' [US]	RSR	RS 21004
'If I Was A Dancer (Dance Pt. 2)'/'Dance' (Instrumental)	RSR	DMD 253
AS 12" SINGLE (PROMOTIONAL ONLY)		

Albums

Sucking In The Seventies [UK]	RSR	CUN 39112
Sucking In The Seventies [US]	RSR	COC 16028
Tattoo You [UK]	RSR	CUN 39114
Tattoo You [US]	RSR	COC 16052

UK Albums

Slow Rollers	Decca	TAB 30*

1982

Singles

'Hang Fire'/'Neighbours' [US ONLY]	RSR	RS 21300
'Hang Fire'/'Worried About You' [SCHEDULED BUT WAS REPLACED BY THE ABOVE]		
'Going To A Go Go'/'Beast of Burden' [UK, PS]	RSR	RSR 110
AS 12" SINGLE [EUROPE ONLY]	RSR	RSR 64820
'Going To A Go Go'/'Beast of Burden' [US, PS, WITHDRAWN]	RSR	RS21301
'Time Is On My Side'/'Twenty Flight Rock' [UK, PS]	RSR	RSR 111
AS 12" SINGLE Bonus track: 'Under My Thumb'	RSR	12RSR 111
Time Is On My Side'/'Twenty Flight Rock' [US]	RSR	RS 21302

UK EPs

'EP Collection 1964–65'	Decca	
RE-ISSUED AS 12" SINGLES, COVERS AND NUMBERS REMAINED THE SAME		

Albums

Still Life (American Concert 1981) [UK]	RSR	CUN 39115
AS PICTURE DISC	RSR	CUN 39115A
Still Life (American Concert 1981) [US]	RSR	COC 39113

UK Albums

Story Of The Stones	K-Tel	NE 1201
History Of Rock Volume 10: The Rolling Stones	Orbis	HRL 010
Rolling Stones	RD	GROL-A 119
READER'S DIGEST BOX SET		

US Albums

The Rolling Stones: The First Eleven London Albums	ABKCO	
LIMITED EDITION IN WOODEN BOX	[boxes numbered]	

1983

UK Singles

'Let's Spend The Night Together'/'Start Me Up' [UK, PS]	RSR	RSR 112
PROMOTIONAL ONLY		
'Undercover Of The Night'/'All The Way Down' [UK, PS]	RSR	RSR 113
AS 12" SINGLE	RSR	12RSR 113
'Undercover Of The Night'/'All The Way Down' [US, PS]	RSR	7-99813
'Undercover Of The Night'/'Feel On Baby'	RSR	0-96978
AS 12" SINGLE ONLY		
'Too Tough'/'Miss You' [US ONLY]	RSR	7-99724
'She Was Hot'/'Think I'm Going Mad' [US ONLY, PS]	RSR	7-99788

Albums

Undercover [UK]	RSR	CUN1654361
Undercover [US]	RSR	90120

UK Albums

Slow Rollers	Decca	TAB 30*

1984

Singles

'She Was Hot'/'Think I'm Going Mad' [UK, PS]	RSR	RSR 114
AS SHADED PICTURE DISC	RSR	RSR P114
'Brown Sugar'/'Bitch' [UK ONLY, PS]	RSR	SUGAR 1
AS SHADED PICTURE DISC	RSR	SUGAR P1
'Too Much Blood' (3 VERSIONS) [US ONLY]	RSR	0-96902
AS 12" SINGLE ONLY		

Albums

Rewind (1971–1984) [UK AND US]	RSR	CUN 1

1986

Singles

'Harlem Shuffle'/'Had It With You' [UK]	RSR	A6864
AS 7" SINGLE WITH WRAP-AROUND POSTER	RSR	QA 6864
AS 12" SINGLE (2 DIFFERENT MIXES)	RSR	TA 6864
Harlem Shuffle'/'Had It With You' [US]	RSR	38-05802
AS 12" SINGLE (2 DIFFERENT MIXES)	RSR	44-05365
'One Hit (To The Body)'/'Fight' [UK]	RSR	A7160
AS 12" SINGLE	RSR	TA 7160
'One Hit (To The Body)'/'Fight'[US]	RSR	38-05906
AS 12" SINGLE (2 DIFFERENT MIXES)	RSR	44-05388

Albums

Dirty Work [UK AND US]	RSR	86321

US Albums

The Rolling Stones: The First 17 Albums	ABKCO
RE-ISSUED ON CD, COVERS AND NUMBERS REMAINED THE SAME	

1987

UK Singles

'Jumpin' Jack Flash'/'Child Of The Moon'	Decca	F102*
'Jumpin' Jack Flash'/'Child Of The Moon'	Decca	FX 102*
ISSUED AS 12" SINGLE TO COINCIDE WITH FILM OF SAME NAME		
Bonus track: 'Sympathy For The Devil'		

1989

Singles

'Mixed Emotions'/'Fancyman Blues' [UK]	RSR	655193-7
AS 12" SINGLE	RSR	TA 655193-8
AS CASSETTE SINGLE	RSR	655193-4
AS 5" CD SINGLE (1ST VERSION)	RSR	655193-2
AS 5" CD SINGLE (2ND VERSION)	RSR	655193-5
LIMITED EDITION IN TIN WITH TONGUE STICKER		
Bonus tracks: 'Tumbling Dice'/'Miss You'		
AS 5" CD SINGLE (3RD VERSION)	RSR	655214-2
2ND LIMITED EDITION IN TIN		
Bonus tracks: 'Shattered'/'Waiting On A Friend'		
'Mixed Emotions'/'Fancyman Blues' [US]	RSR	38-69008
'Rock And A Hard Place'/'Cook Cook Blues' [UK]	RSR	655422-7
AS 12" SINGLE	RSR	655422-8
AS CASSETTE SINGLE	RSR	655422-4
AS 5" CD SINGLE (1ST VERSION)	RSR	655422-2
AS 5" CD SINGLE (2ND VERSION)	RSR	655448-5
LIMITED EDITION IN TONGUE-SHAPED SLEEVE		
Bonus tracks: 'Emotional Rescue'/'Some Girls'		
AS 5" CD SINGLE (3RD VERSION)	RSR	655448-2
2ND LIMITED EDITION IN BOX WITH POSTER		
Bonus tracks: 'It's Only Rock 'N' Roll'/'Rocks Off'		
'Rock And A Hard Place'/'Cook Cook Blues' [US]	RSR	38-73057
AS 12" SINGLE (4 DIFFERENT MIXES)	RSR	44-73133

Albums

Steel Wheels [UK AND US]	RSR	464752

US Albums

The Rolling Stones Singles Collection: The London Years	ABKCO	1218-2

4 ALBUMS

1990

Singles

'Almost Heard You Sigh'/'Wish I'd Never Met You'/		
'Mixed Emotions' [UK]	RSR	656065-7
AS 12" SINGLE (GATEFOLD SLEEVE)	RSR	656065-6
AS CASSETTE SINGLE	RSR	656065-3
AS 5" CD SINGLE (1ST VERSION)	RSR	656065-2
LIMITED EDITION, GOLD CD		
AS 5" CD SINGLE (2ND VERSION)	RSR	656065-5
LIMITED EDITION IN TIN WITH Urban Jungle STICKERS		
Bonus tracks: 'Miss You'/'Waiting For A Friend'		
'Almost Hear You Sigh'/'Break The Spell' [US]	RSR	38-37093
'Terrifying'/'Rock And A Hard Place' [UK]	RSR	656122-7
AS 12" SINGLE	RSR	656122-6
AS CASSETTE SINGLE	RSR	656122-4
AS 5" CD SINGLE (2 VERSIONS OF 'Terrifying'/'Harlem Shuffle')	RSR	656122-2
AS 5" CD SINGLE	RSR	656122-5
Bonus tracks: 'Start Me Up'/'Shattered'/'If You Can't Rock Me'		

UK Singles

'Paint It Black'/'Honky Tonk Women' [RE-ISSUE]	London	LON 264*
AS 12" SINGLE (1ST VERSION)	London	LONX 264*
Bonus track: 'Sympathy For The Devil'		
AS 12" SINGLE (2ND VERSION)	London	LONX12 264*
Bonus track: 'Satisfaction'		
AS CASSETTE SINGLE	London	LONCS 264*

US Albums

The Rolling Stones Collection 1971–1989	CBS	
LIMITED EDITION BOX SET, 14 CDs	[boxes numbered]	

1991

Singles

'Highwire'/'2000 Light Years From Home' [UK]	RSR	656756-7
AS 12" SINGLE (GATEFOLD SLEEVE)	RSR	656756-6
AS CASSETTE SINGLE	RSR	656756-4
AS 5" CD SINGLE (1ST VERSION)	RSR	656756-5
Bonus tracks: 'Play With Fire'/'Factory Girl'		
AS 5" CD SINGLE (2ND VERSION) WITH FOLD-OUT SLEEVE	RSR	656756-2
Bonus tracks: 'Sympathy For The Devil'/		
'I Just Wanna Make Love To You'		
'Highwire'/'2000 Light Years From Home' [US]	RSR	38-73742
'Ruby Tuesday'/'Play With Fire' [UK]	RSR	656892-7
AS 12" SINGLE	RSR	656892-6
AS CASSETTE SINGLE	RSR	656892-4
AS 5" CD SINGLE (1ST VERSION) PICTURE DISC	RSR	656892-5
Bonus tracks: 'Harlem Shuffle'/'Winning Ugly'		
AS 5" CD SINGLE (2ND VERSION)	RSR	656892-2
Bonus tracks: 'You Can't Always Get What You Want'/		
'Undercover Of The Night'		
'Sexdrive'/'Undercover Of The Night' [US]	RSR	38-73789

Albums

Flashpoint [UK AND US]	RSR	468135-1

SOLO ROLLING STONES DISCOGRAPHY 1969–1992

Mick Jagger

1970 Single

'Memo From Turner'/'Natural Magic'	Decca	F13067

1970 Albums

Ned Kelly [SOUNDTRACK]	U.A.	UAS 29108
Performance [SOUNDTRACK]	Warner	WS 2554

1985 Album

She's The Boss	CBS	86310

1986 Album

Ruthless People [SOUNDTRACK]	CBS	EPC-70299

1987 Album

Primitive Cool	CBS	460123-1
CD PICTURE DISCS [WITH FREE 1988 CALENDAR]	CBS	460123-9

1993 Album

Wandering Spirit	Atlantic	7567-87 4361-1

Brian Jones

1971 Album

Brian Jones Presents the Pipes of Pan at Joujouka	RSR	COC 49100

Keith Richards

1979 Single

'Run Rudolph Run'/'The Harder They Come'	RSR	RSR 102

1988 Album

Talk is Cheap	Virgin	V2554
SPECIAL ISSUE AS 3 x 3" CDs IN TIN	Virgin	2-910475
Hail! Hail! Rock 'N' Roll [SOUNDTRACK]		MCF 3411

1992 Album

Live At The Hollywood Paladium [CD ONLY]	Virgin	VSCD 36022
[WITH THE X-Pensive Winos]		
Mean Offender	Virgin	VUSLP 59

Charlie Watts

1980 Album

The People Band	Atlantic	TRA 214

1981 Album

Rocket 88 [FEATURING Charlie Watts AND Ian Stewart]	Atlantic	K50776

1986 Album

The Charlie Watts Orchestra – Live Fulham Town Hall	CBS	4502531

1991 Album

From One Charlie [BOX SET CD & BOOK, Ode to a High Flying Bird]	UFO	2

1992 Album

A Tribute To Charlie Parker [Charlie Watts Quintet WITH STRINGS]	Continuum	19201–2

1995 Album

Warm and Tender	CTUM	3

Ronnie Wood

1974 Album

I've Got My Own Album To Do	Warner	K56065

1975 Albums

Now Look [UK]	Warner	K56145
Tommy [SOUNDTRACK]		2657-014
Mahoney's Last Stand [SOUNDTRACK]	Warner	K50308

1979 Album

Gimme Some Neck [UK]	CBS	83337

1981 Album

1 2 3 4 [UK]	CBS	85277

1984 Album

The Wild Life [SOUNDTRACK]	MCA	25-1523-1

1985 Album

Cancel Everything	Possum	5

1989 Album

Live at The Ritz [WITH Bo Diddley]	Victor	VDP 1329

1992 Album

Slide On This	Continuum	CAT 19120

1993 Album

Slide On Live [PLUGGED IN AND STANDING]	CTUM	3
Unplugged and Seated [WITH Rod Stewart]	Warner	4/2 45289

Bill Wyman

1974 Singles

'Monkey Grip Glue'/'What A Blow' [UK ONLY]	RSR	RS 19112
'White Lightnin' '/'Pussy' [UK ONLY]	RSR	RS 19115

Album

Monkey Grip [UK]	RSR	COC 59102

1975 Album

Stone Alone [UK]	RSR	COC 59105

1976 Singles

'A Quarter To Three'/'Soul Satisfying' [UK AND US]	RSR	RS 19119
'Apache Woman'/'Soul Satisfying' [UK]	RSR	RS 19120

1981 Albums

Drinking TNT 'N' Smoking Dynamite	Red Lightin	RL0034
[Bill Wyman WITH Buddy Guy AND Junior Wells]		
Green Ice [SOUNDTRACK]	Polydor	POLS 1031

1982 Album

Bill Wyman	A & M	AMLH 68540
EP [DISCS HAVE THE SAME NUMBER]		

1983 Album

Digital Dreams [SOUNDTRACK]	Ripple	[NO NUMBER]

1985 Album

Willie and the Poor Boys	Ripple	Bill 1

1993 Album

Stuff [JAPAN ONLY]	Victor	VICP 5202

Stone Collaborations

1972 Album

Jamming with Edward!	RSR	COC 39100
[FEATURING Mick Jagger, Bill Wyman, AND Charlie Watts]		
The London Howlin' Wolf Sessions	RSR	COC 49101
[UK, FEATURING Bill Wyman, AND Charlie Watts]		

Stone's World Tour 1994-5

1994

JULY
19 RPM Club, Toronto

AUGUST
1 JFK Stadium, Washington
3 JFK Stadium, Washington
6 Legion Field, Birmingham
10 Hoosier Doom, Indianapolis
12 Giants Stadium, New York
14 Giants Stadium, New York
15 Giants Stadium, New York
17 Giants Stadium, New York
19 Exhibition Centre, Toronto
20 Exhibition Centre, Toronto
23 Winnipeg Stadium, Winnipeg
26 Camp Randell Stadium, Madison
28 Municipal Stadium, Cleveland
30 Riverfront Stadium, Cincinnati

SEPTEMBER
4 Foxboro Stadium, Boston
5 Foxboro Stadium, Boston
7 Carter-Finley Stadium, Raleigh
9 Spartan Stadium, East Lansing
11 Soldier Field, Chicago
12 Soldier Field, Chicago
15 Mile High Stadium, Denver
18 Faurot Field, Columbia, MO.
22 Veteran Stadium, Philadelphia
23 Veteran Stadium, Philadelphia
27 Liberty Bowl, Memphis
29 Three Rivers Stadium, Pittsburgh

OCTOBER
1 Cyclone Stadium, Ames
4 Commonwealth Stadium, Edmonton
5 Commonwealth Stadium, Edmonton
10 Superdrome, New Orleans
14 MGM Grand Garden, Las Vegas
15` MGM Grand Garden, Las Vegas
17 Jack Murphy Stadium, San Diego
19 Rose Bowl, Pasadena, LA.
21 Rose Bowl, Pasadena, LA.
23 Rice Stadium, Salt Lake City
26 Alameda Stadium, Oakland
28 Alameda Stadium, Oakland
29 Alameda Stadium, Oakland
31 Alameda Stadium, Oakland

NOVEMBER
3 Sun Bowl, El Paso
5 Alamdrone, San Antonio
11 War Memorial, Little Rock
13 Astrodome, Houston
15 Georgia Dome, Atlanta
16 Georgia Dome, Atlanta
18 Cotton Bowl, Dallas
22 Tampa Stadium, Tampa
25 Joe Robbie Stadium, Miami
27 University of Florida, Gainesville

DECEMBER
1 Silverdrome, Detroit
3 Sky Dome, Toronto
5 Olympic Stadium, Montreal
6 Olympic Stadium, Montreal
8 Carrier Dome, Syracuse
11 Metrodome, Minneapolis
15 Kingdome, Seattle
17 BC Place, Vancouver
18 BC Place, Vancouver

1995

JANUARY
14 Autodromo Hermanos Rodriquez, Mexico City
16 Autodromo Hermanos Rodriquez, Mexico City
18 Autodromo Hermanos Rodriquez, Mexico City
27 Murumbi Stadium, Sau Paula

FEBRUARY
2 Rio de Janeiro
9 River Plate Stadium, Buenos Aires
11 River Plate Stadium, Buenos Aires
12 River Plate Stadium, Buenos Aires
14 River Plate Stadium, Buenos Aires
24 Ellis Park Stadium, Johannesburg
25 Ellis Park Stadium, Johannesburg

MARCH
6 Tokyo Dome, Tokyo
8 Tokyo Dome, Tokyo
9 Tokyo Dome, Tokyo
12 Tokyo Dome, Tokyo
14 Tokyo Dome, Tokyo
16 Tokyo Dome, Tokyo
17 Tokyo Dome, Tokyo
27 Melbourne Cricket Ground, Melbourne

APRIL
1 Sydney Cricket Ground, Sydney
5 Adelaide Football Park, Adelaide
8 Perry Lakes, Perth
12 ANZ Stadium, Brisbane
16 Western Springs, Auckland
21 National Stadium, Singapore

EUROPEAN TOUR

JUNE
3 Stockholm
6 Helsinki
9 Oslo
11 Copenhagen
13 Numegan
14 Numegan
17 Landgraff
20 Cologne
22 Hannover
24 Werchter
25 Werchter
30 Paris

JULY
1 Paris
9 Sheffield
11 Wembley (London)
12 Wembley (London)
15 Wembley (London)
16 Wembley (London)
19 Hammersmith (London Charity Show)
22 Guon
24 Lisbon
27 Montpelier
29 Basle

AUGUST
1 Vienna
3 Munich
5 Prague
11 Moscow
15 Warsaw
17 Berlin
19 Hockenheim

At the time of going to press these are the confirmed tour dates for the 1995 leg of the Voodoo Lounge World Tour
There is a provisional two week extension as yet unconfirmed possibly going to Switzerland, Turkey, Greece, etc.

Update on Single/Album Releases as at February 1995

1993
Album
Jump Back   V 2726
   PROMO CD STONES 1
'Start Me Up'/'Angie'/'Brown Sugar'

1994
Album
Voodoo Lounge [DOUBLE ALBUM]   V 7750
   CD   CDV 2750
   8 TRACK PROMO CD   DPRO 14158

UK Singles
'Love is Strong'/'The Storm'   VS 1503
   7" SINGLE LIMITED TO 7000 COPIES
CD 'Love is Strong'/'The Storm'/'So Young'
'Love is Strong' (RE-MIX)   VSCD T 1503
cd 'Love is Strong' 6 VERSIONS   VCDX 1503
Teddy Riley Dance remixes
   CASSETTE SINGLE   VSC 1503

US Singles
'Love is Strong' 4 VERSIONS/'The Storm'   V25H 39446
'Love is Strong' PROMO CD ONE TRACK   DPRO 14180
'Love is Strong' PROMO CD FOUR TRACKS   DPRO 14155
   12" SINGLE 6 MIXES   Y-38446

UK Singles
'You Got Me Rocking'/'Jump on Top of Me'   VS 1518
   7" SINGLE LIMITED TO 7000 COPIES
CD 'You Got Me Rocking/'Jump on Top of Me'
'You Got Me Rocking' x 2 REMIX VERSIONS   VSDG1518
   CASSETTE SINGLE   VSC 1518
   12" SINGLE 3 MIXES   VST 1518

US Singles
'You Got Me Rocking'
   PROMO CD ONE TRACK   DPRO 14229
'You Got Me Rocking'
PROMO CD TWO TRACK   DPRO 12702
NEVER OFFICIALLY RELEASED IN USA
Desert Island Survival Kit   1848-2
   15 TRACK PROMO CD

UK Singles
'Out of Tears'/'I'm Gonna Drive'   VS 1524
   7" SINGLE LIMITED TO 7000 COPIES
CD 'Out of Tears'/'I'm Gonna Drive'   VSCDT 1529
'Sparks Will Fly'/'Out of Tears' RE-MIX
   CD TRACKS AS ABOVE LIMITED EDITION IN TEAR DROP SHAPED COVER   VSCDX 1529
   CASSETTE SINGLE   CSC 1524

US Singles
'Out of Tears'/'Out of Tears' REMIX/'I'm Gonna Drive'/
'So Young'   V25H 38459
'Out of Tears' PROMO CD THREE TRACKS   DPRO-14237
'Sparks Will Fly' PROMO CD ONLY   DPRO-12688

UK
'Gimme Shelter' (live) Appears on a special cassingle EMI/Food TC Order 1. This is an appeal for homeless people UK only. Two CDs and a 12" also issued with 11 versions of Gimme Shelter by various artists such as Tom Jones, Sandy Shaw, Sam Fox, Heaven 17, Jimmy Somerville, Thunder.

CDS Members of the Stones have played on:

Bobby Womak	Resurrection	Keith and Ronnie play
Georgie Jones	The Bradley Barn Sessions	Keith sings on one track
The Chieftains	The Long Black Veil	Mick sings on one track and the Stones play on one track

INDEX

ACKNOWLEDGEMENTS

Geoffrey Giuliano says Praise be to the following remarkably helpful, kind and generous people:

A Current Affair; Meher Baba; Ginger and Karen Baker; Rob Baker; Mirza Beg; Barbara Berkowitz; Pete Best; Keane, Darla and Melissa Bismarck; Tim and Carrie Bismarck; Debroah Lynn Black; Ray and Sadie Black; Fred and Chris Brown; Larry Brown; Jack Bruce; Cheryl Dee Brzezowski; Stefano Castino; Pat Cherry; Matt Conley; Stacee Coyne; Ram Das; Suavasa Dasa; Federico and Kathy Doldan; Michael Downey; Glen Ellis; Entertainment Tonight; Jim Fitzgerald; John R. Ford; Michael Fragnito; Robert John Gallo; Robert Noel Giuliano; Robin Scott Giuliano; Toni Hafkenschied; George Harrison; David Hemmelfarb; *Hinduism Today*; Roger Hitts; Abbie Hoffman; Steve Holly; Howard from Colorado; Gloria Hunniford; William Hushion; ISKCOW; ISKCON Los Angeles; Suneel Jaitly; Carla Johnson; Joseph and Myrna Juliana; Larry Khan; Ben E. King; Marvin Kirshman; Sean Kittrick; Michael Klapper; Charles and Sharon Klotchbach; Arron Kwinter; Allan Lang; Timothy Leary; Leif Leavesley; Lia Leavesley; Pip Leavesley; Donald Lehr; Andrew Lownie; The MGA Agency; Drew Mackenzie; His Divine Grace Bhakti Hirday Mangal Niloy Maharaj; Mark Studios; Peter Max; Judy McGuire; Chris McCarty; David Lloyd McIntyre; Toni Mitchell; The Nolan/Lehr Group; Ralph Nurmella; PETA; His Grace Swami Pasupati; Dave Peabody; Wilder Penfield III; Frank Poole; His Divine Grace A. C. Bhaktivedanta Swami Prabhupada; Jane Price; Vrinda Rani; Ron Ray; Kevin Renken; Promotional Reprint Company; Joan Rivers; Jennifer Romanello; Charles F. Rosenay!!!; Pippa Rubinstein; Rachel Ryder; Dimo Safari; Martin Schiffert; Sesa; Devin, Avalon and India; Siddha Yoga Foundation; Christine; Paula and Kindra Sinclair; Jackie Sinclair; Wendell Lee Smith; Wendell and Joan Smith; Something Fishy Productions Ltd; Spiritual Realization Institute (SRI); The Sri Chaitanya Gaudiya Math; John Sylvano; Alexander Thynn; Enzo of Valentinos; Eddie Veltman; Anthony Violanti; Jack Webb; Ernie Williams; Julia, Robert and Katie Williams; Mike Williams; David Wolotko; Parmahamsa Yogananda; Ronald Zuker.

A very special thank you to James Swick, a rare gentleman and a good friend to everyone.

Finally, I'd like to remember Frank 'The Freak' Ostapczuk, my old mate from Coventry for the (crazy) good times long past. Also Mick the Cripple for the many late-night natters by the fire with Tommy. Hats off to Thomas Gerrard for over twenty years of long-suffering friendship and affection.

Brenda Giuliano has lent her unique talents to all of husband Geoffrey's various literary projects, acting not only as chief researcher but also photo editor, interviewer, and copy consultant.

Chris Eborn would like to thank the following for their kind assistance with this project, and those who have helped to build up his collection: Dave Caryl (Record Cellar, Liverpool); Thomas Grosh (very English, very Rolling Stone); Mark Hayward (Vinyl Experience/UFO Records); Yuji Ikeda (*Stones People*); Mike Koshitani and Bill German (*Beggars Banquet*); Mark and John (*International Record Collector*); Reg Pippet; June Priestley (Ruislip Records); Steve Pullen; Jerry Stone; Ronald Van Slobbe; André Verhoeven; as well as Linda Chandler for replacing the purloined jacket; Graham and Viv for the painstaking photography; Lyndsay Allen for diligent typing; Gered Mankowitz for his help and fascinating conversation; and, of course, his wife Pam, and children Natasha and Rachel for putting up with his obsession.

The Publishers would like to thank the following companies and individuals for the use of their material in this book:

A & M Records; ABC; ABCKO Inc.; Affinity Records; Appaloosa Records; Arcade Records; ATV Music Group; Bally; Bantam Books; BBC; BCL Group; Beat Publications; Beggars Banquet; Belinda (London) Ltd; Blues Interactions Inc.; Boxtree; Carlin Music; Castle Communications; CBS Records; CBS/Fox; Century Hutchinson; Charly Records; CMV Enterprises; Columbia Records; Connoiseur Collection Ltd; Continuum Records; Corgi Books; Curtis Books; Discomagic Records; Dominion Music; Doubleday Dolphin; Downbeat; Edsel Records; Elm Tree Books; Embassy Pictures; EMI Music; EMI Records; Epic Records; Essex Music Group; Faber & Faber; Fleetway; Futura Books; Gered Mankowitz; GM Records; Granada Television; Hamlyn Books; Hanna Barbera Records; Harper & Row Publishers; Hello; Imaginary Records; Immediate Records; Instant Records; Island Records; Jewel Music; K-tel Records; Keys Pops Publications; King Biscuit; Gered Mankowitz; MCA Records; Media America; Methuen Publications; Michael Joseph; Mirage Music; Modern Drummer; Morrow Books, Random House; Music Sales; Musidor bv; Mutual Broadcasting System; Omnibus Press; Panther Books; Dave Peabody; Peermusic UK; Penguin Books; Phantom Music; Philips Records; Plexus; Polydor Records; Putnam Books; Radio Times; Ripple Records; Rolling Stones Records; Scimitar; See For Miles; Sidgwick and Jackson; Silvertone Records; Simon & Schuster; Southern Music; Stateside Records; Sticky Fingers; Stones People; Tara Records; Thunderbolt Records; Time Out; Track Records; Transatlantic Records; TRC Records; United Artists; Vermillion Books; Victor Records; Viking Books; Virgin Records; W. H. Allen; Warner Bros; WEA Records; Westwood One; William Heineman; Wise Publications.